# Success in Academic Writing

**Palgrave Study Skills**

Business Degree Success
Career Skills
Cite Them Right (10th edn)
e-Learning Skills (2nd edn)
Essentials of Essay Writing
Get Sorted
Great Ways to Learn Anatomy and
  Physiology (2nd edn)
How to Begin Studying English Literature
  (4th edn)
How to Study Foreign Languages
How to Study Linguistics (2nd edn)
How to Use Your Reading in Your Essays (2nd edn)
How to Write Better Essays (3rd edn)
How to Write Your Undergraduate
  Dissertation (2nd edn)
Improve Your Grammar (2nd edn)
Information Skills
The International Student Handbook
The Mature Student's Guide to Writing (3rd edn)
The Mature Student's Handbook
The Palgrave Student Planner
The Personal Tutor's Handbook
Practical Criticism
Presentation Skills for Students (3rd edn)
The Principles of Writing in Psychology
Professional Writing (3rd edn)
Researching Online
The Student Phrase Book
The Student's Guide to Writing (3rd edn)
Study Skills for International Postgraduates
Study Skills for Speakers of English as a
  Second Language
Studying History (4th edn)
Studying Law (4th edn)
Studying Modern Drama (2nd edn)
Studying Psychology (2nd edn)
Studying Physics
Success in Academic Writing (2nd edn)
Smart Thinking
The Undergraduate Research Handbook
The Work-Based Learning Student
  Handbook (2nd edn)
Work Placements – A Survival Guide for
  Students
Write it Right (2nd edn)
Writing for Engineers (4th edn)
Writing for Law
Writing for Nursing and Midwifery Students
  (2nd edn)
Writing History Essays (2nd edn)

**Pocket Study Skills**

14 Days to Exam Success
Analyzing a Case Study
Blogs, Wikis, Podcasts and More
Brilliant Writing Tips for Students
Completing Your PhD
Doing Research (2nd edn)
Getting Critical (2nd edn)
Planning Your Dissertation
Planning Your Essay (2nd edn)
Planning Your PhD
Posters and Presentations
Reading and Making Notes (2nd edn)
Referencing and Understanding Plagiarism
  (2nd edn)
Reflective Writing
Report Writing
Science Study Skills
Studying with Dyslexia (2nd edn)
Success in Groupwork
Time Management
Where's Your Argument?
Writing for University (2nd edn)

**Palgrave Research Skills**

Authoring a PhD
The Foundations of Research (2nd edn)
Getting to Grips with Doctoral Research
Getting Published
The Good Supervisor (2nd edn)
PhD by Published Work
The PhD Viva
Planning Your Postgraduate Research
The PhD Writing Handbook
The Postgraduate Research Handbook
  (2nd edn)
The Professional Doctorate
Structuring Your Research Thesis

**Palgrave Career Skills**

Excel at Graduate Interviews
Graduate CVs and Covering Letters
Graduate Entrepreneurship
How to Succeed at Assessment Centres
Social Media for Your Student and Graduate
  Job Search
The Graduate Career Guidebook
Work Experience, Placements and
  Internships

# Success in Academic Writing

## Second edition

Trevor Day

 macmillan international
HIGHER EDUCATION

palgrave

First published 2018 by
PALGRAVE

Palgrave in the UK is an imprint of Macmillan Publishers Limited, registered in England, company number 785998, of 4 Crinan Street, London, N1 9XW.

Palgrave® and Macmillan® are registered trademarks in the United States, the United Kingdom, Europe and other countries.

ISBN 978–1–352–00204–1  paperback

This book is printed on paper suitable for recycling and made from fully managed and sustained forest sources. Logging, pulping and manufacturing processes are expected to conform to the environmental regulations of the country of origin.

A catalogue record for this book is available from the British Library.

A catalog record for this book is available from the Library of Congress.

*To Anthony and Tessa, a continuing source of inspiration*

# Contents

# Preface to the Second Edition

This book is written for university undergraduates in a wide range of disciplines within social sciences, sciences, engineering, arts and humanities. It will be valuable for students writing at university level for the first time as well as those in their final undergraduate year. It will also be useful for postgraduates on taught courses who have had little recent experience of academic writing. The book focuses on coursework assignments, but the principles of good writing apply to examination answers, so the lessons you learn from assignment writing can be used to help prepare for written examinations.

The book works on the principle that academic writing, like other forms of writing, needs to be tailored to its specific context – its purpose and audience. Nevertheless, there are general principles that apply to many kinds of academic writing. Using examples, reflections and self-study activities, the book takes you through the various aspects of academic writing one step at a time. It includes examples from a wide range of disciplines so that you should be able to find some that meet your disciplinary requirements, as well as others that give general principles that you can apply to your discipline.

You do not need to read through this book from beginning to end. Some of you will want to. Others will want to dip into it according to need. Whatever your preference, there are certain chapters and sections that are more vital than others. I suggest that you read Chapter 1 first, as it sets the scene for the rest of the book. All the other chapters assume that you are familiar with the content of the first chapter. Chapters are divided into numbered sections to assist you in navigating through the book.

Most of the book is written in a relaxed style as though I, the writer, am helping you, the reader, work step-by-step through various aspects of academic writing. The writing style is different from that of academic writing itself and is more like a conversation a tutor might have with you when discussing your writing. Although the style is quite casual, it is nevertheless rigorous. For example, I will use appropriate conventions for citing and referencing, so demonstrating the practice expected of you in academic writing. A summary of key points is given at the end of each chapter, along with a list of references cited in that chapter plus any suggested further reading and answers to self-study activities. A glossary of terms and a complete listing of references are given at the end of the book.

This second edition builds upon the first. While keeping most of the structure of the first edition, it has been updated and contains a wider range of examples and activities, including focusing more on creativity and criticality. It takes more account of those for whom English is a second language and those with distinct learning preferences. The second edition has a stronger visual emphasis.

Most of us learn best when we have to apply what we are learning to specific assignments or activities. So, I would expect many of you to read and reread some sections of the book. You may not fully grasp the meaning of certain concepts until you have tried to apply them more than once. You are at university to learn and learning does not happen overnight. This book is intended to help maximise your learning from each assignment you write. I hope you enjoy the journey.

Trevor Day
*December 2017*

# Acknowledgements

I wish to thank many people for helping to bring the first edition of the book to fruition. Students Charles Crawford, Sam Jolly and Tsz Kaai Lam kindly agreed to have their work adapted for educational purposes. The following colleagues read and commented on parts of the manuscript, provided examples, or through helpful discussions clarified and stimulated various directions of thought and practice that find expression in this book: Peter Bradley, Geoff Carr, Hazel Corradi, Matthew Day, Mary Deane, Christine Edmead, Suki Ekaratne, Julianna Féjer, Justin Hodds, Linda Humphreys, Julie Letchford, Geoff Murphy, Tom Rogers and James Wilson. Of course, I take full responsibility for the results of those interactions that appear in this book.

I would particularly like to thank the four scholarly peer reviewers (you know who you are but are anonymous to me) who provided invaluable feedback to fine-tune the first edition.

I also wish to warmly thank Gwen van der Velden, Kate Robinson and Tracey Stead at the University of Bath, Steve Cook and David Swinburne of the Royal Literary Fund, and colleagues at Aston University and Birmingham City University, who together have provided numerous opportunities for me to work with students and staff, the experience of which has informed the writing of this book.

I wish to express my appreciation to Suzannah Burywood who commissioned the book, and to others at Palgrave – Della Oliver, Jocelyn Stockley and Tina Graham – who brought their expertise to bear in creating the first edition.

For the second edition, which builds on the first, I have an additional set of people to acknowledge. Max Adams, Anna Barker, Heather Dyer, Katie Grant, Julia Hathaway, Christina Healey, Karen Ottewell and Anne Wilson have all been sources of inspiration and ideas, spurring me on to include creative activities and to more overtly cater for those from a wide range of backgrounds and learning preferences.

Thanks to the anonymous reviewers and to Helen Caunce, Rosemary Maher, Olivia Lynch, Amy Brownbridge, Margie DeWind and Vidya Venkiteshwaran who between them steered the second edition to fruition.

As ever, greatest thanks to my wife Christina who not only read the manuscripts but endured, or perhaps enjoyed, the many weekends when I was closeted away writing the first edition and the time taken away from vacations when I was penning the second.

The author would like to thank the following:

Facts On File, Inc. for permission to quote and adapt extracts from *Oceans*, Revised Edition, © 2008 by Trevor Day.

Taylor & Francis Group for permission to quote and adapt extracts from Trevor Day and Paul Tosey's 'Beyond SMART? A new framework for goal setting' from the *Curriculum Journal*, December 2011.

# The Nature and Process of Academic Writing

Whatever programme of study you are taking at university, at some point you will need to put words on paper or enter them in an electronic file. You might wish to make notes from a lecture you've attended, a book chapter you've read, a professional organisation's website you've visited, or an academic paper you've studied. And then there are the assignments you need to complete. These might be essays, practical reports, slide presentations, a review of an article, webpages you're designing – the list could be long.

Each kind of communication you create has its own particular cluster of features. It is written for a particular *audience* with a certain *purpose* in mind. For example, in a social sciences, humanities or arts discipline you might be asked to write an essay. In a science or engineering discipline, you might be required to submit a report on a laboratory investigation you'd just completed. In completing either writing task, you would need to follow certain conventions. There are likely to be certain rules to follow about *structure* (how the writing is organised around a beginning, a middle and an end). You will normally be expected to adopt a certain kind of *writing style*; such as how informal or formal the writing is, the viewpoint you are going to adopt, what level of knowledge is assumed for the reader of your writing, how citing and referencing will be used to underpin the argument in your writing, and so on. How you do these things, and more, is what this book is about.

### A note about style

The style in which I'm writing this book is not the style you're likely to use when completing assignments for your course. For one, it is quite a casual style. I use contractions such as 'I've' instead of 'I have' and 'you'll' instead of 'you will'. Also, I write as though I am talking directly to you, the reader. Much of the time I'm writing as though I'm actually sitting with you, talking you through a process. I use 'I', 'we' and 'you'. The use of contractions and direct style is not normally acceptable in academic writing. However, be aware that I am choosing to write in this manner as a means to help you write in a more academic manner, much as a tutor or lecturer might sit with you to discuss writing, and how you can write more effectively.

   Notice the difference between my writing style in guiding you through this book, and the academic and other styles of writing I'm encouraging you to use (and that you'll be expected to use on your course). Noticing these distinctions in structure and style will help you develop your writing overall. Doing so will be invaluable to you now, later in your course and in your future career.

## 1.1    Why is writing so important?

Of course, some people write because they gain a great deal of satisfaction from doing so. It is in their blood. They write to express themselves. Being a writer is a major part of their identity. It is how they express their creativity. Taking that into account, for you as a university student there are, in addition, at least five very good reasons for writing. They are probably so obvious that you've rarely, if ever, stopped to think about them. Robert Barrass, in his book *Students Must Write* (2007), lists four reasons. To me, those first four underpin an all-important fifth reason:

1  **Writing helps you to remember.** By taking notes – whether from a lecture, a video, a book, an article, or some other medium – you are keeping a record of that interaction. In doing so you are being selective about what you record. You are organising your thoughts around that experience. Keeping notes helps you to recall the experience. In fact, if we didn't take notes, which we can review afterwards, many of us would forget much of what we experienced. Fundamentally, therefore, note-taking is keeping a record. As we will see later, it is much more than that. Good notes are dynamic. They can be added to as our knowledge and understanding grows. But more of that when we turn to note-taking in Chapter 5.

2  **Writing helps you to observe and to gather evidence.** Whether observing what is happening during a laboratory experiment, at a tutorial meeting, or when watching a video programme, writing notes (perhaps accompanied by drawings) focuses our attention. It aids our concentration and provides a descriptive record of the event. The recording of observations – concisely but in detail – is key for gathering and analysing evidence in many disciplines, whether in science, engineering, social sciences, humanities or the arts.

3  **Writing helps you to think.** Writing is both an expression of your thinking and a vehicle for helping you think. When writing an essay or preparing a practical report you set down what you know. Doing so helps you identify gaps in your knowledge and encourages you to seek answers and deepen your understanding.

When you write and see your thoughts expressed 'outside of yourself', your relationship with those ideas shifts. You can reflect on what you have written and can evaluate its worth. In so doing, you shape, refine and clarify your ideas. They become transformed through reflection and rewriting.

4 **Writing helps you to communicate.** It is through writing that, in many cases, your academic progress is assessed, whether by coursework or in examinations. Writing, of course, is also the common medium by which academics report their research findings and opinions to the world. And writing may not be the final form of that communication. It could be a stepping stone to another medium of communication, such as a talk, a speech, a video clip streamed on a website, a radio play or a television documentary.

5 **Above all, writing helps you to learn.** Taking all the above points together, writing is a powerful device for helping you to learn. Writing is a key way in which you reveal your knowledge and understanding to yourself, as well as to others. It is a vital ingredient in your learning, both as a process and as a product. Writing is clearly a key part of your educational process. Without writing, most of us would not reach the depth and clarity of thinking required in our discipline. And it is through writing that we reveal some of our thinking to the scrutiny of others. By showing our work to others, gaining feedback and reflecting on it, our thinking and writing develop. Writing can be transformative, changing the way we interpret our world.

Added to these five, of course, is the value of writing for other aspects of your life. Writing is a uniquely powerful, precise and satisfying form of expression. It is also a vital skill for future employment. In the UK, university graduates' writing ability (or lack of it) is a recurrent press story (for example, Paton, 2014). In the latest UK Confederation of British Industry's survey of employers, the Education and Skills Survey 2016 (CBI, 2016), more employers were concerned about graduates' literacy and communication skills than they were with their numeracy. Writing ability is a key concern for employers, and so it should be for you.

Writing for academic purposes, and shaping your communication to match your specific purpose and audience, will stand you in good stead for other kinds of writing. Universities are increasingly aware of the need to cultivate graduates with skills of value to a range of employers, not just those in a specific discipline. With this in mind, some course assignments are likely to require you to write for non-academic audiences.

Most of us have become used to writing from an early age. It is therefore easy for us to take it for granted. Much of the writing we do, we carry out almost automatically, without much thought. If English is not your first language, forming phrases, sentences and paragraphs may require more thought. But over time, drafting flowing text (prose) will become more and more an automatic process.

It is helpful to take stock of the writing you already do. For example, you might text and email your friends every day, and you might have a blog or a Twitter account. These various kinds of communication in technological media each have their own conventions. On Twitter, of course, you are currently limited to 280 characters, and abbreviations are almost essential in getting your message across.

For your study programme the kinds of writing you will be asked to do are usually much more formal. You might be asked to write practical reports, literature reviews, essays, and so on, each according to certain conventions. So, it is likely that you're already involved in writing in a wide range of styles, from casual to formal. Take a moment to think about the range of writing you already do.

---

**ACTIVITY 1.1**

### The writing you already do

Jot down the kinds of writing you do (not all of which might be in English):

- For day-to-day communication with other students
- For academic staff
- For administrative and other university staff
- For wider communication within your university
- For wider communication outside your university (this could be study-related or not)
- For yourself (for example, writing a diary, personal log, short stories or poetry)

---

Making an inventory like this of the kinds of writing you do shows that you are already writing for a wide range of audiences (readerships) and purposes. In other words, you already have a wide range (repertoire) in your writing. This is a strong foundation on which to build.

## 1.2   The nature of academic writing

A major challenge for many students is to write assignments in an appropriate *academic style*, with a suitable *structure*, that develops an *argument* in an appropriate way. As we shall see later, there is no single kind of academic writing. Unless you are taking a generic, introductory writing course, writing academically usually has a specific disciplinary context. Almost invariably you are writing for a particular audience within a certain discipline and with a specific purpose in mind.

### Features of writing that assessors value

Given that academic writing is about developing your learning, and evaluating your learning, the assessors of your academic writing are normally looking for some or all of the following features in your writing:

- That you reveal your *knowledge* and *understanding* of the subject.
- That you show that your work is *original* in the sense that you are not simply copying word for word from someone else. You are crafting your own account.
- That you are following the *conventions* of your discipline, such as document structure, writing style and viewpoint.
- That you are using *scholarly method*. Your account must show accuracy and skill in investigating and discussing its subject. This usually means that you reveal the sources of information you are using by *citing* (referring to sources in the text) and *referencing* (listing full entries for your sources, typically at the end of your document). You are usually expected to show evidence of *critical analysis*, which includes considering the strengths and weaknesses of an argument and coming to your own conclusions about it.

Conventionally, most essays have a structure with a clear beginning (introduction), main body (development of an overall argument) and end (conclusion). This is based on the traditional notion of a lecture, which itself dates back to the conventions of the political debating chambers of ancient Greece and Rome: tell the audience what you're going to talk about, talk about it, and then tell them what you've talked about.

## Tailoring writing to a specific discipline

In reading an essay, what your assessors are looking for to some extent reflects the culture of the discipline. A science lecturer is likely to have different expectations, and use different assessment criteria, compared with a history lecturer.

### Thesis statement or not?

Imagine you are writing an essay in humanities or in a social science. That being the case, your lecturer or tutor might ask you to express a clear opinion about the topic in your assignment. She or he might ask that you make this apparent in the introduction by making a thesis statement.

Commonly, a *thesis statement* is taken to be a sentence or two at or near the end of an assignment's introduction that summarises a student's argument and their point of view on the topic they are considering. For example, consider an essay assignment in Economics or Marketing entitled 'By reference to one or two large companies, and drawing upon appropriate economic or marketing theories, discuss strategies for making best use of the online environment in a business context.' A student might respond with an assignment that includes this thesis statement in its introduction: 'Given that the world wide web offers large companies huge potential for marketing and promotion, businesses should make best use of it. They can do so by taking every opportunity to target their advertising to specific potential customers while at the same time offering strong support online to existing customers.'

- Being asked to include a thesis statement can make for 'stronger' writing, insofar as you are writing to defend your *thesis* (argument). In doing so, you still need to consider both sides of the argument – evidence and reasoning both for and against the position you have chosen to take.
- Be aware, however, that in some disciplines the use of a thesis statement is not encouraged. Instead, in writing your essay it is expected that you allow the evidence and reasoning in support of your overall argument to unfold gradually. You are not expected to give away your conclusion at the beginning. This second approach – not having a thesis statement – is common in scientific and engineering disciplines.

### Personal or impersonal?

Imagine you are writing a practical report for a scientific discipline. The report is likely to have a structure indicated by sections such as: Introduction, Methods, Results, Discussion and Conclusion(s). Commonly, scientific reports are written in a formal, objective style, in which the person carrying out the investigation is not mentioned, but actions are referred to in the impersonal, for example: 'An investigation was carried out ...' rather than 'We investigated ...' or 'I investigated ...'.

In many university programmes, students go out on work placement at some point in their course. When they do so, they are often required to write a reflective report about their experience of the placement. In doing so they are usually encouraged to write a more personal account, using the 'I' form to discuss their experiences, for example, 'In the second month of the placement I encountered a problem with ...'. Clearly, different kinds of academic writing have distinct conventions. Nevertheless, there are generalisations we can make about what many kinds of academic writing have in common.

## Some common features of academic writing

The following features apply to many kinds of academic writing:

- It is usually written for a narrow range of purposes, to develop or assess learning.
- Depending on its purpose, academic writing has particular requirements in terms of structure, organisation and presentation.
- It usually presents a structured argument overall, supported by secondary arguments.
- Arguments are built up from evidence and reasoning, either your own or from what you have read, heard or observed.
- Academic writing adopts an appropriate writing style, usually in formal written English.
- It follows the conventions of a particular discipline, using appropriate technical vocabulary and agreed principles for citing and referencing.

We will now consider some of these features.

## Academic writing as argument

I have used the word 'argument' several times already. I find it helpful to keep in mind that academic writing is almost always about argument. This moves you beyond writing description – recalling a theory or fact, for example. Description is important, but usually it is a starting point to building an argument, or part of an argument. Thinking of your writing as argument encourages you to weave facts, ideas or opinions into a reasoned overall account. Lecturers, tutors and other assessors of your work are often keen that your writing goes beyond mere description, to critical analysis.

As a starting point, I regard an argument as essentially:

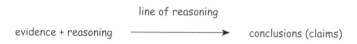

line of reasoning

evidence + reasoning    ——————————→    conclusions (claims)

What different disciplines regard as suitable evidence and reasoning can vary, and different assignments within the same discipline might require different forms of evidence. For example, on a psychology course, an individual's own experience of being a pupil at school might be appropriate evidence to include in an essay about models of behavioural psychology applied to classroom practice. Another assessor, setting a psychology literature review in which there is an emphasis on quantitative research (analysis of numerical data), might not regard personal experience as suitable evidence.

You can recognise an overall argument in a piece of writing because it has the following features:

- The author gives *evidence* and *reasoning*, assembled as *reasons* (sometimes called supporting arguments, premises or propositions) that support the eventual conclusion. For example, in responding to an essay title 'Is it never too late to learn?' one of the supporting arguments might include the statement 'In the last 15 years, government schemes have helped millions of UK senior citizens (here, defined as males and females over 60) to learn to use computers and access the World Wide Web.'
- Reasons are presented in a logical order, an overall *line of reasoning*, which takes the reader convincingly through to the conclusion. For example, by compiling evidence for improvements in literacy, numeracy, health and wellbeing among over 50s who have engaged in government-backed educational initiatives.
- There is a *conclusion* – the position that the author wants the reader to accept. For example, 'The evidence presented suggests that, within certain limitations, it is rarely too late to learn.'

In short, an academic argument contains evidence and reasoning that guide the reader, through an overall line of reasoning, towards a conclusion.

## Which of these is an argument?

By the criteria used above, which of the three items (a)–(c) below is an academic argument, and which is not?

(a) *The main active chemicals in the* Cannabis sativa *plant are two forms of tetrahydrocannabinol (THC) and cannabidiol (CBD), collectively called cannabinoids. A ten-year follow up study of recreational cannabis users, reporting in the* British Medical Journal *in 2011, showed a doubling in the risk of psychosis among cannabis users compared with a control sample. Previous studies suggest that there is great variation in individual susceptibility to onset of psychosis on exposure to cannabinoids. Pre-clinical studies show promise for THC and CBD, on their own or in combination with other medicinal drugs, in halting or at least slowing the growth of specific cancerous tumours in brain or lung tissue. Further pre-clinical testing, and if successful, then clinical testing, is required to establish the value of cannabinoids as anti-cancer agents. Even if their use is indicated, their psycho-active effects need to be considered carefully, and ways found for countering or minimising them. By that time, genetic screening may have determined which patients are likely to be most susceptible to cannabinoids' negative psychoactive effects. Public attitudes to recreational cannabis use, or use of cannabis extracts in a clinical context, are very mixed. However, any public concerns about clinical use may be dwarfed by the potential for cannabinoids to treat aggressive cancers.*

(b) *Medicinal drugs can trigger an allergic reaction – an abnormal response from the body's immune system that can range from mild to life-threatening. The signs and symptoms of drug-induced allergic reactions include wheezing, swelling, an itchy rash, and nausea or diarrhoea. In the worst cases, so-called anaphylactic shock, sometimes brought about by extreme sensitivity to antibiotics such as penicillin, the person's airways narrow dangerously and their blood pressure drops dramatically. If not treated rapidly, normally by injection of adrenaline (epinephrine), the person can die within minutes.*

(c) *Complementary therapies are seen by many people as a valid supplement or alternative to conventional forms of medical treatment provided by doctors. Complementary therapies such as reflexology, homeopathy and chiropractic are provided by trained practitioners, with many patients claiming that they gain great benefit. There is plenty of anecdotal evidence in support of complementary therapies but I have yet to be persuaded by it.*

Is it an argument?

(a) yes/no
(b) yes/no
(c) yes/no

*Check your answers at the end of the chapter.*

## Being critical

In the higher education traditions of developed Western nations, criticism is encouraged. Being critical involves evaluating what you read; in other words, making judgements about how relevant and important it is in relation to your task. Being critical does not just involve being negative about what you have read. It involves weighing up both sides – the pluses and minuses – of what you have read, seen or heard, and then drawing your own conclusion as to its value in relation to your assignment, or to your learning overall.

The best of Western academic traditions encourage you to think for yourself. In such traditions, if your reasoning is flawed or weak this should be noticed by your assessors, and perhaps by other students, who will help guide you in more fruitful directions.

By thinking for yourself, and helped by others' questioning, you are encouraged to develop higher-level skills, including:

- **Analysing.** Reading the work of others and breaking down their arguments into component parts in order to better understand them.
- **Synthesising.** Building your own arguments, drawing upon the work of others.
- **Applying.** Taking facts or ideas and using them in another context, such as a practical, real-world one.
- **Evaluating.** Judging the validity of elements of an argument, whether your own or those of others.

### Being critical, from start to finish

As we shall see, although there are times when you want to put your 'critical mind' on hold and encourage creativity, being critical applies to many stages in completing an assignment. You will want to think critically about how you interpret an assignment, how you begin to devise your response and what materials you need to read. You then need to think critically about the material you are reading, and decide which is strong and relevant and which is weak and irrelevant. As you write the text for your assignment, you will need to check that your writing is building a strong case. Finally, you will need to check that your submitted assignment is written to a high standard, with attention to detail – both in its text and its visual appearance. Being critical is a frame of mind you need to come back to again and again.

## Being formal

I am writing this book, for the most part, in a reasonably casual style. The writing you are asked to do in your assignments is usually much more formal. It normally needs to meet these requirements:

- Employing words that have *precise meaning*; for example, 'analyse' rather than 'think about'.
- *Avoiding jargon or colloquial English*. For example, instead of writing 'ideas were knocked about' or 'everyone pitched in with their ideas', you might write 'ideas were discussed and considered'.
- *Not using contractions*. Instead of 'can't' and 'doesn't', write 'cannot' and 'does not'.
- On many occasions one avoids writing in the personal (for example, 'you', 'I' or 'we'). Instead, the *impersonal* is often encouraged by assessors, such as, 'The analysis was carried out' rather than 'We carried out the analysis'. The use of the impersonal is linked to the use of the *passive voice*, something to which we will return in Chapter 3.
- Academic writing usually *avoids using direct or rhetorical questions*; for example, 'Was the solution to the problem within the hands of the protesters?'

### TIP

### Formal, with clarity

Writing formally does not mean that you cannot write clearly. Aim for formality *and* readability.

## Using words with precision

Academic writing often goes beyond description. It usually involves being critical and making judgements about the worth of sources of information that are used in writing an assignment. In academic writing, words tend to be used with greater precision than in everyday writing.

Here, for example, I have chosen a range of verbs (doing words) that might be used in an assignment brief or in an examination question. Each verb has a specific meaning.

**ACTIVITY 1.3**

## Words and precise meanings

Match the following verbs with their meanings. Draw a line between the verb on the left and its best meaning from the list on the right.

| Verb | Meaning |
|------|---------|
| 1 Compare | A. Make clear the meaning of something. This might include giving a personal judgement. |
| 2 Contrast | B. Set two views in opposition in order to highlight the differences between them. |
| 3 Evaluate | C. Give an overview of the general principles and/or main features of a subject, omitting fine detail. |
| 4 Interpret | D. Give reasons for decisions or conclusions reached, which might include responding to possible objections. |
| 5 Justify | E. Assess the value of something, which might include offering a personal opinion. |
| 6 Outline | F. Point out similarities and differences between two or more views. This might involve coming to a conclusion as to the preferred view. |

*Check your answers at the end of the chapter.*

During a lecture, a member of staff might use the phrase 'Now, let's look at ...' to mean 'Now let us consider ...' rather than 'Now let us observe ...'. Using 'look at' (when it does not mean 'observe') is perfectly acceptable in speech. In academic writing, however, the use of the phrase 'look at' can be replaced by more specific verbs that are more precise in their meaning.

**ACTIVITY 1.4**

## Avoiding 'look at'

Without using the words from Activity 1.3, write down six verbs that could replace the term 'look at', but not in the sense of 'to observe'.

Imagine you are writing the first sentence in part of a report. You've started writing. 'This sections looks at ...' You could replace 'looks at' with 'considers', as in 'This section considers ...'. Think of six other verbs you could use in place of 'looks at'.

*Compare your answers with those at the end of the chapter.*

## 1.3    The process of writing

Different people write in different ways. For example, Creme and Lea (2008) describe four kinds of writer. The 'diver' likes to plunge into writing part of an assignment as soon as possible. The 'patchwork writer' likes to plan, and starts writing sections of an assignment at an early stage, and might then move those sections and their contents around within the written assignment. The 'grand plan writer' likes to do plenty of research and thinking before committing to writing. They seem to hold the structure of the assignment in their head, and commit little to writing until they are ready to write the whole assignment. The 'architect writer' prefers to build a visual structure for their assignment, perhaps a mind map or spider diagram, a flow chart, or a concept map (Chapter 5). They then organise their research and writing around this visual structure.

Not everyone falls into one of these four categories of writer. In fact, a person might be a blend of more than one category or, for example, might behave like a 'diver' for short assignments but be more like an 'architect writer' for longer ones. Even if you don't fall neatly into one or more of these categories, you no doubt have preferences; for example, whether you like to make very detailed plans or like to start writing as soon as possible.

ACTIVITY 1.5

### What kind of academic writer are you?

Which kind of writer (diver, patchwork, grand plan or architect), on balance, do you most closely resemble?

Not only are there different kinds of writer, but the same individual typically writes in different ways depending on the nature of the writing task. If you were to write a casual email to a friend your writing process would almost certainly be very different from the one you'd use when writing a practical report or an essay.

ACTIVITY 1.6

### Different assignments, different approaches

Do you find you behave differently depending on the kind of assignment you are writing? If so, how?

(a) Write down two different kinds of assignment you need to complete for your coursework. Examples you might include are: an essay, a practical report, a review of an academic paper, a reflective account of your experience on a work placement.
(b) Is the way you organise your writing similar for both assignments? If not, in what way(s) is it different?

Despite there being differences between people in the way they like to write, and differences in the way an individual likes to write depending on the task, there are nevertheless recognisable stages in the academic writing process, which I've summarised in Figure 1.1.

| Planning, researching, reading and note-taking | Composing (drafting) | Reviewing and editing |
|---|---|---|
| (everything you do before you actually start writing flowing prose) | (writing flowing prose in sentences and paragraphs) | (evaluating, rethinking, and revising what you have written) |

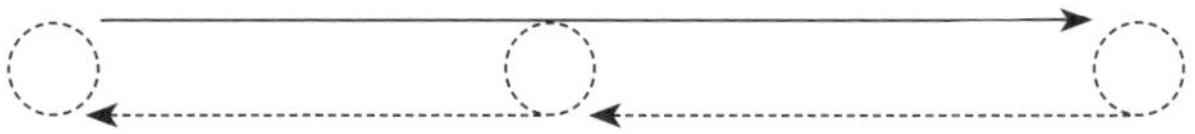

Figure 1.1 **Stages in an academic writing process**

The writing process flows from left to right, but it is not one-way. It is an *iterative* process (stages may be repeated, so that the writing becomes refined through gradual improvement). For example, after a student has planned her essay, and started composing it, she might find that there are gaps in her argument. She may discover this as she composes, or only after she reviews her work after composing. In either case, she will find herself going back to the research stage to gather more information. This is not uncommon. If we remember that writing is a creative process, which develops our thinking, we may only discover gaps in our argument when we start to compose, or when we review our work. That is fine. But we do need to leave ourselves enough time to react to such events, which is why planning our writing is so important. But before that, we need to be sure that we have understood, as best we can, the task we are about to undertake.

## Understanding the task

In a book like this I cannot cover every eventuality, or every writing task you might carry out. But what I can do is help you to ask appropriate questions, so that you can discover for yourself what you need to do to complete a task.

To be sure that you are fulfilling the requirements for a writing task, some of the key items you need to know are the *purpose, scope* and *audience* (readership) for your task. 'Purpose' concerns why you have been given the task. Normally the purpose is framed as one or more learning objectives or learning outcomes (what you are expected to learn or develop, and show evidence of, as a result of completing the task). 'Scope' concerns the detail and breadth of the task. Usually, the assumed reader is your assignment assessor.

Consider a task that has been set late in the first year of an undergraduate Psychology course:

Listen to the three examples of popular song provided and analyse their lyrics in terms of motivational theory. To what extent does each song reflect examples of intrinsic or extrinsic motivation?

The assignment contributes to your ability to: describe and apply motivational theory to everyday contexts; demonstrate your awareness of the significance of motivational theory in relation to contemporary Western society; recognise how cultural context favours or discourages different types of motivation. Your analysis should extend to 1,000 words.

The scope of the task has been made clear in both paragraphs of the assignment description. The purpose of setting the assignment has been given in the second paragraph (and the assessment criteria for the assignment should reflect this). The assumed qualities of the reader of the assignment have not been stated, and the student might need to ask their assessor to clarify who such a person might be. Usually the reader is taken to be at a similar level of experience to the student's own. This means that basic knowledge is assumed, but ideas and terminology that are specific to the assignment may need to be defined and explained. A student might need to check with their assessor what knowledge they should assume on the part of their reader.

To give another example, Narduzzo and Day (2012) describe a Physics lecturer early in the first year of an undergraduate programme setting his students a 200–250-word assignment on a science topic that interests them. He directs them to read certain kinds of publication (such as *New Scientist*, *Scientific American* and *Physics World*) and asks them to write a *clear* and *effective* explanation of the chosen topic. Examples of topics students had chosen included Schrödinger's Cat, Heisenberg's Uncertainty Principle, and hydrogen fusion. To meet the assignment's criteria, students need to include a figure (image) in their account and at least one equation or symbolic expression (using mathematical or chemical notation). They also need to cite and reference 3–5 sources of information they have used. The assumed reader of their work is another student in their year. In other words, they have to write the assignment in a manner that another student in their year would understand.

Taking the information above, the scope of the assignment and the nature of the reader have been outlined. But the purpose of the assignment is not clearly stated in terms of learning objectives or outcomes (although the students are given the assessment criteria for the assignment). If I were a student given such an assignment, some key questions I would want to be able to answer in my own mind would be:

- Why has the lecturer set this assignment? What exactly is he looking for?
- How do I know if what I have written is *clear* and *effective*?
- How do I include mathematical expressions within my text?

- In the text how do I refer to a figure?
- How should I cite my sources and list my references?

If I were completing this assignment, I would also want to choose a topic that I was genuinely curious about, and that I wanted to know more about myself. Motivational theory (for example, Ryan and Deci, 2000) suggests that we are likely to find it easier, and perform better, if we take on a task that is intrinsically motivating (engaging in it because it is inherently interesting or enjoyable).

## Planning and completing the task

For a piece of academic work, most of us plan the work before we write it. This planning might involve both scheduling the *overall process* (such as the time to be given to each part of the writing process) as well as outlining the *structure* of the document we are going to write.

For example, imagine a student is being asked to write an essay responding to the question 'With reference to three examples, how can the benefits of river dams be maximised and their negative impacts minimised?' It is near the end of the first year of a Human Geography degree programme and she has attended relevant lectures, and a tutorial session with several students and her personal tutor during which the assignment was discussed. She has also been given an initial reading list of three books as background reading for the assignment. Knowing that she has three weeks to write the 2,000-word essay, and that she has many other tasks to do, she might schedule the writing of the assignment as in Figure 1.2 (technically called a Gantt chart – a means of displaying parallel activities through time).

| | Wk 1 | Wk 2 | Wk 3 |
|---|---|---|---|
| Planning | | | |
| Literature searching, reading & note-taking | | | |
| Composing | | | |
| Reviewing & editing | | | |
| Final checks | | | |
| Submission | | | |

Figure 1.2  **A schedule for writing a 2,000-word essay: 'With reference to three examples, how can the benefits of river dams be maximised and their negative impacts minimised?'**

Firstly, notice that the different stages of the overall process overlap in time. This makes sense. Planning the structure of the essay, for example, is likely to be influenced by the information the student discovers during the literature searching and reading phase. The plan suggests that this student is not a 'diver'. She is not plunging into composing but is holding back until she has done much of her research and reading. Notice too that she plans to review and edit during the composing phase. In other words, parts of the work are to be checked and improved while other parts of the essay have yet to be completed. Again, this makes good sense and is also the way that many professional writers work.

Notice, too, that in the student's plan she is being realistic about finishing the main research phase more than a week before the assignment is due in, and that she will start composing more than a week before the deadline. She aims to finish writing a near-final version 1–2 days before the deadline, so that she has time to make final checks.

---

**TIP**

### Give yourself enough time

Many students do not leave themselves enough time to do final checks on their work. This includes making sure that they've kept to the word limit of the assignment, have cited and referenced correctly, have checked spelling, grammar and punctuation, and above all, that they've met the brief for the assignment. Completing these final checks can make all the difference between a pass and a fail, and can often improve final marks by 5–15% compared with what is achieved without this careful checking.

---

As for planning a structure for the assignment, doing this goes hand in hand with literature searching, reading and note-taking. After early research, the student might make a plan, either as headings and lists or bullet points (Figure 1.3a), or as a mind map or similar (Figure 1.3b).

One of the essay structure outlines in Figure 1.3 is a starting point. Once the student has carried out further research she will probably fill in more detail (such as which examples of dams to use) and might want to revise the plan, fine-tuning the content. As we shall see in Chapter 3, some students plan the essay in some detail, paragraph by paragraph, once they have finished the bulk of the research phase.

## Literature searching, reading and note-taking

As the student writing the human geography essay is at an early stage in her degree programme, she has been given guidance about books to read and key papers to view, and she has attended relevant lectures and a tutorial. It is rarely too early to reveal curiosity and independence of mind and so she may decide to

(a)

With reference to three examples, how can the benefits of river dams be maximised and their negative impacts minimised? (target 2,000 words)

Introduction:
Importance of topic for wildlife, and human health and wellbeing. Key measures e.g. socio-economic value, biodiversity, ecosystem services. Rationale behind choice of examples e.g. variety, and those for which good data are available. Aim and structure of the essay. (200 words)

Benefits of dams:
Examples from North America. Overview of benefits e.g. flood control; agricultural, industrial and domestic water supplies; power generation; leisure industry; wildlife; fisheries. (500 words)

Negative impacts of dams:
Examples from North America. Effects on migratory aquatic species, wetlands, river topography, irrigation, leisure industry and fisheries. (500 words)

Maximising the benefit and minimising the harm:
High-quality baseline data often lacking. Complex effects of changes in water flow regime. Effects on sedimentation, chemical transformation, water storage, temperature regime and biological dispersal. Environmental impact assessment before siting a dam. Possible mitigation of negative impacts e.g. alter flow regimes. (600 words)

Conclusion:
Drawing upon conclusions from the different sections, the need for better data and action at different time- and geographic-scales. Better scientific knowledge and understanding. Workable water management and policy frameworks. Public awareness-raising. Putting the pieces in place, from local to regional (national and international?). (200 words)

Total: 2,000 words

(b)

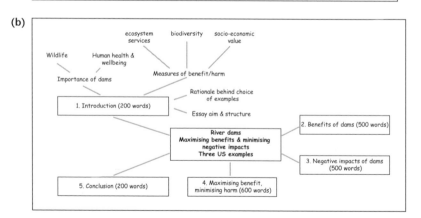

Figure 1.3   An early outline for the structure of the essay 'With reference to three examples, how can the benefits of river dams be maximised and their negative impacts minimised?': (a) using headings; (b) as a simple mind map (only Introduction shown in detail)

read further and delve deeper rather than just restricting herself to the material she has been given or the sources to which she has been directed. Those sources can provide leads to further sources, such as in the reference list at the back of a book or an article. Using web search engines such as Google Scholar or literature databases such as Web of Science, the student can discover more recent articles that have referred to earlier key papers (see Chapter 4).

It is helpful to read with a clear purpose in mind when studying an article, book chapter or reputable website. That way you read strategically, hunting for what you need to complete the task. This is an efficient and flexible approach. It works on the well-established principle that reading a piece of work two or three times, with specific purpose(s) in mind, takes about the same time and is usually much more effective than reading through a source document slowly from beginning to end only once (see Chapter 5).

As for note-taking, this is determined by your purpose in reading your source and your personal preferences. I take relatively few notes from a source article but annotate it with highlighting, underlining, and questions or comments in the margins. I normally do this on a printed copy of the article but you could do so on an electronic copy using appropriate software, such as Adobe Acrobat Professional. Many of the notes I take are comparisons between one source and another, sometimes entered into a table.

Whatever means of note-taking you choose, your plan for an essay often evolves as you learn and understand more about the topic you're writing about. When literature searching, reading and note-taking, it is important to keep referring back to the purpose of your assignment, so that you don't lose focus and waste time in gathering irrelevant information.

## Composing

No matter how elegant your assignment plan, how extensive your reading or how detailed your notes, there comes a time when you have to start composing your assignment. This is the process of writing flowing prose in sentences and paragraphs (see Chapter 7). Having interviewed many academics, professional writers and successful students about their writing processes, I'm aware that there is much we have in common. Most of us do plenty of planning, research and, above all, thinking, but when it comes to composing we give ourselves permission to 'go for it'. What this means in practice is not being too self-critical when writing the first draft. Treat writing the first draft as 'getting your ideas down'.

There is good reason for not spending much time in writing this first draft. Painstakingly writing the first draft, line by line, scrutinising each sentence you write before moving on to the next, means that you may have invested a great deal of time. Having invested so much time at an early stage you will be less likely to revise what you have written. But revising it may be just what you need to do. There are various stages in the revision process, and the first often involves quite substantial changes, such as moving or rearranging whole paragraphs. The more time spent in writing the first draft, the less likely you are to invest time in substantially changing what you have written. But it is through redrafting that many of us come to write with clarity and precision. For most of us, writing with power comes through crafting our writing through several processes of revision (reviewing and editing). If too much time is invested in writing the first draft, and trying to perfect what we have written at an early stage, we are likely to be reluctant to make major changes to the argument and structure of our work; but doing so may be what is needed most.

## They do it differently in English

If you have learnt to write academically in another language you will find that conventions in UK academic English are likely to be different to those with which you are familiar. For example, according to Karen Ottewell in the Language Centre at the University of Cambridge, and others who focus on working with international students, academic English has these characteristics amongst others:

It is **reader-friendly**. It is the responsibility of the writer to make their meaning clear to the reader. In some languages, this is not the case and the reader has to work hard at extracting meaning.

**Context is explained rather than assumed.** In some languages, much is assumed about the context of an academic communication. In UK academic English, context is often made explicit, e.g. in an essay, the breadth and depth of what is to follow is made clear near the beginning of the document.

**Argument is developed cumulatively, in a logical and straightforward manner.** Some languages do not develop an argument in a direct way, but have digressions before returning to the main theme of an argument. Writing in academic English is usually more straightforward. Old information often comes before new and simple before complex. One paragraph builds on another.

**The writing style is concise and direct.** Some languages do not express themselves in a direct manner, but the language is more poetic and philosophical. Some UK academics would describe this style of writing as 'flowery' and with too much 'padding' – unnecessary words. In most academic disciplines, most of the time, those who mark assignments are interested in students 'getting to the point'. Writing in a concise and direct manner means fewer words. It does not mean that the writing is any easier.

Writing text that is reader-friendly, where the context is explained, that develops an argument cumulatively, and that is concise and direct, is what many forms of English academic writing aspire to be.

## Reviewing and editing

Thirty or so years ago, small desktop computers had barely been conceived. Students who typed their assignments used typewriters and had little opportunity to correct their work, other than retyping whole pages or making corrections on the line they had just typed. You have the opportunity to use word-processing software, which enables you to quickly and easily change what you have written. You should make good use of the opportunities your software provides to revise your work.

In publishing, it is common to consider the process of revising what has been written in three stages: developmental editing, copy-editing and proofreading. *Developmental editing* involves moving whole chunks of text around, such as changing the order of paragraphs in your account, rearranging the order of sentences in a paragraph, and substantially rewriting sentences. Significant amounts of material may be added or removed – whole paragraphs, tables, figures, citations and references. Developmental editing is most likely to happen just after you've written the first draft, or part of the first draft, but it can occur at later stages as well.

Developmental editing – to create a complete, cohesive account and powerful argument overall – is often key to effective writing. A key question at this stage should be 'Are you meeting the assignment guidelines (brief)?'

*Copy-editing* involves fine-tuning the sentences in your paragraphs. This includes checking grammar, punctuation and spelling and improving the readability of your text and the strengths of your argument. In your text, have you removed unwanted repetition and unnecessary words? It is an opportunity to check that you have included appropriate sections, subsections, tables and figures. Are the citations and references accurate and do they support your argument? Have you checked that any facts and assertions are correct?

*Proofreading* – these are the final checks to ensure that all is present and correct. This stage focuses on completeness, consistency and fine-scale correctness. Are the sections and subsections, citations and references, figures and tables, complete and consistent? Is the layout and presentation correct? And a final check: Have you met the assignment guidelines?

## Knowing when to stop

A significant proportion of students find it difficult to 'move on' from one stage of the writing process to the next. Some keep researching and reading, wishing to get to the bottom of the topic. In some cases, they might have been delaying composing. About half the undergraduate and postgraduate students I've asked regard composing as the most challenging part of the writing process.

Some students find it difficult to 'let go' of their writing and hand it in, because they don't feel it is good enough. Many students who become the most accomplished writers suffer from feelings of not having done enough or not feeling happy about what they're handing in. However, you do have to hand in your work on time and meet the guidelines (the brief) set for it. The more you are aware of the different stages in the writing process – planning, researching and reading, composing, reviewing and editing – the more likely you are to manage the overall process effectively. That means completing the different stages so that you can be more or less satisfied with your work and finish it in time.

## 1.4    Playing to your strengths and preferences

I've put forward various ideas and suggestions in this chapter about both the nature of academic writing and the process of creating it. Although these suggestions are based on more than a decade of research and coaching in writing development, and drawing upon the practices of many other academics involved in writing development, I am also acutely aware that each person reading this book is different. English may not be your first language. You may have unusual learning preferences. You are different because of your unique gifts, your specific social, cultural and educational background, and because the context in which you are writing is discipline-based. One of the key messages I hope you have gained from this first chapter is that, although there are generalisations we can make about the nature and process of academic writing, it is uniquely expressed because of your nature as an individual and the context in which you find yourself. We will explore this more in the chapters that follow.

## 1.5    In conclusion: the process of academic writing

Academic writing begins with *understanding the nature of the task* you have to undertake. Your writing assignment is normally set within a discipline that has certain conventions for the writing you are expected to do. This, in turn, shapes the *research* you carry out, the *reading* you do, and the *writing style* and *document structure* you will fashion. Writing an assignment usually involves *planning* the structure of the assignment you are going to submit, in order to *build an argument*. Planning shapes the act of *composing* (writing flowing sentences). Writing is normally done in stages, with text gradually being improved through *reviewing* and *editing*. Ultimately, the text and its presentation are *polished* to create the final version.

**Key points in the chapter**

1 Different kinds of academic writing have their own features, including specific forms of structure and style.

2 Writing is important in study because it helps you to: remember; observe and gather evidence; think; communicate; and above all, learn. Through writing, you also develop key skills that enhance your employability.

3 Academic writing has certain features that apply generally but that also need to be tailored to your specific discipline. Features of academic writing include: the use of argument; being critical; being formal; and using words with precision.

4 Different people write in different ways and the same person may write in different ways depending on the nature of the task.

5 The process of academic writing normally involves: planning, researching, reading and note-taking; composing (drafting); and reviewing and editing.

## Cited references

Barrass, R. (2007). *Students Must Write*. 3rd edn. London: Routledge.

CBI (2016). *The Right Combination. Education and Skills Survey 2016*. London: Confederation of British Industry/Pearson. Available from: www.cbi.org.uk/cbi-prod/assets/File/pdf/cbi-education-and-skills-survey2016.pdf [accessed 2 August 2017].

Creme, P. and Lea, M. R. (2008). *Writing at University: A Guide for Students*. 3rd edn. Maidenhead: Open University Press.

Narduzzo, A. and Day, T. (2012). 'Less is More in Physics: A Small-scale Writing in the Disciplines (WiD) Intervention'. *Journal of Learning Development in Higher Education*, 4, Case Study 5.

Paton, G. (2014). 'OECD: UK Graduates "Lacking High-Level Literacy Skills"'. *Telegraph newspaper*, 9 September 2014. Available from: www.telegraph.co.uk/education/educationnews/11082842/OECD-UK-graduates-lacking-high-level-literacy-skills.html [accessed 2 August 2017].

Ryan, R. M. and Deci, E. L. (2000). 'Intrinsic and Extrinsic Motivations: Classic Definitions and New Directions'. *Contemporary Educational Psychology*, 25, pp. 54–67.

### Further reading

Elbow, P. (1998). *Writing with Power: Techniques for Mastering the Writing Process*. New edition. Oxford: Oxford University Press.

Zinsser, W. (2006). *On Writing Well: The Classic Guide to Writing Non-Fiction*. 30th anniversary edition. New York: Harper Perennial.

Zinsser, W. (2009). 'Writing English as a Second Language.' *American Scholar*, Winter 2010. Available from: https://theamericanscholar.org/writing-english-as-a-second-language [accessed 8 August 2017].

# Answers for Chapter 1

## Activity 1.2: Which of these is an argument?

(a) Yes, this is an argument. The writer has sought to use evidence and reasoning, and careful wording, to shape an argument that leads to a conclusion.

(b) No, this is not an argument. It is essentially a description or statement of fact.

(c) No, this is not an argument. It is a description, followed by the expression of an opinion.

## Activity 1.3: Words and precise meanings

| Verb | Meaning |
| --- | --- |
| 1 Compare | F. Point out similarities and differences between two or more views. This might involve coming to a conclusion as to the preferred view. |
| 2 Contrast | B. Set two views in opposition in order to highlight the differences between them. |
| 3 Evaluate | E. Assess the value of something, which might include offering a personal opinion. |
| 4 Interpret | A. Make clear the meaning of something. This might include giving a personal judgement. |
| 5 Justify | D. Give reasons for decisions or conclusions reached, which might include responding to possible objections. |
| 6 Outline | C. Give an overview of the general principles and/or main features of a subject, omitting fine detail. |

## Activity 1.4: Avoiding 'look at'

Possible answers include: analyses, ascertains, assesses, challenges, critiques, deconstructs, determines, establishes, explores, introduces, investigates, judges, ponders, proposes, reflects, reveals, reviews, synthesises, verifies.

# Understanding the Nature of an Assignment

The most common kinds of assignment you are likely to meet on an undergraduate or taught postgraduate degree course include essays, technical reports, practical reports, literature reviews, research papers, presentations and dissertations. Each kind of assignment has its particular purposes and conventions (Chapters 3 and 6).

Academic writing almost always takes place within a disciplinary context. Through understanding the conventions and practices of the discipline, you can develop confidence in writing within it and can ultimately develop your own 'voice'.

In this chapter you are introduced to the IPACE model: identity, purpose, audience, code and experience. This model helps you plan an assignment, with rigour. For example, it is through understanding disciplinary identity, clarifying the purpose of an assignment, and really knowing your audience (readership) that you come to know what kinds of writing style and document structures to use.

## 2.1 The IPACE model

For more than a decade I've been developing a practical model, which I call IPACE, for helping university students and staff plan their writing tasks. It has evolved from a model called SPACE, originally devised by Hickman and Jacobson (1997). IPACE has been tested by hundreds of students and dozens of staff, and many have found it helpful for focusing their thinking on the nature, breadth and depth of a writing task. Here I introduce the model and then detail how it can be used practically in planning an assignment.

I sometimes find that students plunge into a writing task without giving sufficient thought as to why they're writing, what they're writing, and for whom. Developing clarity on these matters at an early stage aids in planning the writing task and helps avoid unnecessary struggle and wasted time later on. Thought and planning at the start yield great dividends later.

IPACE is a mnemonic (memory aid) that refers to five elements: identity, purpose, audience, code and experience. Considering these different aspects of writing sets the context for a writing task. Working your way through IPACE the first time, by reading this section of the chapter, can take 30–50 minutes. But once you have absorbed this approach, you can apply it to a given assignment in 15 minutes or less. The benefits of IPACE outweigh the initial time and effort involved in incorporating it into your practice.

## Identity

In our personal and working lives we have more than one identity. For example, a psychology lecturer in her working life might also be a personal tutor, a research team leader, an editor of an academic journal, and so on. When she publishes in the academic literature, she sometimes writes for research journals (with papers written primarily for other researchers) or in practitioner journals (for example, with articles written mainly for psychologists working in the health sector). In writing for these two kinds of journal, her identity (or persona) is slightly different. In one context she is communicating for and with her research peers. That relationship – in terms of quality and power – is subtly different from one where she is communicating with practitioners in the health field, who may not be part of her peer group of researchers.

A student is likely to express a number of different identities during his or her time at university. She may be a sociology student, a daughter, a sports enthusiast, a valued member of more than one friendship group, and a student representative on a staff–student liaison committee. In any writing she does for these various facets of her life she expresses different identities. And on her sociology course, she is likely to express different identities depending on which module assignment she is completing, and for whom. Her identity when completing an essay for the Gender Studies module is likely to be slightly different from the one she expresses when completing a review of quantitative survey techniques for a Research Methodologies module.

As applied linguist Ken Hyland (2016, p. 44) proposes, in the context of writing, 'identity is a *performance*'. When we write, Hyland adds, we are:

> *constructing ourselves as credible members of a particular social group, so that identity is something we do; not something we have. Almost everything we say or write, in fact, says something about us and the kind of relationship we want to establish with others.* (p. 44)

When writing academically, we are not just writing within a discipline, we are writing for particular kinds of people within that discipline. In fact, for individual assignments on an undergraduate programme, we are likely to be writing for specific individuals – those people who will assess our writing.

Seen this way, identity in writing is an interplay between what we are bringing to a writing task, in terms of what we disclose consciously and unconsciously about ourselves through our writing, and how we are seeking to engage with, and satisfy, the community of readers for whom we are writing. Arguably, there is always a tension between expressing yourself as you might wish to, and conforming to certain conventions of the disciplinary community for whom you are writing. Those, such as myself, who are in the business of supporting students in developing their writing, seek to encourage students to develop their 'voice' within the discipline.

Voice, in writing, is a complex phenomenon, which I will not go into in any depth here. Suffice it to say, voice is your form of written words, within a given context, that someone can recognise as yours. In my view, we do not have one voice when we write but a range of voices for different contexts, which are imbued with a recognisable personal hallmark. In writing this book, I have a recognisable voice. Some of you, should you wish to do so, will no doubt notice my habits in choice of words, turn of phrase, preferred sentence and paragraph constructions, and forms of argument, that mark out this book as written by me.

I am keen to get students to think about the identity they aspire to have when they engage in a specific writing task, such as an assignment on their undergraduate programme. I encourage them to think of one to three words that capture who they think they are (in the sense of 'where they're coming from') when engaged in a specific writing task. I am not seeking an answer such as 'first-year politics student' or 'pharmacist'. Rather, the kinds of description I suggest are more about 'action' and are those that encourage students to think about themselves in relation to the reader of their work. Words they might respond with include 'guide', 'explainer', 'critic', and so on. I use these words as a hook, to encourage the student to consider the kinds of qualities such a person would have and demonstrate. For example, a science student in writing a practical report might express aspects of their intended identity as 'observer', 'reporter' and 'explainer'. The qualities they identify, in themselves and in their writing, might include 'attention to detail', 'being rigorous', 'impersonal', 'authoritative', 'easy to read', 'no nonsense', and so on.

This process of exploring identity, and qualities associated with that identity, encourages the student to think more deeply about their engagement with the writing task, and their relationship with the reader. The process can be transformative, enabling the student to see not only that they do have an identity, even if this might have 'impersonal' qualities, but that their identity shifts in a subtle manner depending on the nature of the writing assignment. Identity also shifts during the course of an undergraduate degree programme so that, by the final year, a student makes finer distinctions (whether consciously or unconsciously) about both the nature of identity in a given context and the qualities associated with that identity.

**ACTIVITY 2.1**

### Exploring your academic identity in an assignment

For an assignment you are about to carry out (or have recently carried out):

(a) Write down the name or short description of the assignment.

(b) Use 1–3 words to describe your identity in writing this assignment.

(c) What qualities would you expect a person with this identity to have?

(d) Which of these qualities do you consider to be well developed?

(e) Which of these qualities are, for you, the least developed? Write down two or three action points (things that you can do) that can help you strengthen these weaker qualities.

## Purpose

The notion of purpose seems straightforward. What was your assessor's intention in having you complete a writing assignment? This is often framed as learning objectives or intended learning outcomes. For example, 'The ability to evaluate various forms of evidence to determine the degree of success of a counselling intervention.' Such a learning objective would seek to encourage high-level thinking – the ability to make judgements about different forms of evidence in order to evaluate the outcome of a complex interaction between people. Completing such an assignment would be associated with a host of skills, not least the ability to write a convincing analysis of a situation.

However, I think it is helpful to consider two further aspects of the notion of purpose. One is your intention for the reader. In other words, what do you expect the reader to gain from reading your account? In relation to the example we've just considered, this might be to convince your assessor that you have a sound and deep knowledge of counselling theory and practice that you can apply in order to judge the effectiveness of a therapeutic intervention. It might even be that you want to present to your assessor new ideas at the forefront of the discipline, but with which he is not yet familiar.

There is a final dimension to purpose that I think is important. What is your own purpose in completing the assignment? An honest, straightforward but not very helpful answer is 'Because I have to.' This does not get us very far. It does not encourage your engagement with, and deeper understanding of, the assignment. Completing the assignment is not just a means to a short-term end. It is a stepping stone on a journey. What abilities will you nurture by completing the assignment? Many of these could be similar to those explicitly stated in the assessor's learning objectives or outcomes, but your response might go beyond these. For example, 'By doing well in this assignment it will convince me that it is worthwhile to undertake further training, and that I have sufficient confidence in my academic as well as professional skills to do so.'

For some of you it will be much more motivating to consider where this assignment lies in the wider scheme of things. Some possible answers might be: 'Do well in this assignment, and this will add to my marks for this module, which will help me gain a good placement next year. Being successful in that placement will open doors for me. I'll make good contacts and have more options about where I might finally find work, whether in the UK or abroad.' So, reminding yourself why you're completing the assignment is helpful in seeing its value to you, both now and in the future. This is likely to help motivate you in completing the task.

As shown in Figure 2.1, I suggest framing purpose in three ways: your assessor's purpose in setting the assignment; your purpose in writing it, in terms of the intended effect on the reader; and your purpose in the wider scheme (specifically, to engage your motivation and encourage your learning).

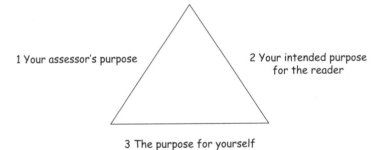

1 Your assessor's purpose          2 Your intended purpose
                                      for the reader

3 The purpose for yourself

**Figure 2.1 An assignment's purpose from three perspectives**

**ACTIVITY 2.2**

## Understanding the purpose of your assignment

For an assignment you are about to do (or have recently carried out):

(a) Write down the name or short description of the assignment.

(b) What is the purpose of this assignment, as indicated by its learning objectives or intended learning outcomes? Note: If you do not know the learning objectives or intended learning outcomes for the assignment, ask your lecturer or tutor what they are.

(c) What is the purpose of the assignment from the point of view of the reader? What would you expect a typical reader to gain from reading your completed assignment?

(d) What abilities will this assignment help you develop? In the wider scheme of things, what is this assignment a stepping stone towards?

At this point you may find yourself thinking more deeply about the reasons for carrying out an assignment than you have ever done before. You may be wondering why you are being asked so many questions. Bear with me. Being clearer about the context for your writing – thinking wider and deeper about what you are doing, why, and for whom – will bring benefits later. Like spending time to learn to read music, learning to use the more advanced functions of word-processing software, or practising developing a drawing skill, some time and effort expended now will be well worth it in the long run.

## Audience

The notion of audience (or readership) seems clear enough. It is the person(s) for whom you are writing. However, it is worth exploring below the surface of this. In an assignment, it is normally your assessor for whom you are writing, and through that writing, developing your own learning. The reader of your assignment, depending on how it is assessed, could be a tutor, a lecturer, or another student.

In my mind, when writing an assignment, you are trying to do two things. You are writing for yourself (so that your communication makes sense to you) and you are writing for your reader. With experience, one does both at one and the same time. Initially, however, you might write to make sense of the assignment for yourself, and then later review and edit the work so that it communicates well to your intended reader. Clarifying the nature of your reader is crucial.

Imagine you are writing an essay or a practical report for a course tutor. Having that person firmly in mind will mean, as you plan, compose, review and edit your work, that you are making checks (consciously and unconsciously) to make sure that you are employing appropriate style, viewpoint, level of explanatory detail, and so on. However, you need to be aware of how your assessor will view your work. The way an assessor will read your work is not in the manner that she might read the work of an established researcher in her field. In most cases, she will read your work to check that you have understood the concepts relating to the subject matter. She might only know that if you have explained them. If she were reading a published paper by a research colleague, she would assume much basic knowledge and would not require that to be explained. She is the same person, but she is reading the two kinds of work in different ways.

In my experience, assessors don't always make clear what persona they are adopting in reading your work. Are they reading your work as though they are a member of the public (in which case they would require you to define or explain basic concepts)? Are they reading your work as though they are reading that of another researcher in the field (they might read a final-year dissertation in this manner)? For many assignments, it seems to me, assessors are reading your work as though they were a student at a similar or slightly more advanced level than your own. By adopting that persona, they require you to explain yourself, and in doing so, to show that you have properly understood what you are writing about so that it can be appropriately assessed.

### Keeping your reader in mind

For an assignment you are about to do (or have recently carried out):
(a) Write down the name or short description of the assignment.
(b) Who assesses your assignment?
(c) In reading and assessing your assignment, what persona are they adopting? Are they reading your work as though they are a member of the public, a student similar to yourself, or who?

**TIP**

### Imagine your reader

Seeking to step into the mind of your reader is a powerful way to improve your work. Have you ever stopped to think about how your assessor reads your work? Let us assume she has 80 scripts of an assignment to mark. How do you think she will mark them? In batches of ten? How much time do you think she will allocate to marking each one? What will she be looking for? What will make your assignment stand out from the rest? What will make your work easier and more interesting for her to read? Thinking about your reader in this way will almost certainly improve your work. When I write, I like to think of the expression on the face of the reader if I have succeeded in my task. Doing so helps imbue my writing with the qualities I think will be attractive to my reader.

## Code (style, structure and format)

You want your writing to look right, sound right and feel right. If you've established your *identity* and your *purpose* in writing, and you can imagine your *audience* and their responses, then you are on the way to establishing the right *code* for your writing. Turning the thoughts in your head into readable prose involves encoding; that is, finding the right language or *writing style*, an appropriate *structure* and a suitable *format*.

### Format

Format relates to the medium and overall appearance of your communication. Is your communication on paper, card, in an electronic format, in sound only, in sound and moving images, and so on? If on paper, is it in colour? What is the page size? Which font styles and sizes will you use? Will the communication be printed on both sides of the paper, what will be the paper quality, how will text be laid out on the page, and will there be images as well as words? A communication on paper could range from poster size, to hang on a wall, to credit card size, to fit in a purse or wallet.

As a student, in most cases the format of an assignment is chosen for you. Commonly, if submitted on paper or as an electronic document, it is A4 or perhaps US letter size. If you have the opportunity to choose your format, think carefully about your purpose and intended audience, and exactly how he or she will engage with your communication. On one occasion I designed instructions to show car drivers how to replace a wheel if they experienced a tyre puncture when driving. I made the communication A2 size, laminated, with printed images on a fluorescent background, and few words. My reasoning was that the instructions could be readily stored in a car boot and taken out and used in poor light conditions and whatever the weather.

On an art course or a computing design course, for example, you might have far greater flexibility in how you might present an assignment. Rather than a poster or slide presentation, you might want to create a three-dimensional sculpture or a three-dimensional virtual model. In most cases these constructs would still be accompanied by text, in the creation itself and/or justifying your approach in completing the assignment.

### Structure

The structure of a document concerns how the various elements of evidence and reasoning are organised to form the beginning, middle and end of a communication. Essays, for example, typically have an introduction (often 5–10% of the whole document), a body (typically 75–85%) and a conclusion (usually 5–15%). In some cases, assessors expect these sections to be clearly indicated by the use of headings; in other cases they may not. You may have the opportunity to indicate the flow of your argument in an assignment through the use of sections, each with its own heading. An essay is often easier to read and mark if it contains thoughtfully chosen sections with appropriate headings. But you will need to be guided by your assessor as to whether this practice is acceptable for his or her assignments. Structure is clearly crucial to developing the argument in your assignment.

There are many kinds of document structure, a subject to which we will return in Chapters 3 and 6. Reports of laboratory investigations in the physical and life sciences, for example, commonly have a structure that is the same as or similar to: introduction (sometimes incorporating a literature review and/or theoretical background), method(s), results, discussion and conclusion. It is true to say that most assignments – except perhaps creative writing assignments such as poems or short stories – have a recognisable beginning, middle and end, and the beginning and end may be indicated by 'introduction' and 'conclusion'.

Clearly, for you as a student completing an assignment, you need to know the structures that are acceptable for the type of assignment you have been asked to complete. While there are some conventions (see Chapters 3 and 6), they always need to be checked in the context of a specific assignment on your particular programme at your particular institution. You may have the opportunity to be creative – and challenge accepted practice – but you need to judge whether this will be acceptable. If you decide to defy convention, you need to be confident about the expectations you are choosing to challenge.

### Writing style

We have touched on writing style several times already. There are numerous facets to style, but some of the most important in relation to completing assignments are: how formal or informal your writing is, how personal or impersonal, what viewpoint is adopted, what conventions of argument are employed, and what knowledge is assumed on the part of the reader.

---

**ACTIVITY 2.4**

### Aspects of style

Here is a sample of writing. Which of the answers (a)–(d) best describes the style of writing used?

> In field experiments using tree species from boreal forests, the removal of soil mycorrhizae revealed a marked diminution in productivity (g fixed C/kg dry biomass/yr) compared with stands of untreated trees used as controls. The mycorrhizae probably make micronutrients available to the trees with which they are associated, and through infiltration of root cells the mycorrhizae may serve to increase effective root surface area. Some mycorrhizae release anti-bacterial agents that may help protect the tree against pathogens. On balance, mycorrhizae appear to benefit the trees with which they are associated.

(a) Written in the third person in an informal style, with technical terms explained.
(b) Written in the first person in a formal style, with relevant technical knowledge assumed on the part of the reader.
(c) Written in the first person in a formal style, with technical terms explained.
(d) Written in the third person in a formal style, with relevant technical knowledge assumed on the part of the reader.
*Check your answer at the end of the chapter.*

---

## Experience

For the final part of the IPACE model, your experience is essentially the *knowledge*, *skills* and *attitudes* you are bringing to the writing task in hand. These apply not just to the *content* of what you are going to write but also to the *process* of writing it.

For example, imagine you are writing an assignment in response to the instruction 'Having viewed the video of the interview (exhibit A), critique the effectiveness of the interviewer Mrs X in carrying out the interview with the job applicant'. Apart from the video itself, possible sources of information for this task might include lecture notes, tutorial notes, textbooks, academic journal articles, radio or TV programmes, conversations with staff or other students, and relevant websites. But what about the process of writing the assignment? To what extent are you familiar with the writing style, structure and format of the assignment you are being asked to create? If required, do you know how to use computer software to draw and then import suitable graphics into your document? Have you experience of the particular referencing system you might be expected to use?

Thinking about content and process at an early stage helps ensure that you build in enough time to gather the information you need, carry out the writing, and then complete the assignment to the required specification. At this early stage, identifying gaps in your knowledge and understanding of content and process gives you enough time to seek the help you need, to address any shortcomings.

You have now used IPACE to consider various aspects of a writing task in some detail. IPACE is a powerful planning tool. By establishing *identity*, *purpose*, *audience*, *writing code*, and *experience* for a writing task, you are now in a much stronger position to carry out the task. You have identified your strengths and weaknesses, and potential gaps in your knowledge of content and process in relation to the task. You are now much clearer about exactly what you are seeking to do. At the very least you are in a more powerful position to seek specific kinds of help and support. Although the IPACE model may appear time-consuming, it will save you time in the long run. You will be more focused and much less likely to waste time gathering inappropriate or irrelevant material. Developing an appropriate style and structure for your writing will be less a process of trial and error. And having worked through IPACE once, you will find it much speedier to use the next time you have something significant to write.

In the next section we will consider how you can you use IPACE in just 15 minutes to help you plan and organise completing an assignment.

## 2.2   Putting IPACE into practice

The next time you have something significant to write, work through items 1–5 below in about 15 minutes to clarify what you are seeking to do, why you are doing it and how you might accomplish it. Further chapters within the book will then enable you to explore any part of the overall writing process in more depth. If you cannot answer all the questions or prompts to your satisfaction, this might indicate areas where you need to obtain further clarification or support.

**1 Identity**

(a) Who do you aspire to be when you are writing this assignment?
(b) What qualities would you expect that person to have?
(c) For you, which of these qualities are strongly developed?
(d) Which qualities do you need to focus on to develop further?

**2 Purpose**

(a) What is your assessor's purpose in setting the assignment (this is often framed in terms of learning objectives or intended learning outcomes)?
(b) What do you want the intended reader to gain from reading your assignment?
(c) In the wider scheme of things, what do you hope to gain in terms of your learning by completing the assignment?
(d) Looking to the future, what is the assignment a stepping stone towards?

**3 Audience (readers)**

(a) Who will be reading and assessing your work?
(b) What is the persona that the reader(s) will adopt (e.g. the assignment assessor(s), in the persona of a member of the general public or of an undergraduate student)?

**4 Code (style, structure and format)**

(a) In what format are you expected to submit your assignment? Do you have any choice?
(b) What structure are you expected to use in your assignment? Do you have any choice?
(c) What writing style should you use? What level of formality will be expected? From whose viewpoint will you be writing? Will you be writing in the personal or impersonal? What knowledge can you assume on the part of your reader?

**5 Experience (knowledge, skills, and attitudes) as it applies to both content and process**

(a) How familiar are you with the content you will be writing about in your assignment? Where are the obvious gaps? What will you do to fill them?
(b) How familiar are you with the process of completing the assignment? Process extends from writing your argument in a particular style, for a particular audience, using an appropriate structure and format, to the mechanics of putting together the document, such as using appropriate word-processing and other kinds of software. It might also include any citing and referencing system you are expected to use. Again, where are the obvious gaps in your knowledge and skills? What will you do to fill them?

**Figure 2.2 The key questions to ask yourself when using IPACE**

Early in your academic career you may not be able to answer all the questions in Figure 2.2 to your satisfaction. But as you progress through your undergraduate programme you should find it easier.

---

**TIP**

**When to use IPACE**

You do not need to use IPACE for every assignment you do. It is most appropriate for those assignments you think will be most challenging or with which you are least familiar.

---

**Key points in the chapter**

1  The IPACE model (**i**dentity, **p**urpose, **a**udience, **c**ode and **e**xperience) is a planning tool that systematically focuses attention on the various aspects of a writing task so that you can complete the task more effectively and with a greater likelihood of success.

2  Identity concerns the *persona* you use, or aspire to use, when writing in a given context. Identity shapes your writing to meet its purpose and audience.

3  Purpose is considered from three perspectives: the intention of the assessor in setting the assignment, your intention in terms of what the intended reader will gain from your writing, and the benefits for you in completing the assignment.

4  Audience (or readership) refers to the people for whom you are writing and who will read, and perhaps assess, your work. An assessor may take on a particular *persona*, such as that of a member of the public, when assessing your writing.

5  Code refers to format, structure and writing style, and is shaped by the writer's identity in responding to the purpose of, and audience for, a given writing assignment.

6  Experience is what you are bringing to a writing task in terms of the knowledge, skills and attitudes for the content of the writing and the process of creating it in its final form.

7  By using the IPACE model you can better prepare yourself for a writing task, completing it in a timely manner and with less likelihood for error.

# Cited references

Hickman, D. E. and Jacobson, S. (1997). *The POWER Process: An NLP Approach to Writing.* Carmarthen: Crown House Publishing.

Hyland, K. (2016). *Teaching and Researching Writing.* 3rd edn. Abingdon: Routledge.

# Answer for Chapter 2

## Activity 2.4: Aspects of style

(d) best describes the style of writing used: Written in the third person in a formal style, with relevant technical knowledge assumed on the part of the reader.

Chapter

# Two Popular Types of Assignment

**3**

Within the realm of academic writing there are many kinds of writing assignment, such as essays, reports, projects and dissertations, each tempered by their particular disciplinary context. Across this range of documents, with different purposes and audiences, I have chosen two styles of writing for this chapter. Essays are common assignments in social science, arts and humanities disciplines, while writing reports of laboratory investigations are frequent in science and engineering disciplines. Other kinds of assignment, including business style reports and critical reflective accounts, are considered in Chapter 6.

It is important at this stage to be familiar with the structure and style of at least one kind of academic writing before progressing to researching literature and reading source material, which are explored in Chapters 4 and 5. All of you reading this chapter are likely to have to write an essay or a laboratory report during your time as a university student; some of you will be writing both. However, before we plunge into the detail of writing essays and practical reports, it is vital you are clear about what is required of you when starting an assignment.

Academic writing almost always takes place within a disciplinary context. And a specific assignment has particular purposes (although these may not always have been made explicit). To really understand a writing task may involve asking your assessor key questions, so that which was hidden or unclear is revealed and made clear.

## 3.1 Questions to ask your assessor

In Chapter 1 we considered that an argument – the basis for most academic writing – involves marshalling evidence and reasoning, and developing a line of reasoning overall, which leads to conclusions. However, what exactly counts as evidence and reasoning will vary from one discipline to another, and even between different sub-disciplines within the same discipline. In educational studies, for example, investigations that observe behaviour in a classroom may analyse qualitatively what people say for emerging themes. Such studies may use quite different forms of evidence and interpretation from those of researchers using scientific methods; for example, where many teachers are surveyed by questionnaire, and quantitative data are analysed. Both kinds of investigation may, however, be equally valid.

Increasingly, teaching staff in higher education seek to make clear what their expectations are for an assignment by giving guidelines, referring to learning objectives or intended learning outcomes, and providing assessment criteria. Even better is if examples of previous students' work, for similar if not the same assignments, are available. These exemplars or models of good practice give you an idea of what you are seeking to achieve. You may even have the opportunity to view a range of completed assignments of varying quality, to gain a sense of common weaknesses or mistakes that students make, and what distinguishes the best work from that of a lesser quality.

However, whether or not this wealth of information is available to you, you may well have questions to ask, perhaps guided by the elements of the IPACE model in Chapter 2. The staff member who set the assignment, or the one who will mark it, is the best person to approach to clarify any outstanding matters. These are among the questions you might wish to ask:

- In writing an essay, should a thesis statement be provided? Should the essay take a particular viewpoint and argue for it?
- Can I use 'I' or 'we'? Or should I write in the third person and impersonal, e.g. 'it is argued that'?
- What knowledge can I assume on the part of the reader?
- Is it appropriate to include sections and subsections?
- What kinds of source material do you expect me to refer to?
- Can I quote from sources? If so, how much?
- Roughly how many sources do you expect me to use?
- Is it appropriate to include tables and figures in my account?
- What citing and referencing system, if any, is required?

## 3.2   Interpreting the nature of the task

When given an assignment, the first step is to interpret the wording of the assignment to decide how to tackle the task. Here is an example of an assignment set on an undergraduate International Development course. Students are expected to write a 2,000-word essay in response to this guidance:

*There is no universally agreed definition of sustainable development. Discuss, with examples, how the diversity of interpretations of the concept can be seen as both adding to and undermining its usefulness.*

If I were responding to this task, I would then underline the key phrases I need to interpret:

*There is no universally agreed definition of sustainable development. Discuss, with examples, how the diversity of interpretations of the concept can be seen as both adding to and undermining its usefulness.*

Putting myself in the place of the assessor, I can see that she has started with a forceful statement and then used wording that encourages me to address both sides of an argument. There is now plentiful opportunity for me (or you) to show criticality and depth of thinking. I would probably start thinking: 'What was the original, influential definition of sustainable development?', 'Who came up with it?', 'How has it developed since?' and 'How has it been interpreted, modified and criticised, and by whom?'. As for the examples I might use, I would want to pick and choose these carefully so that they do show diversity and development of ideas, that I can weigh up both sides of the argument and that I can come to an interesting conclusion that is definitely my own.

The assignment gives plentiful opportunity for students to interpret the guidance, and pick examples, to reflect their own backgrounds and interests. A student from a developing country, with experience of international development, is likely to interpret the assignment in a rather different way compared to a student from a highly industrialised country who does not have practical experience. We will return to this example later in the chapter, to see how the initial ideas evolve into a workable essay.

---

**TIP**

### Your initial thoughts

Once you have interpreted the nature of the task, it's a good idea to write down your initial thoughts. What do you already know? What questions do you have? What do you need to find out? What are the challenges? What are your next steps?

Writing down these initial thoughts achieves many things. It helps clear your mind, opening up space for other thoughts to emerge. Often, you will find you know more about the task than you thought you did. It is good to capture your initial ideas and opinions before you are influenced by what you discover during your literature research and further reading. Your initial thoughts might influence the nature of your research, e.g. the examples you might choose to include in your essay. At the very least, you will ask good questions and can start planning your next steps. You have already started, which can be confidence-building in itself, spurring you on to further action.

---

Although distinct kinds of assignment differ in detail, they do share some common features. One of these is in their overall structure, divided into a beginning, middle and end.

# 3.3 Beginnings, middles and ends

As with an effective talk, lecture or other kind of presentation, a written assignment normally has a clear beginning (introduction), middle (body) and end (conclusion). The introduction sets out for the reader the context of what is to follow, the body delivers it, and the conclusion summarises it in a punchy manner.

## The beginning (introduction)

Some common features of beginnings (introductions) are:

- **Answering the 'Why bother?' or 'Who cares?' question.** This applies to many kinds of written communications, but not all. Why is the topic of the assignment important? Often such questions are pre-empted (or answered) using one or more sentences that set out the background to the assignment and, ideally, grab the reader's attention. This can be done in a variety of ways, such as: giving a real-life example that is relevant to the topic and has wide implications; giving statistics that reveal how important the topic is; revealing some features of the topic that show how important it is to the discipline; perhaps using a quotation that captures the essence of the topic.
- **Moving from wider to narrower context.** This situates the assignment within the context of the discipline or sub-discipline and then moves on to the specific focus of the topic. In moving from the general to the specific, key terms that aren't self-explanatory, are ambiguous or do not have generally agreed meanings may need to be defined as well as explained. For example, even well-used expressions such as 'climate change' or 'global warming' do not have standard definitions. Different international organisations, such as the Intergovernmental Panel on Climate Change (IPCC) and the United Nations Environmental Programme (UNEP), have differing definitions. In writing an essay on such themes, you might wish to give your reasons for using certain definitions and rejecting others.
- **What you are setting out to do.** This states the intention of the assignment, which could be framed as questions to be answered, aims and objectives to be met, or even hypotheses to be tested. You might wish to introduce how you are going to meet your intention. If a thesis statement is to be included (a summary of the writer's argument and point of view on the topic), it is situated here. In larger documents, such as dissertations or a major report, the end of the introduction often sets out the structure of the rest of the document, chapter by chapter or section by section.

In many kinds of assignment, the introduction makes up 5–15% of the whole. An example of a plan for the introduction to an essay is given in Section 3.4.

**TIP**

**An introduction need not be written first**

Although an introduction comes at or near the beginning of a written assignment, that does not mean it has to be written first, before other parts of the document. Often, it is sensible to write the introduction first, to set your direction, knowing that you will probably change its detail after writing the rest of the account. At other times, you may want to leave writing the introduction to the end, until you have fully explored the topic of your assignment. By leaving the introduction 'open' you may be giving yourself more freedom in the way you conduct your research and develop your argument.

## The middle (body)

In the body of the assignment, you use evidence and reasoning to convince the reader of the strength of your argument. This involves selecting relevant evidence and deciding how to present it, evaluating alternatives and weighing up conflicting evidence, and making judgements on the basis of evidence and reasoning.

In scholarly writing, key words and phrases are used to convey to the reader the direction of the argument, location within the argument, or both. Such words or phrases are sometimes called signposts, transitions, connectives or connectors. They connect parts of an argument, linking one part to another and setting each in the context of the whole. These connectors often appear at or near the beginning of sentences and paragraphs, but not always. Connectors or transitions play at least six roles:

- *They may introduce a line of reasoning.* These are words and phrases, such as: at the outset, first, first and foremost, initially, it is apparent, the first point, to begin … In practice, a line of reasoning is quite often begun without resorting to using a connector.
- *Connectors reinforce a line of reasoning.* Suitable words and phrases include: again, also, as well as, besides, equally, furthermore, in addition, in the same manner, likewise, moreover, similarly, such as, what is more …
- *They qualify a previous line of argument,* e.g. There are exceptions, or this situation does not always apply …
- *They introduce alternatives.* Signposts include: alternatively, although, by contrast, conversely, however, nonetheless, notwithstanding, on the one hand, on the other hand, others argue …
- *They signpost consequences or an evaluation.* Possible words and phrases are: as a result, on balance, consequently, hence, therefore, this indicates, this suggests, thus …
- *They signpost the drawing of conclusions.* Connectors include: concluding, in conclusion, in summary, it is apparent, therefore, thus …

In most kinds of assignment, the body makes up 70–80% of the whole. Section 3.4 includes an example of a plan for the body of an essay.

## The end (conclusion)

A conclusion brings your written assignment to a close. It usually has the following features:

- **It is short** and summarises the most important points argued in the body of the assignment, but not in a boring and repetitive way.
- **It weighs up the evidence and reasoning presented in the body of the assignment and makes a concluding statement.** In doing so, it does not simply repeat, word for word, what has been presented earlier. It normally uses different forms of words and highlights the main points of evidence and reasoning. The degree to which it does so depends on the nature of the assignment. In a scientific report, a conclusion could be one or two sentences. In a humanities or social science essay, it could be two or more paragraphs. In a dissertation, the conclusion could be several pages.
- Normally, a conclusion **does not introduce new material** that has not been discussed earlier (but see Section 3.4 for an example of an exception).
- In some kinds of essay or report, a conclusion will include implications and **make recommendations**. In many kinds of assignment, the conclusion makes up 5–15% of the whole document.
- **Usually, the conclusion refers back to the introduction** and demonstrates that any aims have been met, questions set up at the beginning have been answered, or hypotheses have been tested. If not, the conclusion will explain why.

The conclusion is usually the last part of the assignment your assessor reads. As such, it needs to be well written and not rushed. You do not want your parting statements to leave a poor impression. If you can make a parting pithy statement, then do so.

> **TIP**
>
> **A stimulus, not a straitjacket**
>
> The guidance that follows about structures for different types of assignment is just that – guidance. It is not definitive. Wherever you can, check by studying previously completed assignments in your degree programme, or by asking your teaching staff whether the structures they are expecting to see are the same as, or similar to, the ones shown here.

Now we are ready to consider two specific kinds of assignment. Essays are common assignments and exam answers in many disciplines, whereas practical reports have more specialised requirements and tighter guidelines.

# 3.4   Essays

French writer and philosopher Michel de Montaigne (1533–1592) was among the first to use the term 'essay'. In 1580, his book *Essais* (English translation, *Essays*) contained short self-reflections and longer philosophical discussions about human nature. Today, in academic circles, a non-fiction essay is usually taken to be a piece of writing between 500 and 5,000 words in length, structured into paragraphs. Depending on disciplinary and staff preferences, it may or may not have sections and subsections. It might be written for coursework or during an examination. Here we will focus on essays written for coursework.

Typically, an essay has the following broad structure:

- Introduction (5–15% of the whole)
- Body (70–80%)
- Conclusion (5–15%)

## Introduction

The introduction to your essay should encourage your reader to read on. It should also manage your reader's expectations about what is to follow. Commonly, the introduction includes some or all of the following:

- It reveals why the topic or theme of the essay is of interest.
- It defines or interprets relevant technical terms.
- It explains how you have interpreted the essay title.
- It asks questions that you mean to answer or sets aims that you intend to meet.
- It establishes the limits of the essay (what will be included and excluded), perhaps with justification as to why you have made that choice.

In addition, it may:

- Explain the approach you are taking, e.g. 'I give greater weight to those studies that report on the voice of the practitioner.'
- Include a thesis statement (one or two sentences that summarise the conclusion that will be reached).
- Outline the structure of the rest of the essay (particularly if it is a long one).

### A plan for an essay's introduction

In response to the 2,000-word essay assignment:
*There is no universally agreed definition of sustainable development. Discuss, with examples, how the diversity of interpretations of the concept can be seen as both adding to and undermining its usefulness.*

A plan for the 200-word introduction might look something like this:

- Why the concept of sustainable development is important. Its influence on international development policy and practice in the last 30 years.
- Origins of the concept of sustainable development (e.g. Bruntland Report, 1987). Deconstructing key elements of initial definitions and their interpretation, e.g. 'development' and 'needs'.
- The diversity of interpretations is based on how key words are conceptualised and expanded upon by different governments, non-governmental organisations (NGOs) and transnational agencies.
- The rationale behind the essay's chosen examples.
- A statement about the nature of the analysis and the conclusion to be drawn (thesis statement).

## Body

The middle part of your essay normally makes up 70–80% of the whole. It gives the line of reasoning that connects the various parts of your argument. The body will include:

- a series of paragraphs, each of which contains one idea or a closely related set of ideas and is likely to be less than 250 words long; and
- transitional words or phrases that connect one paragraph with another and explain to the reader at which point in the overall argument the paragraph lies.

The body may include:

- headings and subheadings that signpost the reader to different stages of the argument; and
- images or other kinds of material, e.g. graphs or tables, that complement the text (see Chapter 8).

### A plan for an essay's body

In response to the 2,000-word essay assignment:

There is no universally agreed definition of sustainable development. Discuss, with examples, how the diversity of interpretations of the concept can be seen as both adding to and undermining its usefulness.

A plan for a 1,600-word body might look like this:

- Unpacking further the Bruntland Report's (1987) definition, and its focus on alleviating poverty internationally.

- On the international scale, however, interpretations of SD vary according to the nature of the organisation and their remit. Compare for, example, interpretations by the World Bank, the World Wide Fund for Nature and the World Health Organisation.
- What are the socio-economic and environmental assumptions that underlie these different worldviews? And do these interpretations depend on whether you are members of a developing or developed nation? For example, the UK government's recent definitions of SD, despite their wording, are interpreted so as to focus more on national needs and economic growth. Contrast with, say, Sri Lanka.
- Examples where differences in interpretation and emphasis by industrialised and developing nations have held back progress.
- Despite differences in interpretation and emphasis, industrialised and developing nations can collaborate to effect change which has a demonstrable effect on the global environment and human quality of life. Use the example of the Montreal Protocol (1987) and Kyoto Protocol (1997) and subsequent agreed action to curb greenhouse gas emissions.
- Nevertheless, the imbalance in the power to effect change exerted by industrialised as opposed to developing countries remains. Use agreements within the United Nations Framework Convention on Climate Change (UNFCCC) as examples.

## Conclusion

The conclusion typically makes up the final 5–15% of the essay's length. Overall, the conclusion should relate well to the expectations set up in the introduction.

Being the last part your assessor reads, the conclusion performs several vitally important functions. A conclusion typically:

- reminds the reader how the essay has interpreted and responded to the essay title or the assigned task;
- summarises the main points in the argument; and
- includes a final judgement based on evaluation of evidence and reasoning.

In addition, it might:

- state the limitations of the analysis of evidence and reasoning;
- suggest related areas for further work; and
- give recommendations.

If you can, finish on a final punchy sentence that captures the theme of the essay, perhaps alluding to a key statement made in the introduction.

---

**TIP**

### Does an essay's conclusion contain something new?

This depends. Many assessors prefer that the conclusion of an essay draws upon only what has come before. However, I occasionally come across an assessor who says, 'You might want to introduce a new piece of evidence or an idea into the conclusion, to add a twist.' If possible, find out from your assessor if this is acceptable. Doing so can certainly add punch.

---

### An example of an essay's conclusion

Here is a long conclusion to a 2,000-word essay titled 'Is the writer Sid Chaplin underrated?'

*The North-East English writer Sid Chaplin is less well known than other 'angry young men' authors of the 1950s and 1960s – among them Stan Barstow, John Braine and Alan Sillitoe – who Chaplin had inspired through his short stories in* The Leaping Lad *(1946). Some literary critics have dismissed Chaplin as a 'regional writer', with only a short entry in* The Oxford Companion to English Literature *(Birch & Drabble, 2009, pp. 823–833). However, his most acclaimed novel,* The Day of the Sardine, *is seen by some as 'the definitive novel about a young working class lad growing up in an industrial heartland' (Nelsson, 2011). In terms of plot, narrative, characterisation, dialogue and contemporary social themes, it ranks well against books by other English social realist novelists of the time.* The Leaping Lad *and the critically-acclaimed novel,* The Thin Seam, *both feature the gritty working lives of miners and their families – subjects that may not have wide popular appeal. His tight regional loyalty and commitment to authenticity meant his characters spoke in Newcastle (Geordie) and other local dialects, which may not have endeared him to readers unfamiliar with these strong speech patterns. However, his lack of popular literary success is probably due to misperceptions about his public persona, and bad timing. According to Stan Barstow (2004), 'Chaplin was a man of warmth and sincerity, with a lack of pretentiousness which could be misleading ...'. He was underappreciated by literary critics.*

*The vehicles for his writing – while invariably set in North-East England – were varied, including episodes in two ground-breaking TV series,* When the Boat Comes In *and* The Wednesday Play *(IMDb, 2017). But his landmark Newcastle novels came too late –* The Day of the Sardine *in 1961 and* The Watchers and the Watched *in 1962 – when film-makers were beginning to tire of screening gritty northern novels. Tellingly, unlike the more famous contemporaries he had inspired, none of his writings were turned into feature films.*

This conclusion brings together what has been discussed earlier in the essay, but in a concise and engaging manner. Unusually, the conclusion does incorporate new ideas: that the way a writer's work is perceived may not just be attributable to the quality of the writing, but how fashionable and appealing the topics they write about are and, indeed, the public persona the author projects. And serendipity.

---

**TIP**

**What kind of essay?**

Some writing specialists classify essays into different kinds, for example: technical, review, theory-based, argumentative, critique, issue-based. The problem with this approach is that different disciplines interpret the meaning of words differently, as do various lecturers within the same department. Also, there are overlaps between the categories, and an essay may have a blend of approaches. You need to become aware of the precise interpretation of an essay description as used by your assessor.

## 3.5    Practical reports

Undergraduate degree programmes in science and engineering normally include practical investigations such as laboratory experiments or experimental or observational fieldwork. Such investigations carried out in the first or second year of a degree programme are usually educational exercises designed to improve students' practical and report-writing skills, and to reinforce their understanding of the more theoretical parts of the course. The practical investigation and its associated report requires the student to gather, collate and analyse research data, discuss findings and draw conclusions. The practical report is typically written up formally, following scientific convention. It is modelled on a peer-reviewed research paper, the high-status channel by which researchers report their findings to a wide audience.

As in the case of a scientific research paper, a practical report is organised logically into sections that follow strict conventions. The sections allow the reader to swiftly locate the information they are seeking. A full report has most or all of the sections below. At the other extreme, a routine practical where the method has been standardised by a staff member may require only a short report with a title, results, discussion and conclusion. In a full report, the name of a given section, and its coverage, may vary slightly depending on the discipline:

- Title
- Abstract or Summary (sometimes)

- Introduction
- Method, Materials and Methods, or Procedure
- Results
- Discussion
- Conclusion (sometimes Discussion and Conclusion are combined)
- References
- Appendices (rarely)
- Acknowledgements (occasionally)

## Title

A practical report title is short – customarily no more than 15 words. It precisely and concisely refers to the investigation's topic and its scope. For example:

*Applying transtheoretical models of behaviour change to increase physical activity in males aged 35–55*

*Raised atmospheric sulphur dioxide concentrations and their effect on photosynthesis in Geranium leaves*

---

**ACTIVITY 3.1**

### Effective practical report titles

**(a)** Based on the criteria of being clear, precise and concise, which of these four is the best title for a practical report?
  (i)  Finding out which warm-down regime works best for hockey players after a match
  (ii) Establishing an effective post-match, 'warm-down' protocol for hockey players
  (iii) Finding which warm-down method works best for hockey players
  (iv) Which is the best way for hockey players to warm down after a match?
**(b)** Make this practical report title clearer and more concise:
  An investigation into the effects of drought on the growth rate of the English oak as evidenced from tree rings
*Check your answers against those at the end of the chapter.*

---

## Abstract

An abstract summarises the investigation's context, aim, method, results and conclusion for the investigation. As in a published research paper, an abstract captures the important features. It gives the reader sufficient information to decide whether the report is of interest and should be read. An abstract is normally between 150 and 300 words (check the precise requirements for your assignment). Typically, the abstract summarises:

- the **context** for the investigation
- the **aim**(s) of the investigation
- what was carried out (**method**)
- what was discovered (**results**) and
- what was concluded (**conclusion**)

A well-written abstract has a balance of the above features. Being brief, the abstract does not include a discussion. Traditionally, it does not cite references.

## Introduction

The introduction provides the context for the rest of the practical report. Typically, it contains some or all of the following elements:

- Why the investigation is **important or useful**.
- **The theoretical and/or practical context** for the investigation, citing relevant literature.
- Key **definitions and abbreviations**.
- The **aim**(s) of the investigation, **questions** it seeks to answer or **hypotheses** it seeks to test.

---

**TIP**

### Use of tenses in practical reports

A practical report is written largely in the past tense. As a general rule, use the past tense when describing what was done and then reporting the results. Exceptions to the 'past tense' rule include:

- Using the **present tense** if you are making a general statement about something that applies through time. For example, 'Standard practice is to allow the calorimeter to cool overnight to equilibrate to ambient conditions.'
- Employing the **present tense** in the Method or Results section if you refer to a table or graph. For example, 'The table shows ...'.
- Adopting the **present tense** in the Discussion or Conclusion if commenting on some aspect of your results or making suggestions for improvement. For example, 'Taken overall, the results show ...' or 'It is suggested that ...'.
- Using the **future tense** in the Discussion if referring to something that will take place in the future. For example, 'In the next growing season the procedure will be repeated but with modifications, taking into account ...'.

## Method

Conventionally, a Method section (sometimes called Materials and Methods, or Procedure) gives enough detail so that a reader can repeat the investigation using the information provided. In your studies, your tutor may not wish you to write up a full method for each and every practical investigation you undertake, particularly if the instructions for the method have been given to you in detail. However, you will be expected to write up a full method account on occasion, and particularly as you progress through your degree and devise your own investigations.

A **full Method section** typically contains:

- **Experimental subjects**. Microbes, plants, animals or people that are the subjects of the investigation. Where appropriate, give precise information about their characteristics and how samples were obtained.
- **Materials**. Chemicals (including detail of amounts, concentrations, physical form, and so on) and other media (such as a particular growth medium for microbes or plants).
- **Conditions**. Physical factors, such as temperature and pressure, and any other factors that are likely to influence the outcome of the investigation.
- **Apparatus**. Equipment of all kinds, including measuring and recording devices, used in carrying out the investigation.
- **Procedure**. What was done, how and, where appropriate, why.

Sometimes the various elements of the section are listed separately under subsection headings. Check the precise guidelines for your assignment.

## Results

Unless specifically requested by your assessor, a results section does not normally contain raw data. Rather, it contains data that are presented and analysed in ways that respond to the investigation's aim(s). It is usual to guide the reader through the presented data, highlighting the points you wish to bring to the reader's attention, which will be referred to in the discussion and conclusion. The data are typically presented in numbered tables, graphs, or both, which are referred to in the text. A table is a means of arranging summaries of data (often in the form of numbers) in columns and rows to enable ready comparison. A graph or chart – such as line graphs, scatter plots, bar charts and histograms – reveals relationships between variables in a visual form. Data presented in tables or graphs may be accompanied by statistical analyses, together with their interpretation. See Chapter 8 for information about creating tables, graphs and charts of various kinds.

## Discussion

The discussion of a practical report is typically a distinct section after the data have been presented. It includes some or all of the following items (with slight variations according to the discipline):

- It **discusses the results** in response to the aim and in relation to other people's findings from the research literature.
- It **critiques** the investigation, revealing any **limitations** or **errors**, where possible with suggestions as to how they might be overcome.
- It might give **implications** for practice within the discipline.
- It may give **recommendations** for further investigations.

## Conclusion

A conclusion in a short practical report is typically a single paragraph or even a single sentence. It may come at the end of the discussion or in a separate section with its own heading, just after the discussion. The conclusion makes closing statements that draw together findings from the results and discussion.

---

**TIP**

### Reporting objectively

Traditionally, practical reports in science are written in an impersonal style that supports the notion of being objective. The procedure, for example, is written impersonally: 'The calorimeter was calibrated ...' and 'After crystallisation, the purple residue was dissolved in ...'. By avoiding any reference to a specific investigator, the report seeks to convey that the investigation has been carried out and reported on objectively, in an unbiased manner. The implication is that given the same circumstances, any competent person carrying out the same investigation should obtain similar results and reach similar conclusions.

Writing practical reports in this impersonal style is demanded in most undergraduate and taught postgraduate courses in science and engineering. In fact, the practice in peer-reviewed science journals of high standing is less clear-cut. Sometimes, authors of articles in the leading journals *Nature* and *Science* refer to 'we', especially in article introductions and discussions, although they use the impersonal when explaining methods and reporting results. It is worth pointing out that Watson and Crick's (1953) famous article in *Nature* on the structure of DNA begins (p. 737), 'We wish to suggest a structure for the salt of deoxyribose nucleic acid ...'.

---

**TIP**

### Active or passive?

The active voice emphasises the subject of the sentence, who or what carries out the action, e.g. 'Heath and Field (2017) analysed the beam's loading characteristics.' Using the passive voice, the sentence emphasises the object that is acted upon, e.g. 'The beam's loading characteristics were analysed by Health and Field (2017).' Using the passive voice, the source of the action, the actor(s), can be left out entirely: 'The beam's loading characteristics were analysed.'

Scientists and engineers commonly use the passive voice in writing technical documents. As we have seen, doing so gives the work objectivity and authority and avoids the writer having to say who did what. However, writing that way throughout makes documents rather 'dry' to read. Where you are able – for example, in a literature review – injecting sentences with an active voice brings vitality. Instead of having a document full of passive people or objects having things done to them, you have a document that has (at least some) people or objects engaging in action.

**ACTIVITY 3.2**

### Passive and active

In the table below, enter the missing passive or active form of the sentence. The first one has been done for you:

| Passive | Active |
| --- | --- |
| Five students were interviewed. *Or* Five students were interviewed by Sally. | Sally interviewed five students. |
| | A team using a platform and hoist painted the underside of the bridge. |
| | The project team's latest research revealed an error in the original findings. |
| The beneficial use of regular exercise in reducing blood pressure is reported by Smith and Jones (2017). | |

*Check your answers at the end of the chapter.*

## Key points in the chapter

1  You may need to ask your assessor specific questions to clarify the purpose, audience and code for a given writing assignment.
2  Interpreting the task usually involves deconstructing the title or guidance for its precise meaning, to uncover the assessor's intention in setting the assignment.

3 Most kinds of communication involving academic writing have recognised structures with a beginning (introduction), middle (body) and end (conclusion).

4 Essays and practical reports normally have clear structures; in the case of practical reports, these tend to be modelled on the style of research papers in peer-reviewed scientific journals.

## Cited references

Watson, J. D. and Crick, F. H. C. (1953). 'Molecular Structure of Nucleic Acids. A Structure for Deoxyribose Nucleic Acid'. *Nature*, 171, pp. 737–738.

### Further reading

Barker, A. (2017). *Alex Essay Writing Tool.* London: Royal Literary Fund. Available from: https://alexessaytool.com [accessed 29 August 2017].

Barrass, R. (2002). *Scientists Must Write: A Guide to Better Writing for Scientists, Engineers and Students.* 2nd edn. London: Routledge.

Godwin, J. (2014). *Planning Your Essay.* 2nd edn. Basingstoke: Palgrave Macmillan.

Greetham, B. (2018). *How to Write Better Essays.* 4th edn. London: Palgrave Macmillan.

Morley, J. (2017). *The Academic Phrasebank.* Manchester: University of Manchester. Available from: www.phrasebank.manchester.ac.uk/ [accessed 29 August 2017].

Swatridge, C. (2014). *Effective Argument and Critical Thinking.* Oxford: Oxford University Press.

Taylor, G. (2009). *A Student's Writing Guide: How to Plan and Write Successful Essays.* Cambridge: Cambridge University Press.

Young, T. M. (2005). *Technical Writing A–Z: A Commonsense Guide to Engineering Reports and Theses.* British English Edition. New York: ASME.

## Answers for Chapter 3

### Activity 3.1: Effective practical report titles

(a) (ii) and (iv) are the best answers, with (ii) the more formal. Whether to use a report title that is a question (iv) is a matter of taste and style (check with your assessor).

(b) One possible answer: Tree ring evidence for the effects of drought on the growth of the English oak tree.

## Activity 3.2: Passive and active

| Passive | Active |
|---|---|
| *The underside of the bridge was painted using a platform and hoist.* Or: *The underside of the bridge was painted by a team using a platform and hoist.* | A team using a platform and hoist painted the underside of the bridge. |
| *An error in the original findings was revealed by the latest research.* Or: *An error in the original findings was revealed by the project team's latest research.* | The project team's latest research revealed an error in the original findings. |
| The beneficial use of regular exercise in reducing blood pressure is reported by Smith and Jones (2017). | *Smith and Jones (2017) reported on the beneficial use of regular exercise in reducing blood pressure.* |

# Researching an Assignment

There is no single way to research an assignment. It depends on the nature of the assignment. But a wise researcher knows where to look, asks for help when they need it and then knows when to stop. Researching, like writing, is not about reaching perfection (although we might strive for it). When researching and writing in some professions, such as law and medicine, the consequences of inaccuracy or miscommunication could result in miscarriages of justice and even be life threatening. Nevertheless, whether you are a professional working in the discipline, or a student on the way to becoming such a professional, researching, reading and writing concerns doing the best job you can with the time and resources available. When researching the literature for an assignment, following the guidance in this chapter should save you time and focus your attention on gathering high-quality material that is most relevant to your task.

## 4.1 Being strategic

In carrying out research you need to be strategic. You need to quickly gain a sense of the information that is available, how it relates specifically to your task, and how to judge its value in completing your assignment. It is easy to waste time gathering information that is not exactly relevant to your task or is of poor quality. You also need to be prepared to change direction, based on the information you are finding. In many cases you start out with preconceived ideas (and this allows you to make a preliminary plan), but often it is only when you have gathered material that your response to an assignment takes shape – and perhaps in unexpected ways. This is as it should be. After all, if you knew the answers before you carried out the research, why carry out the research? An assignment is intended to stretch your learning, not simply to reinforce what you already knew and understood.

Taking online information alone, as you are no doubt aware, there is a huge volume of material on almost any topic. Searching the World Wide Web using a search engine such as Google and the phrase 'global climate change' will find many millions of relevant webpages. The problem is, from the wealth of material available to you, to quickly find and evaluate the best sources for a given writing task. That is what this chapter is about. Given that you have understood the nature of a task, as outlined in Chapters 2 and 3, then your next step is to find the information you need to write the assignment. Identifying key words, phrases and underlying themes, while understanding the scope of the assignment, is key to carrying out an efficient literature search. These parameters set the boundaries for what you do and don't need to find.

---

**YOUR UNIVERSITY LIBRARY**

Your university library, information centre or resource centre (for convenience, we'll call it a library) is much more than a repository of information on paper. It is an electronic gateway to a world of online material, much of it in peer-reviewed journals, which is accessible from on or off campus. The library is also an invaluable source of expertise. It normally provides:

- computing terminals, printers, scanners and photocopiers
- an online catalogue of resources held by the library, or to which the library has access
- paper (hard copy) information such as books, journal articles, newspapers, magazines, dissertations and theses
- online resources, including those for which the library pays a subscription, such as electronic journals and e-books
- resources in media other than paper or electronic print, including CDs, DVDs and photographic slides
- bibliographic databases to help you search for relevant information, including interdisciplinary databases such as Web of Science and disciplinary ones such as Eric, Psychinfo or Pubmed
- subject librarians, who provide one-to-one assistance and may also run courses on various aspects of information literacy
- online tutorials to help you develop your literature-searching and other information skills, including evaluating information, citing and referencing, avoiding plagiarism, copyright issues and managing references

It may hold specialist collections of artefacts as well as the kinds of materials listed above.

---

## 4.2   Different strategies for different assignments

Exactly what strategy you need to use for gathering information depends on the nature of the task and the level at which you are working. As a first-year student at university, for an early task you may not be required to read the latest peer-reviewed research journals on a topic. But by your final year, that is exactly what you might need to do.

A sensible approach to researching an assignment is to move from the general to the specific; that is, to find and read relevant textbooks and review articles and then, if appropriate, read research articles on specific aspects of the topic (Figure 4.1). In a sense, you are mapping the territory, checking your general understanding of a topic, before you narrow down to what is most relevant to your assignment.

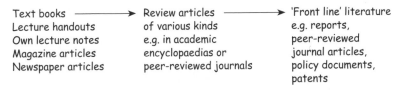

| Text books | Review articles | 'Front line' literature |
| Lecture handouts | of various kinds | e.g. reports, |
| Own lecture notes | e.g. in academic | peer-reviewed |
| Magazine articles | encyclopaedias or | journal articles, |
| Newspaper articles | peer-reviewed journals | policy documents, |
| | | patents |

**Figure 4.1    The overall strategy for a literature search often moves from the general to the specific, depending on the nature of the task**

In your first and perhaps second year as an undergraduate you are likely to rely more on textbooks, journalistic articles, and review articles in academic journals. In the final year you are likely to be reading research papers on specific aspects of the topic in academic journals – what I call 'front line' literature. In some degree programmes, you will start reading such leading-edge research papers in your first year.

> **TIP**
>
> **Online academic journals**
> Many peer-reviewed academic journals provide articles in an electronic format, which are downloadable, often as a PDF (in Adobe Portable Document Format). These are equivalent to a paper copy of the journal article, and can be cited and referenced in the same manner as a paper document (see Chapter 11). Such documents are not the same as information freely available on the World Wide Web. They usually carry much higher academic authority.

Nevertheless, whether you are just starting out at university, or whether you are in your final year, there are three key questions you need to be able to answer:

- What resources (books, articles in peer-reviewed journals, and so on) are available that are best suited to the task?
- How do I find the sources I need?
- How do I judge whether what I have found is suitable?

It is easy to waste hours searching through hundreds of sources that are not exactly relevant to your task or are of poor quality. You need to quickly work out strategies to avoid falling into these traps.

**TIP**

**Making good use of your library**

Learning to made good use of your university library, information centre or resource centre, and the staff within it, can make an enormous difference to your productivity and success on your course.

Key information skills you will need to develop in your time at university include:

- Using your library's electronic catalogue.
- Understanding the classification and shelving system your library employs, such as Dewey Decimal Classification or the Library of Congress system, so that you can locate items.
- Finding a book, academic journal or other library resource, whether on paper or in an electronic form.
- How to access a distant library, to borrow a book or journal or to obtain a printed or scanned copy of an article or book chapter.
- How to cite and reference correctly (see Chapter 9).
- How to identify appropriate tools to set up an efficient and effective search strategy to gather literature for an assignment (this chapter and Chapter 11).
- How to narrow your search, if you have too many responses to your enquiry, or broaden it if you have too few responses (this chapter and Chapter 11).
- How to evaluate what you have found (this chapter and Chapter 5).
- How to keep records of your search strategy and sources (this chapter, Chapter 5 and Chapter 11).
- How to avoid plagiarism and deal with copyright issues (Chapter 9).

Early in your first year at university, you could be asked to carry out an introductory task to enable your tutors to find out whether you are skilful at finding material and judging its suitability for the task. They might well, of course, be interested in knowing how well you can write an essay. We won't go into great detail about what criteria they might use in assessing your assignment (which, in any case, will vary according to the discipline). Let us assume you've been asked to write a 1,000-word essay in response to the question:

*Mobile phones: are they bad for your health?*

The scope of such an essay could vary depending on who set the task. One tutor might wish you to focus on the physics of radio waves and the likelihood of a mobile frying your brain. Another tutor might wish you to consider the effect of the mobile phone in the round, such as its impact on your posture, attention span, likelihood of being involved in a car accident (if you were driving and using a mobile at the same time), risk of repetitive strain injury from too much texting, the psychological impact of spending hours each day viewing a smartphone screen, and so on. Nevertheless, whatever the scope of the assignment, you need to find information and you need to assess its value in relation to your task.

As it is an assignment early in your first year, let us assume you are asked to gather the material by searching online. In fact, for health and medical topics, there is a considerable volume of high-quality material published online by reputable organisations.

> **WARNING**
>
> Depending on your discipline, some teaching staff may not wish you to use sources that are freely available on the World Wide Web because the quality of much of the material on the web might be poor. For example, a Wikipedia article – although it might give a useful initial overview of a topic – cannot be assumed to be accurate or reliable and normally should not be used as a source in academic writing. In many disciplines, the most authoritative articles are found in peer-reviewed journals and other publications for which your university library may pay a subscription. As such, many of these publications are not freely available on the web but you gain access to them through your university's registration or by paying a fee for the article.
>
> There are exceptions. In health and medicine, for example, there is increasing pressure from research funders for published research, even in the best peer-reviewed journals, to be freely available online. This is partly so that those in developing countries, whose institutions may not have the funds to subscribe to journals, are not disadvantaged by the lack of access to information that could be vital for improving healthcare.

A useful way to start any search of the literature is to define your brief, what is sometimes called a search profile. In this you set down the scope of your search. It narrows down what you are seeking to find. Figure 4.2 shows an example of a student's literature search profile for the current task.

| Search profile for *Mobile phones: are they bad for your health?* | |
|---|---|
| Scope (level, dates, languages, country) | *Authoritative online and other sources. Review articles within the last 5 years, with preference for the latest and most authoritative. English language. UK & US.* |
| Exclusions | *Effects on children* |
| Key words | *Mobile phone, cell phone, cellular phone, safe, safety, unsafe, harm, harmful, harmless* |
| Known references | - |
| Notes | - |

**Figure 4.2  A search profile for an assignment**

Google is the world's most popular online search engine. Simply typing 'mobile phone' into the Google search engine will inundate you with responses, many of which would be unsuitable. Many of the responses would probably be trying to sell you a mobile phone service or might be giving you reviews of the latest mobile phone models. You need to narrow your search.

Even when using a generic search engine such as Google, you can dramatically improve your search by including qualifiers: terms that narrow down your search. Using Google Advanced Search, I entered the following terms:

The exact word or phrase: 'mobile phone' (in quotes)
Any of these words (are acceptable): safe safety unsafe harm harmful harmless

When I carried out this search using www.google.co.uk/advanced_ search in the summer of 2017, the first page of results listed webpages that included those from the UK's National Health Service, NetDoctor UK, the US National Cancer Institute and the online encyclopaedia Wikipedia. Once you have found such sources, you need to judge their usefulness.

To find more specialist sources, you could use a discipline-specific database such as PubMed. This is a free-to-use database on biomedical and life science topics. It is maintained by the US National Library of Medicine at the National Institutes of Health. In response to your search, it will list the most relevant sources, in most cases with their abstracts (summaries). In many cases, you will need to then go to another resource to access the full article. In some cases, your university will need to already subscribe to the relevant journal for you to obtain the article, or a specific fee may be payable.

---

**TIP**

**Be aware of synonyms**

Be aware that the items you are searching for may have synonyms (different words that mean the same thing). The terms 'cell phone' or 'cellular phone' are synonyms of 'mobile phone'. Some bibliographic databases, including PubMed, automatically incorporate synonyms of key words or phrases in a search. In other cases, you may need to manually enter the different possibilities.

---

## 4.3 Being selective (using RABT)

Much of the information you find during your literature search may not be relevant or it could be of poor quality. You need to make judgements about which material to use as a suitable source and which to exclude.

> **TIP**
>
> **Swiftly evaluating a source**
>
> When evaluating an academic source, read its abstract (summary) if there is one. Note its authors. Are they affiliated to well-recognised institutions? View the publication's reference list, if provided. Are the listed references of high quality? In some cases you may be able to quickly judge whether the source is relevant, authoritative and worthy of further reading.

The mnemonic (memory aid) **RABT** is a prompt for the four features that are likely to characterise a good source for your task:

- **R**elevant?
- **A**uthoritative?
- **B**alanced or biased?
- **T**imely?

Let us consider each of these elements in turn:

## Relevant?

In judging the suitability of material for your task, key questions to ask are:

- Is the material relevant to my assignment?
- Does it focus on the issues that are part of my task?
- For example, does the material relate to an appropriate group of people or a suitable geographic location?
- Is it a broad overview or does it focus on only part of my task?

In the case of the introductory assignment 'Mobile phones: are they bad for your health?' let us assume that the tutor has asked you to exclude the effects of mobile phones on children, and asked you to consider only adults. In my Google search, three of the ten website entries on the first page of results concentrated on the effect of mobiles on children. For this task, these three can therefore be excluded.

> **ACTIVITY 4.1**
>
> **Relevant?**
>
> You are in your first year at university and you are asked to write an essay entitled 'Is the Antarctic (South polar) ice sheet retreating?' Decide whether each of the sources below is:
>
> 1  Relevant but aimed at too low a level for university use (although it may be appropriate for gaining an overview when you are starting research on the topic)
>
> 2  Not geographically relevant

3   Probably too specialised and technical

4   Relevant, recent and probably aimed at an appropriate scholarly level

Enter 1, 2, 3 or 4 alongside each of the following:

**(a)** A recent, peer-reviewed article on fluctuations in area of the North polar ice sheet.

**(b)** A recent article titled 'Disappearing Antarctic Ice', written by a scientific institute and aimed at school pupils aged 14–16.

**(c)** A recent review article in a leading scientific journal, focusing on the decreasing area of Antarctic summer sea ice.

**(d)** An up-to-date technical article on improving the equipment used for measuring the thickness of sheet ice.

*Check your answers at the end of the chapter.*

## Authoritative?

'Authoritative' means that what you are reading comes from a reputable source. It carries authority. In judging material for your task, questions to ask include:

- Are the authors from an organisation that is well recognised?
- Do the authors have credibility in their field?
- Does the publication give its sources of information?

A reputable website, such as one for an academic institution or professional organisation, will give organisational addresses and contact information on its webpages. A reputable website for an individual should give information about that person; for example, their qualifications and experience, and any organisations with which they are affiliated.

---

**TIP**

### Grey literature

Published or unpublished material of potential academic importance that does not come with bibliographic information, such as an ISBN (international standard book number) or ISSN (international standard serial number), is called grey literature. Such material includes technical reports from government agencies or research groups, patents, newspaper articles and editorials, personal letters and diaries, and even trade catalogues. Because such material may be difficult to catalogue and archive, it can be challenging to find. OpenGrey, the official System for Information on Grey Literature in Europe (www.opengrey.eu/), holds bibliographical references for more than 700,000 paper sources of grey literature. In recent years, grey literature is increasingly published online and has therefore become easier to find.

Grey literature is of importance in many disciplines in the humanities and social sciences, because 'unofficial' or 'less official' sources of information can be artefacts, serving as significant items of evidence for analysis. Some grey literature reveals the latest developments in a field, before more official communications are published, and so is of interest in scientific and technological disciplines as well.

Returning to the initial research findings for 'Mobile phones: are they bad for your health?', websites for the UK's National Health Service and the US National Cancer Institute can be regarded as authoritative. On both these sites you can find more information about who is responsible for the content and you can see what their editorial policy is or judge what it might be. The UK NetDoctor link was to an article published in 2010 (so, quite dated). Also, that website carries heavy advertising for a wide variety of health products, has links to other websites of dubious quality, and does not clearly state its editorial policy. I would reject this website as a source of up-to-date, authoritative information.

The extent to which you might rely on sources of variable quality would depend on the exact nature of the task. If you were criticising information given to the general public about the use of mobile phones, you might want to include the NetDoctor article but critique it. In your first year of undergraduate study you might be less critical about sources, but by the second and third years you should be subjecting them to detailed scrutiny, and rejecting them or criticising their content. Wikipedia is not an authoritative source of information, but it does have its uses.

**TIP**

### If and when to use Wikipedia

Using the online encyclopaedia Wikipedia is problematic. You cannot easily judge the reliability of a Wikipedia article unless you already have in-depth knowledge of that topic. A Wikipedia article might give a useful overview at the beginning of a literature search, but you cannot be confident about the article's accuracy. A Wikipedia article might help you decide which search terms to use to find out more about a topic. Also, the sources to which a Wikipedia article refers could be sought, and provide useful information, but you still need to judge their reliability. As a general rule, do not cite Wikipedia articles but find more authoritative sources.

The most authoritative sources are written by experts and peer-reviewed by other experts. 'Peer-reviewed' means that the item has been scrutinised, normally by at least two independent checkers, who have passed it as of suitable quality, often after appropriate changes have been made.

Publications that are peer-reviewed include academic journals, the websites and published reports of professional institutions, and some academic books. High-status academic journals list the status and affiliation of their editors, and their peer-review policy is normally given in a section called 'guidelines for authors' or similar. A book's title page or acknowledgements section normally reveals who has checked the author's work.

---

**ACTIVITY 4.2**

### Authoritative?

You are asked to write a 1,500-word assignment on the benefits and potential dangers of genetically-modified (GM) crops. Which sources of information below are likely to be appropriate (A), in terms of being authoritative for use as a source for the essay? Which are likely to be inappropriate (I)?

Indicate with an A or I as appropriate.

**(a)** a Wikipedia article on GM crops
**(b)** a review article on GM crops by the Royal Society (the UK's national academy of science)
**(c)** a recent article on GM crops published in the academic journal *Nature*
**(d)** a blog campaigning against the spread of GM crops, signed by someone called 'antiJim'.

*Check your answer at the end of the chapter.*

## Balanced or biased?

Is the material you have found balanced (in that it seeks to represent many sides of an argument) or is it biased (putting forward only particular points of view)? Key questions to ask are:

- Does the author or publisher hold a particular view on the subject?
- Is the publication sponsored by a person or organisation that takes a particular stance?
- Why was the publication produced?

Authors may have a complex mix of motives for being published, such as: their passion for writing, their compulsion to be read by others, their curiosity about a topic, their wish to promote a particular view, or simply, economic survival. If it is a commercial writer, they are probably writing for their daily living. If it is an academic writer, they may have a longer-term view. Academic researchers are influenced by the need to publish in prestigious academic journals in order to secure further funding for their work. The writer's institution, and their publisher, will also have agendas that might influence the nature of the work published.

Judging whether, and to what extent, a publication source is biased is part of assessing its suitability for your task. In order to present a balanced view of your topic, you may decide to refer to publications produced by campaigning organisations (both for and against) as well as academic or official publications. If you choose to promote one side of the argument, at the expense of the other, you would need to justify that decision.

---

**ACTIVITY 4.3**

### Biased or balanced?

Imagine you were asked to write the essay 'The effect of sunlight on the skin. How much is enough?' This is a question with a potentially complex answer.

Sunlight can have positive effects (e.g. promoting vitamin D synthesis in the skin or raising a person's psychological mood) and potentially harmful ones (e.g. triggering skin cancer). People from different ethnic backgrounds have skin with different sensitivities to sunlight, and the pattern of solar radiation (intensity, hours of daylight per day, and so on) varies across the world.

Putting aside such matters, of the sources of information below, which is likely to favour a positive view (P) of the value of sunlight, a negative view (N), or a balanced view (B)? Indicate with a P, N or B as appropriate.

(a) the website for a manufacturer of suntanning beds
(b) the collection of related articles published on the British Broadcasting Corporation's (BBC's) news, nature and science webpages
(c) a consumer website for those who have recovered from surgery for skin cancer
(d) the website for a 'healthy lifestyle' magazine.

*Check your answers at the end of the chapter.*

---

## Timely?

Key questions to ask about the material you find:

- How up to date is the publication?
- Have developments since publication meant that the findings and conclusions are now out of date?

Information and ideas can quickly become outdated. Many fields of research – including communications and the media, energy-related engineering, medicine and international finance – are fast moving. For a given assignment you need to judge whether a source is sufficiently up to date as to still be current and appropriate for your task.

For example, international concerns about human pandemics (disease epidemics that are geographically widespread) have shifted markedly in the last decade or so. In 2003, outbreaks of the SARS virus (responsible for fatal human respiratory infections) and the avian flu virus were international causes of concern. The swine flu virus came to the fore in 2008. Publications that are only a few years old may give levels of risk for different kinds of disease that have changed significantly since. In the case of AIDS (acquired immune deficiency syndrome) caused by HIV (the human immunodeficiency virus), the likelihood of contracting the disease and the long-term survival rate of those affected have shifted dramatically since the late 1980s and continue to do so.

For an assignment, your tutor may list sources that are several years old, in the knowledge that the more diligent students will use these sources to track down more recent ones. This can be done using Google Scholar, or bibliographic databases such as Web of Science, to find recent sources that cite earlier ones that the student has identified (see Chapter 11).

---

**TIP**

### Primary or secondary source?

In most disciplines, a '**primary source**' (part of the primary literature) refers to a publication in which original information or ideas are first communicated. The commonest primary sources are research papers in peer-reviewed academic journals and conference papers. A '**secondary source**' (part of the secondary literature) is a publication that reports on, summarises, or otherwise reviews one or more primary sources. A review article or a chapter in an academic book are typical secondary sources. They might refer to both primary and secondary sources, which are cited and referenced. As you progress through your degree, you are likely to spend more time reading primary sources and less time reading secondary sources.

The use of the terms primary and secondary literature sources should not be confused with primary or secondary sources of evidence, as referred to in some disciplines, such as history or archaeology. In such instances, a **primary source of evidence** is an artefact or document. An example of an artefact would be an unearthed human bone that, on chemical analysis, reveals information about the diet of the person from which it came. An original signed copy of the American Declaration of Independence would be another primary source. **Secondary sources of evidence** are then documents that refer to aspects of the primary sources of evidence. If a staff member refers to a primary or secondary source, make sure in what sense it is being used. Is it a primary or secondary source of literature or a primary or secondary source of evidence?

**President Obama and the US economy. Relevant and timely?**

Imagine you have found an authoritative article in a national US newspaper from January 2013, in which President Obama's administration's handling of the US economy is reviewed for the president's first term (January 2009 to January 2013). Other factors aside, would you consider this article to be 'timely' (Y, yes; N, no) for each of the following assignments?

**(a)** An essay comparing and contrasting the economic success of US presidents since 1989.

**(b)** An essay about President Obama's handling of the US economy (2009–2013), in comparison with the second term (2005–2009) of the previous president, George Bush II.

**(c)** An essay reviewing the successes and failures of President Obama's two administrations.

*Check your answers at the end of the chapter.*

In conclusion, by using **RABT** (Relevant? Authoritative? Balanced? Timely?) you can check that a source is relevant and of appropriate quality for your task. Such sources will also shape your further research.

## 4.4   Becoming more discerning

Earlier in this chapter, we considered a simple example – finding online sources to inform the writing of an assignment in response to the question 'Mobile phones: are they bad for your health?' What if your tutor wished you to use only sources that appear in peer-reviewed publications?

You could narrow your search by using a disciplinary database such as PubMed. When I tried this search in the summer of 2017, this is what I found:

- The search term 'mobile phones' yielded 10,636 results. PubMed is 'intelligent' insofar as it will automatically search for synonyms such as 'cell phones'.
- The search string 'mobile phones AND (harm OR safe)' gave 286 results.

Quickly reviewing what I had found so far, I decided that I wanted to include a further research term 'risk' but concentrate on recent review articles only. So I adjusted the search terms:

- Selecting 'mobile phones AND (risk OR safety OR harm)', plus 'review articles only', still yielded 243 results so I adjusted it further by adding 'within the last five years', which gave me 160 results.

- Removing the reference to child studies 'mobile phones AND (risk OR safety OR harm) NOT child' plus 'review articles only' and 'within the last five years' still gave me 147 hits. I discovered that many of these articles concerned using mobile phones in positive ways, such as phoning for emergency help or smartphone apps that helped people manage their healthcare.
- Excluding articles focusing on positive aspects of mobile phones reduced the number of relevant articles to just 30, of which just a handful I judged to be relevant, authoritative and timely for the task. This included a 2017 article 'Prevalence and risk factors associated with musculoskeletal complaints among users of mobile handheld devices: A systematic review' and a provocative article 'Mobile phone radiation causes brain tumors and should be classified as a probable human carcinogen'.

Now is the time to read those sources you have selected, and the strategies for doing so are considered in the next chapter. For further advice on carrying out literature searches see *Section 11.2 Using bibliographic databases* in Chapter 11.

---

**TIP**

**Free-to-use scholarly search engines and databases**

These focus on scholarly sources, rather than listing a very wide range of public sources as Google does, and so are likely to source higher quality material, thus narrowing the breadth of your search. Google Scholar (http://scholar.google.co.uk) is a free-to-use search engine that indexes scholarly sources, including books, conference papers, journal articles and theses. Some of these sources are downloadable from links provided in the results list. PubMed (www.ncbi.nlm.nih.gov/pubmed) is a free-to-use database listing sources on life sciences and biomedical topics.

---

**Key points in the chapter**

1. Knowing what kinds of sources of information are suitable for your task, being able to narrow your search for information among those sources, and then judging the value of what you have found, are key research skills.

2. In most cases, a useful search strategy is to move from the general to the specific.

3. Using qualifiers is key to narrowing or expanding your search for information.

4. Use RABT (Relevant? Authoritative? Balanced or biased? Timely?) to judge the value of the material you find.

**Further reading**

Cardiff University Information Services (2006). *Evaluating Information Flowchart*. Cardiff: University of Cardiff. Available from: https://ilrb.cf.ac.uk/evalinfo/evalinfo.html [accessed 7 August 2017].

Deane, M. (2010). *Academic Research, Writing and Referencing*. Harlow: Pearson Education.

Dochartaigh, N. O. (2012). *Internet Research Skills*. 3rd edn. London: Sage.

Ridley, D. (2012). *The Literature Review: A Step-By-Step Guide for Students*. 2nd edn. London: Sage.

University of Southampton (2017). *Introduction to Research Skills*. Southampton: University of Southampton. Available from: http://library.soton.ac.uk/sash/introduction-to-research-skills [accessed 7 August 2017].

# Answers for Chapter 4

## Activity 4.1: Relevant?

(a) 2. This article does not specifically cover the geographic region of the assignment. However, it may be of interest for comparing the North polar ice cap with the South polar equivalent.

(b) 1. This article is at a simple level but may provide a good overview and act as a suitable starting point for further research.

(c) 4. This article is relevant and recent and is probably aimed at the right level.

(d) 3. This article is probably too specialised and technical.

## Activity 4.2: Authoritative?

(a) I. Wikipedia articles are not authoritative sources. They are compiled for no fee by normally well-intentioned but not necessarily expert contributors. Contributors' identities may not be given and so their credibility cannot be verified. The information in the article could be of high or low quality, but it is difficult to verify which. However, Wikipedia articles may cite authoritative sources, which can then be found and read.

(b) A. The article is published by a reputable scientific organisation.

(c) A. The article is published in a reputable, peer-reviewed scientific journal.

(d) I. The blog does not appear to be an authoritative source of information. The author does not give their proper name nor, presumably, their relevant experience or links to any organisation against which their credibility might be judged.

## Activity 4.3: Biased or balanced?

**(a)** P. Suntanning beds use ultraviolet light, also a component of sunlight (solar radiation), to tan skin. Manufacturers of suntanning beds are likely to promote a favourable view of the effect of sunlight on skin, although they should warn of the dangers of overexposure to sunlight and to ultraviolet light specifically.

**(b)** B. The BBC has a remit to represent a wide spectrum of views on a particular topic.

**(c)** N is the most likely, but possibly B. Such a website is likely to warn of the dangers of excessive exposure to sunlight, but could nevertheless seek to give a balanced view of sunlight's benefits and dangers, promoting moderate exposure.

**(d)** B. Hopefully, a good health magazine would represent both the positive and negative effects of sunlight on human health. However, this would depend on the editorial stance of the magazine.

## Activity 4.4: President Obama and the US economy. Relevant and timely?

**(a)** Possibly Y. Depending on which other sources were available, and what had been published since, this authoritative review could be used as a source for President Obama's first term of office.

**(b)** Y. Depending on which other sources were available, and what had been published since, this authoritative review could well be a suitable source for making a comparison between the two administrations.

**(c)** Possibly Y. Depending on which other sources were available, the article could still be relevant. It would depend on what had been published since, and whether later sources were better choices for the task.

# Being a Purposeful Reader and Note-taker

You might read many kinds of text on an academic programme – webpages, newspaper and magazine articles, academic journal papers, textbooks and source documents, for example. How you read this material depends on your purpose.

## 5.1 Kinds of reading

There are, of course, many kinds of reading, including reading solely for pleasure. When checking your own academic writing you may review your work in different ways prior to developmental editing, copy-editing and proofreading (Chapter 10). This chapter places emphasis on reading as a forerunner to academic writing (see Table 5.1).

As reading plays such a major part in your university programme, finding ways to improve your reading efficiency yields great benefits. If you read for study for some 10 hours a week on average, increasing your efficiency by 25% will save you 2–3 hours a week, giving you more free time or perhaps enabling you to put it to use in further study to gain better grades.

By its very nature, reading for academic purposes normally requires in-depth knowledge and understanding of the material you read. This may only come about through several rereadings over days, weeks, months and even years. What I seek to do in this chapter is bring together flexible, holistic approaches to reading. Practise only half of the ideas presented here and you could radically transform your reading, saving a great deal of time and effort in the long run, and freeing up your time to be more creative and productive.

We are all different, so some reading techniques may not suit you. For example, a few students find they prefer to read slowly line-by-line or even word-by-word. Nevertheless, most students find that they can learn to read more flexibly, varying their reading speed between slow, moderate and fast. They can vary the speed between one document and another, and within different parts of the same document, depending on their purpose.

Of course, if analysing the intent and construction of prose is the focus of your reading – as on a literature or language course – then your style of reading will be rather different from that described in this chapter.

**Table 5.1   Some reading techniques in relation to academic writing**

| Intention | Reading technique | Method |
|---|---|---|
| Searching for key words or phrases to determine if the material contains information of relevance. | Scanning | Rapidly searching for key words or phrases, e.g. 'Smith and Jones (2016)', 'action research', 'global warming' (Section 5.3). |
| Gaining an overview, e.g. to determine whether the material is worth reading and, if so, how. | Skimming | Rapidly searching the text and other features for items that reveal the structure and content of the material, e.g. summaries, headings and subheadings, beginnings and endings of paragraphs and sections, visual elements (Section 5.3). |
| For a variety of purposes, but all concerned with developing a thorough grasp of some or all of the material. | In-depth reading | Using a method such as SP3R (Section 5.6) to read text in detail, more than once, while annotating and/or taking notes. |
| Consolidating existing knowledge, e.g. when checking notes and annotations made from work previously read. | Rapid rereading | Using a moving pen or pencil as a guide to rapidly re-familiarise yourself with work previously read. |

**TIP**

**Paper or onscreen?**

Most tutors and lecturers recommend reading important, detailed written material from a printed copy rather than solely onscreen. Given the current state of technology, most people find it easier and more efficient to read by light reflecting off a paper's surface than by light emitted from a computer screen. For the moment, the balance of evidence is that most students comprehend material on paper better than they do from a screen (Jabr, 2013; Baron, 2016). If you are concerned about wasting paper, you can always print off electronic material at a size smaller than the original, and print on both sides of the paper. It is easier to highlight, underline and annotate a paper copy than using Adobe Acrobat or other kinds of software to mark up an electronic copy. However, we all work differently. You may find that using an electronic copy is sufficient. Whether using paper or electronic versions, most people find it essential to interact with what they read, marking it up and/or taking notes to suit their purpose.

> **TIP**
>
> **Creating the right environment and state of mind**
>
> Creating the right environment and getting into the right state of mind and body to read can make a great deal of difference to your efficiency. Incidentally, many of these suggestions apply equally to writing:
>
> - Read under natural daylight, or failing that, use a source of light that is as close to daylight as possible. Position the light to avoid sharp contrasts and deep shadows.
> - Normally, your reading material should be laid flat on a horizontal or slightly tilted surface directly in front of you.
> - Establish a regular work place that is as uncluttered and attractive as possible.
> - Use a high-backed chair to maintain a straight back, with your feet flat on the floor.
> - Your eyes should be about 18–20 inches (46–50 cm) from the material you are reading.
> - Create or choose an environment where you can avoid interruptions and distractions.
> - Use whatever technique is appropriate for you (stretching, slow breathing, visualisation or another approach) to encourage a relaxed but alert state of mind and body.
> - The above approaches will also help maintain your health and wellbeing in the longer term.

## 5.2   Beginning with the end in mind

Most of us have been reading for so long (for many of us since the age of five or younger) that we take for granted what a remarkable process it is. Also, because reading tends to be an automatic process that we do without thinking, we may not be aware of what our reading habits are, or how we might go about improving them. If we wish to change our habits, a good place to start is to consider the process of reading itself.

According to Tony Buzan, developer of the mind map approach to note-taking, reading involves at least seven steps (Buzan, 2010). It is a multi-level process. As you read this book, light is reflecting off the page and entering your eyes. The light is focused onto the retina, the layer at the back of each eye, where it triggers sensory cells to generate nerve impulses. These travel through the optic nerve to visual-processing parts of the brain, which link, in turn, to language-interpreting regions and areas where higher-level thinking processes occur. It is a surprisingly complex process, with many parts of the brain involved (Smith, 2004). This is perhaps not surprising when you consider the numerous effects that reading has, whether it is words evoking mental pictures, sounds, tastes, smells and powerful feelings, or sentences and paragraphs triggering deep thought.

From a practical point of view, considering reading in relation to writing (and learning more generally), it is convenient to consider the reading process as adapted from Buzan's (2010) seven-stage model:

1 **Assimilating** some part of what is on the page. This is the physical process of light transfer from page to eye, and then message transfer through the optic nerve to the brain. This takes just a few hundredths of a second.
2 **Recognising** letters and words. This too takes place quickly. Providing you are well versed in the appropriate written language, in less than a second you can recognise that you are seeing letters and words. This is the case, whether the words are written horizontally or vertically, or are printed or in longhand (providing the writer's handwriting is legible!).
3 **Intra-integrating (inner-integrating)** what you are reading. This means comprehending what you are reading within its context. This applies to words in a sentence (such as this one), and their context within this paragraph, this section, this chapter, and in the wider context of this book. Similar sentences to these could be projected on a slide, or depicted on a poster, or posted on a webpage. Compared with this book, they are different contexts and the meanings of such words and sentences might be interpreted slightly differently as a result.
4 **Extra-integrating** (outer-integrating) involves relating what you are reading to your previous knowledge and understanding. It entails making connections and employs processes that might be described as analysing, critiquing, reviewing and selecting. This is 'thinking', and happens both within our awareness (consciously) and outside it (subconsciously or unconsciously).
5 **Retaining** (storing) the information in some form of longer-term memory in our brain. Retaining information can be helped by rereading the material, annotating it, taking notes or mentally rehearsing aspects of what you have read.
6 **Recalling** what you have retained. Retaining (storing) information is of little use unless you can recall it when you need it. Reviewing your notes or your annotations (marking up) of a text can help your recall.
7 **Communicating** what you have read and understood in some form: in speech, in writing, as visual art, as music, or whatever.

If reading is seen this way, as a complex, seven-stage process, it becomes clear that to be an effective academic reader, it helps to read 'with the end in mind'. In other words, just before you start reading something for study purposes, to ask yourself 'What am I seeking to gain from reading this?' A more powerful question to ask is 'What will I be able to do as a result of reading this, that I couldn't do before?' Asking such questions transforms the reading process, making it more purposeful. It turns you into a hunter of information rather than a passive sponge seeking to soak up information.

'OK', you might say, 'but how do I know what I expect to gain from reading something if I haven't read it yet?' This is a good question. And that is where scanning and skimming come in.

## 5.3    Surveying (scanning and skimming)

Surveying something you intend to read, before you read it in detail, serves several purposes:

- It helps you choose whether the item is actually worth reading.
- It assists you in creating a mental map of the document in preparation for more detailed reading.
- If you have not already done so, it helps you decide why you are reading the item, i.e. your purpose.
- It assists you in devising a strategy for reading the item.

Surveying spans two processes: **scanning** the writing for specific items and **skimming** it to gain a general overview.

### Scanning

Scanning involves searching for a specific word, phrase or type of information. Providing you know the structure of what you are reading, you can scan at high speed and perhaps restrict your search to only parts of the document. This approach is useful when you're trying to find out, for example, 'Does the article make any mention of climate change?' or 'Smith and Jones (2016) is a key reference for my assignment. Where does this book chapter make mention of this source?'

It is possible to scan an article or book chapter of several thousand words – looking for one or more phrases – in only a very few minutes. You can do so by using your finger, or better still a pen or pencil, as a guide to help direct your eyes as you swiftly scan through the document. This can be done when reading either a paper item or an electronic document onscreen. Alternatively, in an electronic document, you can move the cursor just ahead of the line you're reading. Using the 'find' function, of course, is one way of hunting down specific words or phrases in an electronic document.

Scanning can help determine the usefulness of an item in your search for information to apply to a writing task. Even though you might be looking for specific items, you cannot help but take in other information about the document – consciously or subconsciously; features such as the document's structure, its organisation and emphasis.

However, while scanning is an appropriate method for finding mention of a particular phrase, it is less useful at locating a particular idea if it is framed in more than one way. Even the phrases 'climate change' and 'global warming' could be described in other ways – 'regional temperature shift', 'decadal temperature rise', and so on – and these other descriptions might be missed in a fast scan of text. 'Action research' is a particular approach to researching people in organisations, but other phrases could be used to describe it, such as 'participatory research' and 'self-reflective, collaborative research'. Unless your scanning is carefully set up, it is easy to miss an idea expressed in a variety of ways.

Scanning is one approach to making some sense of a document before choosing to read it further and deciding on how to do so. The other approach, which is even more popular, is skimming.

---

**TIP**

**Let your pen or pencil be your guide**

When we first learnt to read, many of us started using a finger to mark out each word. As we became more proficient readers we were encouraged to stop using a finger to guide our reading. However, evidence and practice suggests that using a guide can be beneficial. Using a pen or pencil to guide the movement of our eyes down and across the page as we read has many beneficial effects. These include smoothing our eye movements, so reducing fatigue, and controlling the speed of our reading based on degree of interest and difficulty in reading the material.

---

## Skimming

Skimming involves gaining a general overview of a document you intend to read. Through skimming you gain a sense of its structure and content. Skimming involves paying particular attention to:

- contents lists
- summaries or abstracts
- introductions
- conclusions
- headings and subheadings
- charts, tables, diagrams and other visual elements
- the key sentence(s) in a paragraph that summarise(s) the paragraph's theme (often near the beginning or end of the paragraph).

As with scanning, skimming is best done using a pen or pencil moving just ahead of the text you are viewing. Commonly, a book chapter or an article of several thousand words can be skimmed in 5–15 minutes. By doing so you can decide whether the item is appropriate for your task and, if it is, which parts to read and how to go about doing so. If you have not already set yourself a purpose, skimming should enable you to do so. Most importantly, skimming helps you begin to build a construct of the document in your mind. This construct serves to guide your reading and acts as a foundation on which further reading can build. When you now read the document, it is no longer 'unknown territory'.

At the skimming stage, you can begin to mark up the printout or photocopy of a document, or the chapter of a book (providing, of course, the document or book is your own property). You might wish to underline key sentences or phrases. Questions or thoughts might already begin coming to you, and you might wish to note them in the margins of the document – another reason why you should have a pencil or pen to hand.

By the end of skimming, you will have some sense of the structure and content of the material. If you had not already set yourself a purpose for reading the document, by now you should be able to do so. You will probably have decided how much of the document you should read, and in doing so, worked out a strategy for reading it.

---

**TIP**

**Skim and/or scan?**

You can choose whether to scan a document, skim it, or do both. In my experience, most people choose to skim and use scanning as a way of helping decide whether they should skim the document.

---

## 5.4   Establishing a purpose

The argument in this chapter is that knowing why you are reading something helps you, in many cases, to read it more efficiently. That is where purpose comes in.

Purpose, applied to reading, concerns what you're going to be able to do as a result of having done the reading. What will you now have, or be able to do, that you couldn't do before?

Consciously setting a purpose gives you *reason* and *motivation* for reading. It also enables you to devise an effective strategy for carrying out the reading. Without purpose, your reading runs a greater risk of being carried out aimlessly and inefficiently.

---

**Reminder:** You may need to survey a document, i.e. skim it, scan it, or both, before you can establish a purpose in reading it.

### Examples of 'purpose' applied to reading

It helps if your purpose is about action. Here are three examples:

*I am reading this 2,000-word article to find out whether it adds anything to my previous knowledge of critical academic reading. If it does, I will highlight or make notes about the new material, and will consider how I can use this new information to help fine-tune my strategy for reading sources for assignments.*

*I am reading these three articles to compare and contrast the ideas of their authors for the 'Current models' section of the essay I'm writing.*

*I am reading this 5,000-word report so that I can present its key findings in a 5-minute slide presentation at my next tutorial meeting.*

So, a purpose is best framed in terms of what you will now be able to do as a result of reading a document. In some cases, however, reading may simply involve checking that you are up to date in a topic or that you have considered a topic from all angles. Even in such cases, your purpose can be framed so that it is still about action. For example:

*After reading this latest review article I can be confident that I am up to date on this topic and that I have gathered and reviewed the material I need, whether to:*

- *answer relevant questions from my tutor at our next meeting*

- *write about this topic in my forthcoming essay*

- *use the material as the basis for preparing revision notes for the forthcoming module exam.*

---

**ACTIVITY 5.1**

**Purpose in reading**

For an assignment you are about to carry out, choose some source material you intend to read. Decide what your purpose is in reading it. The statement 'To complete the assignment' will almost certainly not be sufficiently precise. What will you gain from reading the source material that you can apply to completing the assignment? Working out what this might be may require you to survey (skim and/or scan) the material first.

---

## 5.5   Deciding on a reading strategy

Murray's (2008) paper entitled *Writer's Retreat: Reshaping Academic Writing Practices* promotes the use of writing retreats by staff to improve their confidence

and productivity in academic writing. The article is available at www.seda.ac.
uk/?p=5_4_1&pID=9.2. Download the article to undertake the following activity.

---

**ACTIVITY 5.2**

### Writing retreats

Choose one of the following purposes in reading Murray's (2008) article:

(a) I am reading it to decide whether it is worthwhile organising a mini writing retreat for some of my fellow students, to help us with writing our final-year dissertations.

(b) I am reading it to weigh up the benefits and challenges of organising a writing retreat.

(c) I am reading it to find out how to run a writing retreat, so that I can organise one. Now, skim the article with your chosen purpose in mind. To what extent would this article meet your purpose?

*Check your answers at the end of the chapter.*

---

Depending on your purpose you would read the article in different ways. In fact, you might read it one way (to find out whether it is worthwhile organising a writing retreat) and then another way (to gather information to help organise a retreat). During your degree programme you may find that there are certain key papers or textbook chapters that you will want to read more than once, in different ways and with different purposes in mind.

---

**TIP**

### You don't have to read everything!

It is my belief that some lecturers – having come through a university education in which they were encouraged to read numerous books from cover to cover – now expect this of their own students. A degree programme in literature, the classics or a modern language may require the detailed reading of dozens of books from cover to cover. However, in most degree programmes there are just a few key texts that you are encouraged to purchase, read and reread. When I write a peer-reviewed journal paper, or write a book such as this one, I draw upon my reading of hundreds of books and articles. But it does not mean that I have read every single word in all those books or articles. In some cases I have, but in other cases I will have read them selectively, to meet a particular purpose. I know that most of my colleagues do this too. Even if you are reading a core text, I encourage you to be thoughtful and selective about how you read it.

## 5.6  In-depth reading (using SP3R)

To gain an in-depth understanding of material, I recommend a technique I've developed that I call SP3R. It is a variation on a traditional study method called SQ3R, which dates back to the 1940s (Rowntree, 1998). SP3R is shorthand for the five steps of an in-depth reading process (Survey, Purpose, Read once, Read again, Review). Using the SP3R method you hunt for information to meet your purpose. Reading material slowly, once only, from beginning to end, takes about the same time as using the SP3R method. Using SP3R, however, you are likely to have a much better grasp of the material.

### SP3R

#### Survey (scan and/or skim)

As we have seen earlier, scanning is searching for specific items. Skimming is gaining a general overview of the structure and content. Skimming involves noting the headings and subheadings within the document, any summaries or conclusions, key sentences in paragraphs and any visual elements. Surveying helps you decide whether the item is worth reading and, if so, how. Do you need to read it all, or only parts? Surveying assists you in creating a mental map of the document in preparation for further reading. It also helps you work out a purpose in reading it if you had not already done so.

#### Purpose

As we have seen, setting a purpose involves answering key questions: Why am I reading this? What do I hope to get out of it? Purpose is about action, what you will be able to do as a result of reading the material. I find this approach is more fruitful than the traditional SQ3R method, where Q stands for 'question' and does not mention purpose. I would encourage you to ask yourself questions about the text but not at the expense of setting a purpose as well.

#### Read once

This is reading for understanding, in response to the purpose you have set. At this stage – and assuming the book or document is your personal property, or a photocopy or printout – you could mark up key points by underlining them in pencil or using a highlighter. You could also annotate the margins with questions and comments.

#### Read again

This is to deepen your understanding, check whether you have answers to the questions you've asked, and to take notes to meet your purpose.

#### Review

Read a third time to check you have understood, and to ensure that any notes and annotations are accurate and complete. If there is any follow-up action you need to take, such as getting answers to questions that were not resolved, or following up on any references cited in the text, then make a note of them and follow them up.

## 5.7   Annotating and note-taking

As we considered earlier in the chapter, reading is a complex process. In order to understand and learn from what we are reading, and then apply it in our writing, it pays to read actively with a purpose in mind. Engaging with what we are reading can involve marking up (annotating) text and/or note-taking. Both involve us asking questions about what we are reading, selecting key information and ideas, and interpreting them.

Note-taking and annotating can help you:

- focus your attention as you read
- create a record of what you have read
- link new information and ideas with what you previously knew
- organise and develop your ideas
- research and plan your assignments
- revise for your exams.

You can, of course, take notes in many situations, whether reading a webpage, article or book, or viewing or listening to a lecture, a video, a radio broadcast, or some other audiovisual medium. In most cases, notes are for your own use. We all have our preferences about how we like to learn, so develop ways of note-taking that work well for you. Some suggestions are considered below.

### General guidance on note-taking

Note-taking is, for most of us, a key part of academic reading and writing. I am keen on taking notes that are brief and focused. The best notes can be transformative, involving capturing aspects of the original material and shaping them into something of great value to you, the reader. Like reading itself, note-taking is often best done strategically to meet a purpose. Such a strategy involves:

- Reminding yourself, 'What is my purpose in taking notes or annotating this document?' 'What will this enable me to do?'
- Answering such questions encourages you to take notes or annotate efficiently to meet your purpose, without wasting time recording unnecessary information.
- Reading using a strategy such as SP3R, and taking notes and/or annotating to capture the key points to meet your purpose. Write your own comments, criticisms or queries about what you are reading.
- Making your notes brief but sufficiently detailed that you will understand them when you return to them days or weeks later.
- Finally, checking that your notes have achieved their purpose.

---

**TIP**

**Taking notes in combination with annotating**

Notes, of whatever form, tend to work best when they are visually appealing and have a clear logic. Consider combining annotating with note-taking. If the original material is your own copy, annotate it and then refer to the annotations in your notes, using a numbering or lettering system to refer between the two. Here are some suggestions:

- Systematically use CAPITAL LETTERS, underlining, highlighting and colour to draw attention to key words and phrases in your notes and annotations.
- Ask yourself questions about the new material, in particular relating it to what you previously knew.
- Notes and annotations are dynamic, subject to change.
- Include plenty of white space to make your notes more appealing and to provide opportunities for adding material later.

Your notes and annotations are precious resources. Well-written, they will allow you to return to quickly pick up the thread of what you were reading. Make a note of your purpose(s) and record the date of your reading, note-taking and annotating. This information will be invaluable when you return to the source material days or weeks later, perhaps with a different purpose in mind.

---

## Forms of note-taking

Effective notes contain key words, short phrases, abbreviations and many visual elements, rather than sentences and paragraphs. Notes can be broadly classified into linear or patterned, or combinations of the two.

Linear notes are arranged down the page, from top to bottom. They contain phrases and summaries arranged at different levels such as:

- headings and subheadings
- with items listed in number (1, 2, 3 ...) or letter (a, b, c ...) order and bullet points.

**Patterned notes** are more visual and use space in a more fluid manner. Common types of patterned notes include:

- **Mind maps** (sometimes called brainstorms or spider diagrams). These show ideas branching out from a topic image, word or phrase in the centre of a landscape page. Part of a mind map is shown in Chapter 1, Section 1.3. The mind map concept was originally developed by Tony Buzan in the 1960s (Buzan, 2010) and seeks to engage with the mind holistically, encouraging imaginative and associative thinking (linking one idea with another). See Illumine Training's Mind Mapping Site (www. mind-mapping.co.uk/) for examples of Buzan-style mind maps and how to create them.
- **Concept maps** (sometimes called tree hierarchies). These show ideas branching down from the top of the page in a more hierarchical manner, which can be like the arrangement in a family tree. A line between one idea and the next usually has a verb or phrase explaining the connection. Figure 5.1 shows a concept map in response to the question 'Why does the U.S. have a human space exploration program?'. Free software for creating your own concept maps is available from the University of West Florida's Institute for Human and Machine Cognition (http://cmap. ihmc.us/).
- **Flow diagrams** (flow charts). These show items, usually contained within geometric shapes, linked by arrows in a sequence. Flow diagrams are particularly effective at depicting cyclic and step-by-step processes.
- **Matrices.** A matrix is a table in which items or themes are identified in the headings of rows and columns. Information is placed in the cells where columns and rows intersect. Matrices are particularly useful for summarising and comparing data or themes from different viewpoints or sources.

The Open University has useful webpages and activities on note-taking at www2. open.ac.uk/students/skillsforstudy/notetaking-techniques.php. McMillan and Weyers (2012) give examples of different kinds of notes, with guidance on how to create them.

Patterned and linear notes are not mutually exclusive. You can often pick and choose flexibly between the two approaches, using them in combination, when note-taking for a particular purpose.

> **TIP**
>
> ## Note-taking to avoid plagiarism
>
> Plagiarism is the act of taking the words and/or ideas of others, and not properly attributing those sources in your writing. To avoid plagiarism, you need to ensure that you keep full records of the sources from which you have gathered information, and properly cite and quote them in your writing. If you ever copy and paste material from a source, record the full reference details along with the relevant page number, and mark the copied text in some way (for example, by colour coding or enclosing in quotation marks) to show that these words are not your own. See Chapter 9 for detailed strategies for avoiding plagiarism.

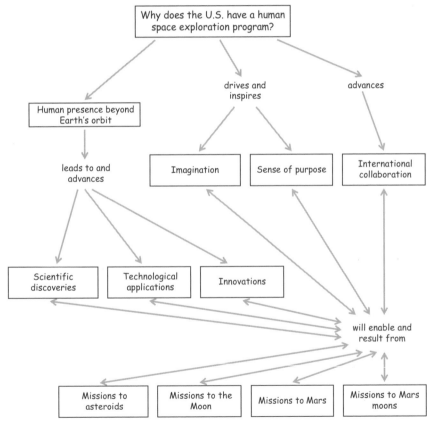

**Figure 5.1  A concept map drawn in response to the question 'Why does the U.S. have a human space exploration program?**

*Source*: Adapted from Cañas et al. (2012)

TIP

**Thinking big using colour**

Do you find organising your reading, note-taking and planning a struggle? Here is an approach some students find useful. Put your notes and ideas on coloured sticky notelets and arrange them on a large sheet of paper – brown parcel paper is cheap and convenient. Rather like the police investigator's case summary displayed on a board, items can be moved about and notes added as ideas develop. You can use various coloured pens to classify your notes and ideas into themes by colour. Try using this 'big picture' approach. Tearing yourself away from the computer keyboard can make organising your note-taking, thinking and planning more flexible, creative and enjoyable.

## Key points in the chapter

1   There are different kinds of reading, such as scanning, skimming and various forms of in-depth reading. Exactly how you read source material depends on its nature, your purpose, your preferences and your familiarity with the content.

2   Reading is a complex skill, involving assimilation, recognition, inner-integration and extra-integration. Note-taking and/or annotating while you read can improve retention and recall.

3   Reading for academic writing is, in most cases, best done purposefully. A purpose involves establishing the reasons for reading the material, and the likely benefits in doing so. To establish a purpose may involve surveying (scanning and/or skimming).

4   Scanning entails reading at high speed to identify specific items.

5   Skimming involves reading at speed to gain an overview of the structure and content of the written material. It confirms or establishes the purpose in reading. It also assists in determining a suitable reading strategy to meet the purpose.

6   In-depth reading using the SP3R method involves surveying the material, setting a purpose, and then reading the material selectively three times to meet the purpose. This includes annotating and/or taking notes and then reviewing them together with the text to check whether the purpose has been met.

7   An electronic or paper copy of the text (assuming it is your property) can be annotated with highlighting, underlining, brief notes, observations and questions.

**8** Annotating the text can be combined with note-taking. There are many different methods of note-taking, both linear and patterned, and they can be combined according to your purpose, your preferences and the nature of the material.

# Cited references

Baron, N. (2016). 'Do Students Lose Depth in Digital Reading?' *The Conversation*, 20 July 2016. Available from: https://theconversation.com/do-students-lose-depth-in-digital-reading-61897 [accessed 8 August 2017].

Buzan, T. (2010). *The Speed Reading Book*. Revised edn. Harlow: BBC Active.

Cañas, A. J., Carff, R., and Marcon, M. (2012). 'Knowledge Model Viewers for the iPad and the Web.' In A. J. Cañas, J. D. Novak, and J. Vanhear eds., *Concept Maps: Theory, Methodology, Technology – Proceedings of the Fifth International Conference on Concept Mapping*. Malta: University of Malta. Available from: http://cmc.ihmc.us/cmc2012papers/cmc2012-p193.pdf [accessed 8 August 2017].

Illumine Training. (2017). *The Mind Mapping Site*. Windsor: Illumine. Available from: www.mind-mapping.co.uk/ [accessed 8 August 2017].

Institute for Human & Machine Cognition. (2017). *CMAP*. Florida: Institute for Human and Machine Cognition (IHMC), University of West Florida. Available from: http://cmap.ihmc.us/ [accessed 8 August 2017].

Jabr, F. (2013). 'The Reading Brain in the Digital Age: The Science of Paper versus Screens.' *Scientific American*, 11 April 2013. Available from: www.scientificamerican.com/article/reading-paper-screens/ [accessed 8 August 2017].

McMillan, K. and Weyers, J. (2012). *The Smarter Study Skills Companion*. 3rd edn. Harlow: Pearson.

Murray, R. (2008). 'Writer's Retreat: Reshaping Academic Writing Practices'. *Educational Developments*, 9(2), pp. 14–16. Available from: www.seda.ac.uk/?p=5_4_1&pID=9.2 [accessed 8 August 2017].

Rowntree, D. (1998). *Learn How to Study: A Realistic Approach*. London: TimeWarner.

Smith, F. (2004). *Understanding Reading: A Psycholinguistic Analysis of Reading and Learning to Read*. 6th edn. London: Routledge.

The Open University. (2013). *Skills for OU Study: Note-taking Techniques*. Milton Keynes: The Open University. Available from: www2.open.ac.uk/students/skillsforstudy/notetaking-techniques.php [accessed 8 August 2017].

## Further reading

Buzan, T. and Buzan, B. (2010). *The Mind Map Book*. Revised edn. Harlow: BBC Active.

Cottrell, S. (2017). *Critical Thinking Skills*. 3rd edn. London: Palgrave Macmillan.

Fairbairn, G. J. and Winch, C. (2011). *Reading, Writing and Reasoning: A Guide for Students*. 3rd edn. Maidenhead: Open University Press.

# Answers for Chapter 5

## Activity 5.2: Writing retreats

Depending on your purpose, you would read Murray's (2008) article in different ways. If you had chosen (a), you would have discovered that the article emphasises the merits of writing retreats. If you had chosen (a) or (b), you would have noticed that the article does not consider the challenges or difficulties of running writing retreats. You would need to read more articles about writing retreats (including perhaps some selected from the reference list at the end of the article) to gain a more balanced view of the drawbacks as well as the benefits of writing retreats. Finally, had you chosen (c), you might only have needed to read parts of the article – those parts that concerned the operational parts of running a writing retreat. In choosing (c), this article alone is unlikely to provide all the information you need. Again, you would need to gather more information. You might even wish to contact the article's author to find out more about how she currently organises writing retreats.

# Planning and Structuring More Assignments

Chapter **6**

As we have seen, researching your assignment, and carrying out the reading required for it, are part of an iterative process. You learn as you go along. You find out about the literature that exists – and that you can gain access to – and this shapes your further searching. You read the best and most appropriate material that you find for your assignment, and annotate and make notes on what you find, and doing so shapes your further searching and reading. All this can be a delightful exploration of a topic, but you don't have unlimited time. And even while you are carrying out your searches, and reading, annotating and note-taking, you need to be thinking about the structure for the assignment you are going to write and begin writing it.

Chapter 3 explored the structure of essays and the structure and writing style of practical reports. This chapter considers five kinds of assignment: business-style reports, critical reflective accounts, presentations, posters and dissertations. Business-style reports writing and critical reflective accounts are almost at two ends of an academic writing spectrum. Business-style report writing usually has a highly structured, no-nonsense approach, often being written in an impersonal style. Critical reflective writing, on the other hand, is likely to be written, at least in part, from a subjective viewpoint and in a personal style. Both kinds of assignment have become commonplace on some vocational degrees. Critical reflective writing has gained momentum as a means of integrating personal experience with academic knowledge, so promoting deep learning.

Presentations and posters are both highly visual forms of communication and any words used need to be thoughtfully integrated with visual elements. In the case of presentations, words spoken need to complement, not simply repeat, any written text that accompanies images.

Dissertations tend to be the longest and most detailed documents that undergraduates and taught Master's students write. They are usually highly structured, with chapters, sections and subsections, and with clear navigation to enable the reader to find their way flexibly through such a long document.

## 6.1    Business-style report writing

A report, as its name suggests, reports on some well-defined area of investigation. A report has a clear structure and adopts many conventions appropriate to the discipline in which it is written. There are numerous kinds of report, for example:

- a practical report on a scientific experiment (see Section 3.5)
- a technical review of a topic in engineering
- a report on the findings of a questionnaire survey
- a business-style report that gives recommendations based on analysis of a situation.

It is the analytical, business-style report that is considered here. Business-style reports are unusual in that apart from being highly structured, they may use more overt tactics to persuade the reader. Words are kept to a minimum, and the 'facts' or data and their interpretation and analysis are kept concise.

### Analytical report structures

Analytical reports often contain all or most of the following elements (although the order of elements in the front and end matter may vary):

**Front matter:**

Title page

Acknowledgements

Glossary

Table of contents

**Main part of the report:**

1    **Executive summary.** One or a few paragraphs summarising: context; the purpose of the report; the report's scope, aims and objectives; methods (sometimes); main findings; conclusions and recommendations.
2    **Introduction/Background/Context.** A few paragraphs giving: the context that triggered the need for the report; the report's purpose, scope, aims and objectives.

   2.1

   2.2 ...
3    **Methods/Methodology.** Present in most but not all business reports.

   The validity of the results obtained depends on the methods used. This section should help convince the reader of the strength and validity of the results.

   3.1

   3.2 ...

4 **Findings/Results.** Presents the data collected: it shows summary data, not raw data; the data is usually presented in charts and/or tables; text introduces the charts and tables and refers to them; text draws out key points from the charts and tables.

4.1

4.2

4.3 ...

5 **Discussion.** This interprets, explains and analyses the results with respect to other sources of information: it may evaluate the strength and validity of the findings on the basis of the methods used; depending on the nature of the report, it may give several options, giving the risks and benefits of each, finishing with the preferred option.

5.1

5.2 ...

6 **Conclusions and Recommendations.** These may occupy separate sections or be combined. The conclusions refer to the original purpose of the report, summarise the main findings rather than simply repeating them, highlight the significance of the findings and their implications, and may suggest further research. If recommendations are included, they suggest what action should be taken.

**End matter:**

References

Appendices. Contain detailed information that would disrupt the flow of the argument in the main part of the report. Such information is needed to convince the reader that the investigation was properly carried out. Material in an appendix might include raw data, statistical analyses, sample questionnaires or interview transcripts.

Notice that in the main part of the report, the sections are numbered. This is a common convention in business and technical reports, and the specific form used here is called decimal numbering. Main sections have a single number (e.g. 3), subsections have two numbers (e.g. 3.2) and subdivisions of subsections, three or more numbers (e.g. 3.2.1). Decimal numbering organises the parts of the report into a clear hierarchy, which follows a logical structure. This makes it easy for the writer to cross-reference between different parts of the document and for the reader to navigate through the document and locate, refer to and discuss specific parts with colleagues.

Most people who read a business report, whether it is an assessor on your course or a manager who is reading the document to help with her work, will first read the contents list, the executive summary, the conclusions and any recommendations. Your assessor should, of course, read your report in detail, but it is those sections that summarise the content, and that are often read first, which will shape the assessor's view. First impressions count.

---

**TIP**

**Aim or objective?**

In a report, there is normally a distinction between the two. An aim is *what* is being sought overall. Objectives are the means of achieving the aim (the *how*). For example:

**Brief**: Investigate whether the university library should install group-study rooms. If so, what is the likely demand and how could it be met?

Part of the response to this brief could involve:

**Aim**: Determine whether there is student and/or staff interest for group-study rooms in the library.

**Objectives:**

**(a)** Raise the issue at Students' Union, Teaching & Learning Staff Committee and Library Staff meetings to gauge the level of support for group-study rooms, before proceeding further.

**(b)** Based on the findings of (a), if appropriate, assess the demand and specific requirements for group-study rooms by undertaking interviews with selected students and staff.

---

## Other analytical report structures

A business-style report may have a different structure from the one above. Business reports tend to be driven by the pragmatic needs of the organisation, and the organisation may have its own standard template for reports. In any case, if you are set an assignment for a business-style report, you may not have been given detailed guidelines for the structure (although I suggest you ask for them). If that is the case, you could structure the main part of the report to respond logically to the guidelines (the brief). You would 'top and tail' the report as normal, with an executive summary, and conclusions and recommendations, but the main part of the report would follow a logical narrative. For example, if you were asked to write a report on the need to upgrade the virtual learning environment (VLE) of an organisation, and the implications of doing so, the main part might look like this:

1  Executive summary
2  The need for change
   2.1 Critical events
   2.2 Limitations

2.3 Missed opportunities
2.4 The need for expansion and modernisation
3 Option A. Upgrading existing VLE
3.1 Requirements
3.2 Implications
3.3 Benefits
3.4 Risks
3.5 Conclusion
4 Option B. Changing to a new VLE
4.1 Requirements
4.2 Implications
4.3 Benefits
4.4 Risks
4.5 Conclusion
5 Summary comparison of options
6 Conclusions and recommendations

---

**TIP**

**A report or a proposal?**

Strictly, a report contains information about what has happened in the past. It records and interprets 'facts' and it seeks primarily to inform the reader. A proposal considers what might happen in the future. It puts forward arguments, usually making one or more recommendations to help persuade the reader to make a decision. It may well express opinions. In practice, analytical reports may contain elements of reports and proposals, as in the alternative analytical report structure example above. The more like a proposal a business document is, the more likely it is to contain overtly persuasive argument.

## Analytical report writing style

As we have seen, business-style reports are formally structured:

- With clear headings and subheadings
- Often employing decimal numbering to aid navigation
- May include tables or graphs.

The direct, no-nonsense approach is also reflected in the writing style:

- Is largely in the past tense, to report on what has happened, but using the present tense to refer to figures and tables, what the findings show, and what applies now. The future tense is used to point to what will, or could, happen.

- A report is often written in the impersonal or third person, using the passive voice: 'The survey was carried out …' rather than the active voice: 'The project team carried out the survey …'.
- Often assumes that the reader has some relevant technical knowledge, so that basic terminology does not need to be explained. Technical terms may be listed and defined in the Glossary.
- Uses abbreviations (acronyms), with the word or phrase being given in full at its first appearance, e.g. 'natural language processing (NLP)', but then abbreviated thereafter.
- Is written with clarity and precision, avoiding vagueness. For example, 'Frontline staff were emailed and directed to complete and submit the online questionnaire survey within seven days,' instead of 'Various kinds of staff member were asked to fill in the online questionnaire survey.' The need for clarity and precision applies to most forms of academic writing.
- Is concise, with any unnecessary words removed.
- Wherever possible, sentences and paragraphs are kept short.
- May use bullet points to summarise items, rather than flowing prose.

As always, be acutely aware of the purpose of your report and its audience. Match the language you use to your audience.

---

**ACTIVITY 6.1**

### Keep it short and simple (KISS)

In business and technical reports, writing clearly and concisely is encouraged. Imagine you have been given the information below by a teacher and you want to simplify it for other teachers. Using bullet points, reduce this 185 words to 100 words or less.

*The rules for using clay in class are designed to meet health and safety requirements, enable effective classroom management and ensure that children have an enjoyable experience and can produce objects of which they can be proud. Among the rules relating to health, safety and hygiene are: children must wear protective aprons; no eating of clay; avoid getting clay in hair; and cleaning all work surfaces thoroughly with water and sponge to remove clay deposits, which would otherwise dry and become dust. Those relating to classroom management include: children not making objects that are offensive to others; no throwing of clay; and no handling of other people's clay objects. Those concerning the proper use of clay are: the need to wedge (knead) the clay to make it pliable and to remove air; making objects with clay that have no parts thicker than a thumb; covering clay in plastic bags or cellophane to keep it moist; joining modelled clay pieces by scoring and slipping while moist; ensuring objects to be fired are thin or hollow; and not glazing the underside of clay objects to be fired.*

One solution to this task is given at the end of the chapter. How does yours compare?

---

**ACTIVITY 6.2**

### Putting the pieces together

Clear and concise sentences are a key feature of good report writing. Shorten this account of 101 words to fewer than 75 and make it easier to comprehend. Do so by using the active voice, removing unnecessary words or phrases, and splitting long sentences into two or more shorter ones.

*The use of the new remote server and its associated management system was found by the project teams to circumvent three of the problems apparent in the original system: project teams could now routinely access the latest version of the software, they could see who had changed which features of the software, and they could track people's comments about the software as it was being developed. We envisage, in the future, implementing most aspects of the new system, but we will have to review the system for providing commentary, so that commentators can choose who they wish to view their comments. (101)*

When you've finished, compare your solution with the example given at the end of the chapter.

## 6.2 Critical reflective writing

Reflective writing has become popular in many disciplines, from architecture and engineering to medicine and media studies. It involves documenting a personal view, focusing on recent experience. It usually entails moving beyond mere description, to explaining and justifying what has taken place. Often, particularly if the work is to be assessed, it involves critical reflection, in which the individual seeks to learn from their experience. Such critical reflection commonly refers to theory referred to and practice developed during a course. It is this latter type of reflective writing – critical reflective writing – that is considered here.

Reflective thinking and writing as a way of improving practice within a discipline has a well-documented tradition dating back to Dewey (1938), Lewin (1946) and, more recently, Schön (1983, 1987) and Boud et al. (1985). The University of New South Wales (2016) in its guidelines highlights the value of critical reflective thinking and writing. Paraphrasing the guidelines, reflecting critically helps you by:

**Building on previous knowledge**, both formal and informal, to make connections:

- between what you knew and what is new
- between your practice and the theory that lies behind it
- between what you are doing now and what you may wish to do differently in the future.

**Examining how you learn** by writing reflectively about your learning experiences, and what and how you have learnt from them.

**Integrating and extending** what you are learning by:

- combining new knowledge with old
- identifying questions you have yet to answer
- and so revealing what you have yet to learn.

**Reflecting on both successes and failures** so as to:

- gain a more balanced awareness of your practice
- learn from your mistakes
- support you in building on your successful practice.

In summary, critical reflective writing should help you become a more 'active, aware and critical learner' (University of New South Wales, 2016). It also helps embed reflective thinking in your practice as a student, and later as a professional in your discipline.

## Reflective writing in action

Notes taken at or around the time of an experience, perhaps recorded in a learning (reflective) journal or logbook, can be highly subjective, with descriptions of what happened and perhaps what the writer thought or felt at the time. Depending on the course and context, such material may be highly personal and for the writer's eyes only. Or it may be evidence that can be shown to an assessor. Such writing may include emotive (emotional) language, exclamations, casual expressions – the very things that are not encouraged in academic writing. Such writing, however, is material for more considered reflection later, which informs a critically reflective account that can justly be called academic writing.

Here are two samples of written work, the first from the experience of a trainee teacher writing a learning journal about what had just happened in a classroom when working with three students. The second draws upon that experience in the student's critical account of how they improved their practice after reflection.

Today, tutorial time, I tried out the action planning exercise with three students. Disastrous! Students hadn't thought about it beforehand. They weren't used to doing this kind of thing. And I wasn't too sure either. By the third student it had dawned on me that the students and I needed to prepare for the meeting and be very clear about what we were seeking to achieve. If the students had known that they had choices, and it wasn't simply a box-ticking or rubber-stamping exercise, that would have helped too! Back to the drawing board. I'll be better prepared next time. This one-to-one stuff can be harder than working with the whole class.

Action planning, as part of making a personal learning plan (PLP), can help empower students. At its best action planning promotes students' 'learning, self-awareness and self-confidence, opportunity awareness and the development of planning skills' (Bullock and Wikeley, 1999, p. 19). As is evident from my experience with class 11, PLP sessions need to be well planned so that both tutor and tutee are clear about aims, process and potential benefits. Both need to prepare before the session. The PLP process dramatically improved when I ...

## The challenges of critical reflective writing

Many students find critical reflective writing difficult, because it combines documenting personal experience and its interpretation with standing back and taking a critical view. Despite writing about personal matters, and using 'I' or 'we', the writing still needs to be well structured, develop an argument, and be written in an appropriate academic style.

## Structure

Exactly how critical reflective writing is organised in a document will depend on the nature of the assignment. In degree courses in health, social work or education, students are required to reflect on critical incidents – dramatic events that they have observed or been directly involved in, which raise important questions from which they can learn. At the same time, they may also be writing reflective accounts about how their practice has improved, looking back over weeks or months. However the account is structured, the account of learning can benefit from drawing upon Kolb's (1984) experiential learning cycle (Figure 6.1). The stages in this cycle can be reflected in the narrative of your writing.

In your account, you will set the context for the experience you wish to analyse and learn from (and explain to an assessor). You cannot critically reflect on everything you experience, so you need to be selective in order to maximise

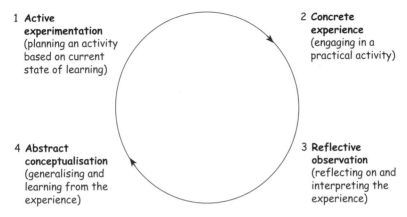

1 **Active experimentation** (planning an activity based on current state of learning)

2 **Concrete experience** (engaging in a practical activity)

4 **Abstract conceptualisation** (generalising and learning from the experience)

3 **Reflective observation** (reflecting on and interpreting the experience)

Figure 6.1  **An interpretation of Kolb's (1984) experiential learning cycle**

your opportunities to learn, and you will often be guided in this by your supervisor. Setting the context and describing the experience involves setting down just the right amount of background information so that the reader appreciates the context, but doesn't get distracted by unnecessary detail. Your skill lies in knowing your reader and what she or he recognises about your situation. For example, here is what a trainee physiotherapist might write about a particular incident with a patient (step 2 in Figure 6.1):

> *I accompanied a local physiotherapist, Mr Smith, who was treating a 35 year old man with a severe ankle sprain. The clinic's conventional treatment regime was followed which involved, in the short term, a self-management programme of compression bandaging, limb elevation, ice packs, anti-inflammatory drugs and resting the joint. Longer term treatment included strengthening exercises. At a review appointment three weeks later, the patient's ankle was still weak, lacking strength and joint movement, with resultant poor mobility.*

The next step involves reflecting upon and interpreting the incident (step 3). For example:

> *In the light of this outcome, and reflecting on advice from my tutor, I approached Mr Smith. I suggested I might review with him recent research literature and case studies for this type of problem and consider what alternative treatment options were available. He agreed, seeing this as an opportunity to improve the clinical outcome for his service when dealing with this common condition.*

This analysis might draw upon background theory from a taught course, so that you are interpreting the specific incident in terms of general principles, or it might prompt a review of relevant literature. For example:

> *Prompted by the guidance notes from Unit 3.4 of the university course, I reviewed the recent literature on best practice for the management of acute ankle sprains[1,2,3,4]. In the light of new research and approaches to treatment documented in the literature, I discussed my findings with Mr Smith, who suggested I prepare a short presentation for the next practice meeting. Drawing upon my review, I proposed that joint manipulation, orthotic joint strapping with non-elastic tape, together with acupuncture, would probably improve the therapeutic outcome for this type of severe ankle injury.*

Finally, critical reflection normally involves applying what has been learnt (step 4), to inform the planning of future actions (step 1). For example:

> *Discussion at the practice meeting resulted in an agreement that Mr Smith, and his physiotherapist colleague Mr Kline, would implement two of the suggested treatment alternatives, namely joint manipulation and strapping. This would be on a trial basis with suitable patients followed by clinical audit to assess any change in outcome. The use of acupuncture (which would involve further staff training and/or bringing in a qualified acupuncturist) would be considered once the results of the initial trial were clear.*

These different stages in the experiential learning cycle need not be neatly separated in your account. But in formal critically reflective accounts, which are assessed, the four steps are normally represented.

## Style

In critical reflective writing, tenses commonly shift swiftly from past, to present, to future, as the writer reflects on what has happened, generalises about how this informs their practice, and then considers how it will shape their future practice. For example, here some of the verbs are shown in bold to make the changes in tense easier to follow:

> *On several occasions over the ten weeks, one student or another **missed** our 2-hour weekly session. The impact of this **was** quite disruptive on the class as a whole, and especially for any sub-group the student **joined**. I **consider** this disruption **came about** because:*

> - *The student had to be brought up to date by other students in the class.*
> - *The student was not skilled in contributing to the practical exercises that built on the previous week.*

*In the future, **I shall make** three changes in response:*

- *Stress the importance for students to attend all sessions.*
- *Post descriptions of that week's activities online, immediately after the session.*
- *If need be, spend time one-to-one with a student on their return, while other students are carrying out group exercises.*

In critical reflective writing, the style should not be too casual or judgemental:

*The choice of employer for my 6-month placement wasn't great, because he wasn't bothered about teaching me new skills. He just wanted me to do the boring 'dogsbody' work.*

Instead:

*In retrospect, I might have influenced my employer's choice of tasks for me if I had reminded him regularly of his obligations within the scheme.*

As the account is about drawing upon personal experience, the use of 'I' is appropriate for at least some of the time. For example:

*My work placement was enjoyable and instructive, but it has confirmed for me that I would prefer to specialise in data management, rather than be employed in the more general design aspects of mechanical engineering.*

And when you then reflect upon practice and refer to professional guidance or the literature to support your argument, you need to adopt the conventions of reflective academic writing:

*During my second session counselling client D, I found it extremely difficult to disassociate from her remembered experience of having a panic attack. However, I recalled the advice offered by Dr Alec Curruthers, citing Chang and Ho (2012, p. 12), and …*

---

**ACTIVITY 6.3**

### Putting the 'I' in reflective

Consider the text below as part of a critical reflective account by a trainee teacher who has taught three consecutive sessions with a Biology class, and later interviewed four of the students about the experience. The account is written in the impersonal. How would you personalise it?

*When working with the Year 11 Biology Class, and interviewing four students afterwards, it was apparent that three of the weaknesses found previously still applied:*

- *Failing to adjust teaching content and process to the students' starting levels.*
- *Not always setting out clearly the aims for each session.*

> ● *Not providing enough opportunities to accommodate the range of ability within the class.*
>
> *These three items will form the major focus of the next review with the university course tutor. ...*
>
> One solution is given at the end of the chapter. How does yours compare?

The two examples of writing style considered so far in this chapter – business-style report writing and critical reflective writing – reveal that the two approaches, both forms of academic writing, have rather different conventions. And each style of writing must be considered within its specific context. A business-style report might even include an element of critical reflective writing if, for example, the report concerned a general medical practice and drew upon the reflective accounts of staff or patients.

## 6.3   Presentations

On your degree programme you might be asked to give a presentation, from 5 to 30 minutes long, reporting on some research you'd done – either singly or as a group. The audience is normally made up of your fellow students and one or more members of staff who assess you. Most such presentations are performed using accompanying slides, created using presentation software such as Microsoft Powerpoint, Apple Keynote or Prezi. Such software can be used to give yourself prompts during the presentation, and to create notes that you can hand out to the audience.

Writing for a presentation is very different from writing a paper or electronic assignment that will be read by an assessor in his or her own time. A presentation is a much more multi-sensory experience in which the words you say need to complement anything the audience sees displayed in writing. This means that you may need to write material to display, often with accompanying images, as well as prepare material to be spoken. Sometimes, you might also need to write an associated report. The focus here is on spoken words and the accompanying visual material.

### Getting started

As with other writing tasks, a good starting point if you are unfamiliar with the type of task is to use the IPACE model (Chapter 2) to identify key elements:

1  **Identity**. Who am I expected to be? What is my persona? What qualities should such a person have? The task guidelines and assessment criteria should help determine the persona you should adopt. As for qualities, think about the

presentations you've experienced and presenters you've admired. This should give you some insight into the qualities you are aspiring to achieve.

2  **Purpose**. Again, the task guidelines and assessment criteria should help you determine this. But go beyond these to consider what you are seeking to convey to your audience. Consider also the benefits for you, in the short to medium term, in developing appropriate skills in designing and carrying out an effective presentation.

3  **Audience**. You need to know, of course, who will be at the presentation, and whether they will be adopting a particular persona (such as a business person, a specific type of practitioner in your discipline, or a member of the general public).

4  **Code**. Encompassing format, structure and style, this will include elements such as: the location of the presentation; the facilities available; whether you are expected to use Microsoft Powerpoint, or can use posters and props; whether you need to produce handouts; and whether there will be a question and answer session at the end of the presentation.

5  **Experience**. This includes what experience you are bringing to the task in terms of content and process. The information that follows should help with process if you are unfamiliar with presenting.

---

**TIP**

**Model yourself on presenters you admire**

Think about presentations – lectures, seminars, videos – you've seen. What, in your opinion, works well? What doesn't work well? What could you apply to your own presenting?

---

## Keep it short and simple

Commonly, students try to pack too much material into a short presentation. In 10–20 minutes you can normally cover only five to eight major items. It helps to work out, early on, what the three key 'take home' messages might be. For example, an undergraduate giving a presentation about the value for students in assessing and giving each other feedback on written work might wish to address issues such as:

- *Vygotsky's zone of proximal development, and the benefits of the process to both the person giving the feedback and the recipient of the feedback*
- *The value of seeing a range of work of different quality*
- *The learning and other benefits that come from better interpretation of the assessment criteria*
- *The degree to which students should be empowered to determine the process and nature of the feedback they give*

- *How students can be supported by staff in giving better quality feedback*
- *How to manage the peer assessment and feedback process so that it maximises benefit for students and staff*

That student would then need to decide which aspects of these points are the key 'take home' messages she wants to convey to the audience (normally, no more than three).

## Overall structure

Your presentation typically follows the traditional maxim: tell the audience what you're going to talk about (**introduction**); tell them (the **body** of the talk); remind the audience what you've talked about (**close**):

The **introduction**. This includes: introducing who you are (unless the audience knows already), what your topic and approach is, any relevant background, and your aim(s) in giving the presentation.

The **body**. If you were talking about an investigation you'd carried out, this might include methods, results, discussion and conclusion (but with more interesting headings!).

The **close**. Ending your presentation with 'take home' messages, and thanking your audience. There may then be an opportunity for questions and answers.

## Planning speech to complement displayed words and images

Whether you show slides, give a practical demonstration, talk about a poster, or any combination of these, the words you say need to complement any words and images you display. You should avoid simply reading out or repeating what is shown in a slide or poster. What you say should summarise, explain or breathe life into what you have displayed visually. Achieving this requires planning.

When giving a presentation, the ideal is to make your audience come away thinking that the experience has been spontaneous yet well planned:

- Make a plan of what you wish to cover in your presentation, basing your structure around an introduction, body and close. Make notes using headings and subheadings, bullet points, key phrases, a flow chart, mind map or concept map, or whatever works best for you (see Section 5.7).
- Sequence your ideas logically, creating notes for each section. Use these as a basis for designing your visual material. At an early stage, decide what you will display visually, perhaps on slides or in a poster.
- Once you have designed the visual material (see below) you need to consider how your commentary will relate to this. If you are unused to giving presentations, you may wish to write a detailed script. Producing a script may be an assessed requirement for your assignment.

- However, it is not normally good practice to read out a detailed script at a presentation. Instead, reduce your script to key words, phrases or bullet points. These are prompts that you can glance at during your presentation. Talking around these is what will make your presentation spontaneous and not leaden.

## Guidelines for presenting slides

By using presentation software such as Microsoft Powerpoint, Apple Keynote or Prezi you can create presentations that elegantly combine words and images. Seeking to use all the functions of the software, including animation, is often unnecessary. Simple but elegant design is often most effective. It is easy to make slides too busy, with too much text, or images that carry too much detail. You can provide weblinks or contact details to direct the audience to further information, rather than using valuable space on the slide.

Suggestions for designing and presenting slides:

- Make sure the projected image is at least 2 metres across (unless the presentation is being displayed on a television screen or computer monitor to a small group of people).
- Develop an overall design concept, but with some variation from slide to slide.
- Avoid gimmicks that might distract the audience.
- The first slide normally shows the title of the presentation, with your name(s).
- For text, choose a non-serif font such as Arial, Helvetica or Tahoma, of at least 24-point size.
- Avoid using more than three or four font styles and sizes on one slide.
- In general, keep to fewer than 80 words per slide (often far fewer).
- Employ short sentences, bullet points, questions, quotes, photos, illustrations, graphs, charts and summary tables to get your points across.
- Avoid overcrowding your slide. Leave clear spaces.
- Ensure there is strong contrast between text and background.
- Each slide is normally displayed for between 20 and 120 seconds.
- The last slide typically gives the 'take home' messages or a striking image that captures a sense of the whole presentation.

## Rehearsing

It pays to rehearse. Doing so boosts confidence. You can check that you are putting across the key messages within the required time:

- If possible, practise using appropriate equipment in a room that is the same as, or similar to, the one where you will be presenting.
- Get a trusted fellow student to watch and listen to your presentation and offer constructive feedback.
- Use prompts, written on index cards or displayed on your computer screen (but not displayed to the audience), to guide your talk.

- Fine-tune your presentation, using your experience of the rehearsal and any feedback received.
- Prepare answers to tricky questions you might be asked.

---

**TIP**

**Prepare for the unexpected**

On the day, arrive in good time to check that the facilities, and your presentation, are in place. It pays to have backup plans should equipment fail. For example, if you are using your laptop for your presentation make sure you have a backup of your presentation file on a memory stick so that you can use the university's built-in computer or can borrow a friend's laptop. Saving your slides as PDF files is one way of ensuring you can display copies of the slides (without any animation) even if you experience compatibility problems using Powerpoint or Keynote.

---

## Presenting

Being an effective presenter depends on good preparation, and on ensuring that what you say complements what you show. Writing a script, which is reduced to prompts, will help give you the confidence to engage with the audience in your presentation, rather than reading out prepared material in a mechanical fashion.

Speak directly and enthusiastically to your audience. Notice your audience's responses and adjust accordingly. If people look confused, be prepared to rephrase what you have said. If they look bored, engage them more by asking questions.

---

**TIP**

**The right degree of nervousness**

Being slightly nervous is an appropriate state to be in when giving a presentation. It will help give your presentation edge and sparkle. If you are very nervous, your speech may become garbled or erratic. Slow down. Taking a few deep breaths before you start speaking is one way to help control your nerves.

---

**ACTIVITY 6.4**

**What makes a good presenter?**

Consider the items below. Tick those you consider to be signs of a good presenter of a slide show:

**(a)** Sticks to a few main points.

**(b)** Engages with the audience by asking and answering questions.

**(c)** Reads from notes or a script.

**(d)** Speaks quickly and quietly.

**(e)** Is enthusiastic.

**(f)** Looks at the screen rather than the audience.

*Check your answers against those at the end of the chapter.*

---

**TIP**

**Answering questions**

Give yourself thinking time when answering questions. You could ask the questioner to repeat what they said. And if you don't know the answer (yet), then say so.

---

## Follow up

To help maximise your learning from the experience of presenting, reflect afterwards:

- What went well?
- What went less well?
- What would I do differently next time?

If there is anything from the presentation that you need to follow up on, such as getting back to a questioner, then make sure you do.

## 6.4    Posters

Designing posters at A1, A2 or A3 size is sometimes used as an assignment on undergraduate or postgraduate programmes. As with designing slides, seeking to include too much detail is a common failing. Simple yet elegant design often works well. As always, the guidance given here should be tempered in the light of the specific guidelines for your assignment.

Guidelines for designing posters:

- If permissible, consider using a provocative title to capture audience interest, e.g. *What makes students lazy?*
- Author's details are usually given just beneath the title or at the bottom of the poster.
- Use letters at least 25 mm tall for headings, at least 15 mm tall for subheadings, and 5 mm plus for body text.
- Non-serif fonts are popular in posters and make for easy reading. Don't overuse different fonts and sizes (6–8 styles are usually sufficient).

- Bear in mind how your design might relate to your subject matter.
- Background images, unusual shapes as text boxes, flow diagrams, or scans or photos of examples can *show* the audience what you are describing rather than you having to *tell* them in words.
- Use colour to set a tone and highlight your poster's features. Make sure that your text contrasts well with any background colour.
- Use fewer than 500 words (perhaps far fewer).
- Employ short sentences, bullet points, questions, quotes, photos, illustrations, graphs, charts and summary tables to get your points across.
- Avoid overcrowding your poster. Leave clear spaces.
- A poster is often read from top left to bottom right. Do you want the reader to follow this pattern, or move in a zig zag pattern or by reading down a column? Or do you want the audience to read the poster in a different way? Provide clear headings and signposting, perhaps using numbers or arrows, to help your audience navigate through the poster (Figure 6.2).

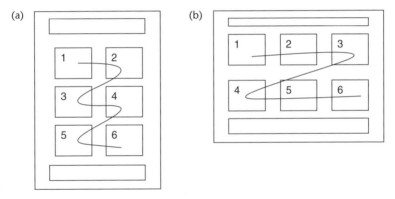

**Figure 6.2  Whether your poster's layout is (a) portrait, or (b) landscape, it is usually helpful to provide signposting to guide your audience through the poster's elements in the right order**

# 6.5   Dissertations

Dissertations are the largest documents you are likely to write on your undergraduate or postgraduate course. Many are 10,000–20,000 words in length, although on a course with a strong design or mathematical element, they could be shorter. Commonly, you will be writing your dissertation in your final year of undergraduate or taught postgraduate study and, together with your final examinations, the dissertation is the culmination of your degree. Certainly, it is an opportunity to bring together many of the skills you have developed during your time at university.

As Levin (2011) suggests, it is important to distinguish between the study (the investigation you are carrying out) and the dissertation (the writing up of that investigation). The two go hand in hand, with the study itself slightly preceding the writing up. Both need to be carefully planned to leave sufficient time for you to write the dissertation so that it properly reflects the study you have carried out. In most cases, the dissertation carries all or most of the marks that are used to assess the quality of your investigation. You could have carried out a brilliant piece of laboratory work, but unless it is written up well, you will not gain maximum benefit from your ingenuity.

There are many good reasons for writing a dissertation of which you can be proud; not least, because it will contribute substantially to your final class of degree. A strong dissertation will make it easier for your assessor to write a glowing reference to accompany your job applications. It will also give you something tangible to talk about at an interview. Along with your final examinations, it is perhaps the best opportunity for you to demonstrate the professional identity you have developed in your training within the discipline.

## Kinds of dissertation

It is not possible in the scope of this book to consider the wide range of dissertations possible in the different disciplines. Rather, I have sought to pick out key issues that need to be considered. Walliman (2014) distinguishes between studies that are theoretical and those that are practical (Table 6.1). These distinctions are not hard and fast; for example, a laboratory experiment will be set within the context of background theory. Deciding which category and subcategory your dissertation falls within is more a matter of emphasis. It is possible that your dissertation could be quite evenly balanced between the theoretical and the practical; for example, if you had considered a theoretical concept in depth, modifying or tailoring it for a particular context, and then tested it out in a small-scale practical study.

The particular blend of approaches (theoretical and practical) will shape the code – the format, structure and writing style (Section 2.1) – you employ in writing your dissertation. For example, practical investigations could employ quantitative approaches, qualitative approaches, or a blend of the two (mixed

| Table 6.1   Types of dissertation (drawing upon Walliman, 2014, Figure 2.4) | | |
| --- | --- | --- |
| **Category** | **Subcategory** | **Examples** |
| Theoretical | Conceptual/ abstract | Discourses on:<br>• aesthetics<br>• capitalism<br>• feminism<br>• sustainability |
| | Applied | Conceptual models and values (economic, ethical, environmental and/or social) applied to:<br>• feminism and classroom practice<br>• leadership theory and hospital management<br>• sustainability in building design |
| Practical | Constructed | Computer models or simulations<br>Field experiments<br>Laboratory experiments |
| | Explored | Action research to improve practice<br>Case studies<br>Field observations<br>Interviews<br>Questionnaire surveys |

methods). When reporting on quantitative data you may wish to be objective ('An analysis was carried out …'). When reporting on qualitative findings, you may adopt a more personal style ('I analysed …' or 'We analysed …'). If you have used mixed methods, you may find yourself reporting in distinct styles in different parts of the dissertation (see Figure 6.3). The acceptability of reporting in such a manner is something you should check beforehand with your assessor.

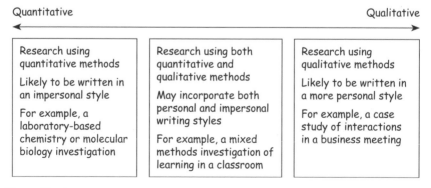

Quantitative                                                                          Qualitative

Research using quantitative methods

Likely to be written in an impersonal style

For example, a laboratory-based chemistry or molecular biology investigation

Research using both quantitative and qualitative methods

May incorporate both personal and impersonal writing styles

For example, a mixed methods investigation of learning in a classroom

Research using qualitative methods

Likely to be written in a more personal style

For example, a case study of interactions in a business meeting

**Figure 6.3  The nature of your research methodology and its theoretical foundations will inform your writing style**

## Structure of a dissertation

A dissertation is an extended form of report, and like a business-style report (Section 6.1) it has front and end matter, with the main part sandwiched in between. However, the writing style and other conventions of a dissertation are likely to be rather different – more academic, less direct and more measured in its use of language.

A dissertation is likely to include all or most of the following sections (with some variation based on discipline). The main part of the dissertation shown here assumes a practically-orientated study:

**Front matter:**

Title page

Abstract or summary

Acknowledgements

Glossary (sometimes)

Table of contents

Lists of figures and tables

**Main part of the dissertation:**

**Introduction.** A few paragraphs introducing the context of the dissertation. Usually the introduction follows this pattern:

- Why this study is of interest
- The study's wider context (locating it within the discipline)
- The study's narrower context (locating it within the sub-discipline)
- The study's aims, sometimes with objectives (how the aims will be achieved). Sometimes the study's intention will be framed as questions to be answered and/or hypotheses to be tested.
- The introduction may finish with an overview of the structure of the rest of the dissertation.

**Background/Context.** This is a literature review, which, in most practically-based dissertations, is up to 25–30% of the dissertation's main text. The purpose of the literature review is, through citing and referencing, to locate the investigation within the context of work done by others. This is the opportunity for you to show your careful judgement in selecting, citing and commenting on the relevant literature (see Chapter 9).

**Methods/Methodology.** This should contain sufficient detail to enable the reader to repeat the procedure of your investigation, and your assessor to know that the investigation has been carried out with due diligence.

Results or findings are only as valid as the methods used to obtain them. In qualitative work, this section goes beyond being a Method. It also gives the reasons why those methods were chosen. It then becomes a Methodology.

**Findings/Results.** This section gathers together the data collected in a systematic manner with an ongoing narrative. If it is a quantitative study, the data is usually presented in graphs, charts and/or tables. If a qualitative study, direct quotations from interviews, descriptions of videorecorded interactions at a meeting, or other sources of field data might be reported on, to develop and illustrate themes. The narrative that accompanies any presented data is written to develop a line of reasoning. The text does not just refer to charts, graphs and figures, it interprets them and highlights points of interest.

**Discussion.** This section interprets, explains and analyses the findings with respect to the aim(s) of the investigation and in relation to the wider literature. It may evaluate the validity of the findings on the basis of methods used. It should discuss any limitations and how these might be avoided in future investigations. The Conclusion might be in a separate section, or may make up the final few paragraphs of the Discussion.

**Conclusion.** This refers to the original purpose of the report and summarises the main findings rather than simply repeating them. It may give recommendations for further work and reveal the implications of the study's findings for future practice, which might, for example, be applied to the work of practitioners or the general public. If recommendations are included, they suggest what action should be taken.

**End matter:**

**References.** The full list of publications cited in the dissertation, each with full bibliographic information.

**Appendices.** Containing detailed information that would interrupt the line of reasoning in the main part of the dissertation (e.g. raw data, computer code, statistical analyses, sample questionnaires, interview transcripts). It may be needed to convince the assessor that the investigation was conducted appropriately.

---

**TIP**

**Following precise instructions**

Following the detailed instructions for an assignment is always important, but is brought into sharp relief when creating a large document such as a dissertation. Creating a long document, with all its features correctly in place, including citing, referencing, lists of contents, use of tables and figures and so on, requires careful planning at the outset. Make sure you build in plenty of time to incorporate and check all these features.

## 6.6   Planning: from large- to small-scale

Planning, always helpful whatever size the communication, becomes even more important when dealing with a large document such as a dissertation. In the case of a dissertation, you can begin creating a plan of your document at an early stage, suggesting likely chapters and their provisional titles and contents. The same approach applies when dealing with a smaller document, such as an essay or practical report, but then you are not dealing with chapters but with sections and parts of them. However, the same general principles apply. The description that follows is for a dissertation, but can be readily scaled down for a smaller assignment.

The overall approach, which draws some parallels with that of Orna and Stevens (2009), is to plan in steps from whole document, to chapter, to section, to subsection, to paragraph. The planning does not all need to be done in one go. Indeed, it is likely that the plan will be built up over time. For a smaller document, such as a practical report, the likely steps are: from report, to section, (perhaps to subsection), and then to paragraph. The process can be conceptualised as planning in steps or layers (see Figure 6.4).

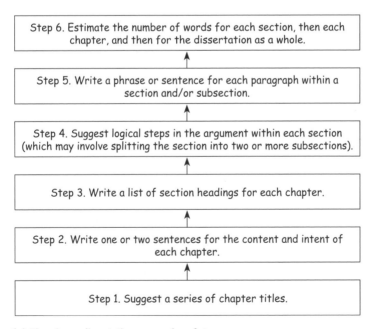

Figure 6.4  **Planning a dissertation as a series of steps**

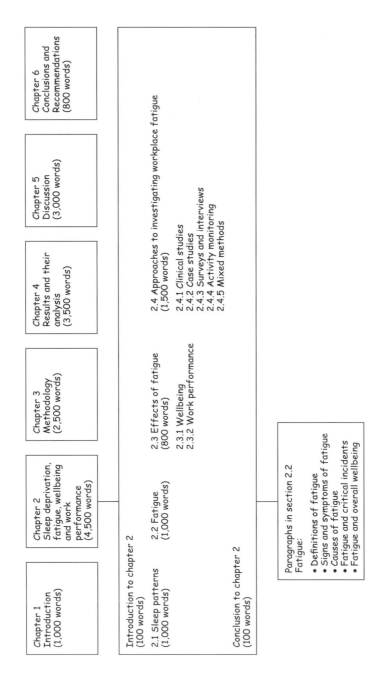

**Figure 6.5** An early plan for a dissertation entitled 'Sleep deprivation and its effect on wellbeing and work-related performance among shift workers in a residential home'. Target length: 15,000 words. Estimated running total: 15,300 words

The outline plan is very fluid, in that the details become filled in as the background research and thinking develop. The outline performs several functions, including:

- keeping you on track, insofar as you know the word limits you are writing to
- allowing you to shape the document as your thoughts emerge
- boosting your confidence insofar as you can see that you are making progress
- providing a 'map' onto which to hang your thoughts as they develop
- helping you to plan so that you achieve all parts of the writing process in good time.

Figure 6.5 shows an early plan for a 15,000-word dissertation on an investigation of sleep deprivation and its effect on shift workers. At this early stage, each chapter has estimated word lengths. Detail is shown for Chapter 2, revealing how the chapter is split into four numbered sections, two of which have subsections. In turn, one of the sections is shown in detail, with the topic of each paragraph indicated. Each part of a dissertation, or a smaller assignment such as an essay or practical report, can be planned down to the paragraph level.

In this chapter, we have considered several kinds of document and modes of communication. Following the approach developed in Chapters 1–3, each kind of writing is situated within a particular disciplinary context. It adopts certain conventions, which are shaped to the particular kind of assignment, its purpose and audience.

## Key points in the chapter

1   Business-style report writing usually involves analysing a situation and giving recommendations. Such reports normally have front and end matter, between which the report begins with an executive summary and finishes with conclusions and recommendations. The bulk of the report may have sections such as an introduction, methods, findings and discussion, or variations on these.

2   Business-style analytical reports usually have a no-nonsense, direct writing style, with concise text, bullet points or numbered lists, and with visual elements such as tables or charts. Sections have clear headings and subheadings, which, like the visual elements, are usually numbered for ease of navigation and comment.

3   Critical reflective writing is a powerful approach to support systematic learning from experience. The writing often reflects stages of an experiential learning cycle: engaging in an activity; reflecting on and interpreting the experience; generalising and learning from the experience; and then planning further action.

4  A key challenge in critical reflective writing is combining a personal voice with academic rigour.

5  Slide presentations and posters seek to engage a group audience. They combine strong visual elements with minimal text. In presentations, spoken words complement rather than repeat displayed text.

6  Dissertations are the most extended forms of writing on undergraduate or Master's programmes. Given their size and complexity, they require detailed planning in order to meet a wide range of assessment criteria.

7  Planning a document can be done as a series of steps, from large- to small-scale, from whole document to paragraph.

## Cited references

Boud, K., Keogh, R. and Walker, D. (1985). *Reflection: Turning Experience into Learning*. London: Kogan Page.

Bullock, K. and Wikeley, F. (1999). 'Improving Learning in Year 9: Making Use of Personal Learning Plans'. *Educational Studies*, 25(1), pp. 19–33.

Dewey, J. (1938). *Experience and Education*. New York: Collier.

Kolb, D. A. (1984). *Experiential Learning: Experience as a Source of Learning and Development*. Englewood Cliffs: Prentice Hall.

Levin, P. (2011). *Excellent Dissertations!* 2nd edn. Maidenhead: Open University Press.

Lewin, K. (1946). 'Action Research and Minority Problems'. *Journal of Social Issues*, 2(4), pp. 34–46.

Orna, E. and Stevens, G. (2009). *Managing Information for Research: Practical Help in Researching, Writing and Designing Dissertations*. 2nd edn. Maidenhead: Open University Press.

Schön, D. (1983). *The Reflective Practitioner: How Professionals Think in Action*. London: Temple Smith.

Schön, D. (1987). *Educating the Reflective Practitioner*. San Francisco: Josey-Bass.

University of New South Wales (2016). *Reflective Writing*. New South Wales: University of New South Wales. Available from: https://student.unsw.edu.au/reflective-writing and links [accessed 16 August 2017].

Walliman, N. (2014). *Your Undergraduate Dissertation: The Essential Guide for Success*. 2nd edn. London: Sage.

## Further reading

Chivers, B. and Shoolbred, M. (2007). *A Student's Guide to Presentations: Making Your Presentations Count*. London: Sage.

Forsyth, P. (2016). *How to Write Reports and Proposals*. 4th edn. London: Kogan Page.

LearnHigher. (–). *Report Writing*. LearnHigher/Association for Learning Development in Higher Education. Available from: www.learnhigher.ac.uk/writing-for-university/report-writing/ [accessed 16 August 2017].

LearnHigher. (2007). *Oral Communication*. Liverpool: Liverpool Hope University/ London: Brunel University. Available at: www.brunel.ac.uk/learnhigher/ giving-oral-presentations/delivering-your-presentation.shtml [accessed 16 August 2017].

Levin, P. and Topping, G. (2006). *Perfect Presentations!* Maidenhead: Open University Press.

Marsen, S. (2013). *Professional Writing*. 3rd edn. Basingstoke: Palgrave Macmillan.

McMillan, K. and Weyers, J. (2011). *How to Write Dissertations and Project Reports*. 2nd edn. Harlow: Prentice Hall.

Morley, J. (2017). *Academic Phrasebank*. Manchester: University of Manchester Press. Available from: www.phrasebank.manchester.ac.uk/ [accessed 29 August 2017].

Reid, M. (2012). *Report Writing*. Basingstoke: Palgrave Macmillan.

Williams, K., Woolliams, M. and Spiro, J. (2012). *Reflective Writing*. Basingstoke: Palgrave Macmillan.

# Answers for Chapter 6

## Activity 6.1: Keep it short and simple (KISS)

A possible solution:

**Rules for clay in class**

Make sure children *do*:

- wear protective aprons
- wedge (knead) the clay to make it pliable and to remove air
- make objects that are thin or hollow (no part thicker than a thumb)
- cover clay in plastic for storing
- join modelled, moist pieces of clay by scoring and slipping
- clean all work surfaces thoroughly with water.

Make sure children *do not*:

- throw or eat clay
- get clay in hair
- make offensive objects
- handle other people's clay objects
- glaze the underside of objects to be fired. (100 words)

## Activity 6.2: Putting the pieces together

A possible solution: The project teams found the new remote server and its management system was an improvement on the old. Firstly, they could now routinely access the latest version of the software. Secondly, they could see who had changed which features. And thirdly, they could track people's comments about the software. We intend to implement most aspects of the new system but will consider how comments can be targeted at selected viewers only. (71)

## Activity 6.3: Putting the 'I' in reflective

A possible solution: When I worked with the Year 11 Biology Class, and later interviewed four of the students, it was apparent that three of my weaknesses still applied:

- Failing to adequately adjust teaching content and process to the students' starting levels.
- Not always setting out clearly the aims for each session.
- Not providing enough opportunities to accommodate the range of ability within the class.

These three items will form the major focus of my next review with the university course tutor. …

## Activity 6.4: What makes a good presenter?

(a), (b) and (e) are characteristics of an effective presenter. The presenter should avoid: reading from notes or a script, speaking quickly or quietly, and looking mainly at the screen.

# Composing

In non-fiction writing, composing is the act of writing in complete sentences that build into paragraphs. In most forms of academic writing, there comes a time when you have to move from planning, researching, reading and note-taking to writing flowing sentences (Figure 7.1). For many, this is the most challenging part of the writing process. This chapter explains approaches for making the shift to composing easier.

| Planning, researching, reading and note-taking | Composing (drafting) | Reviewing and editing |
|---|---|---|
| (everything you do before you actually start writing flowing prose) | (drafting: writing flowing prose in sentences and paragraphs) | (evaluating, rethinking, and revising what you have written) |

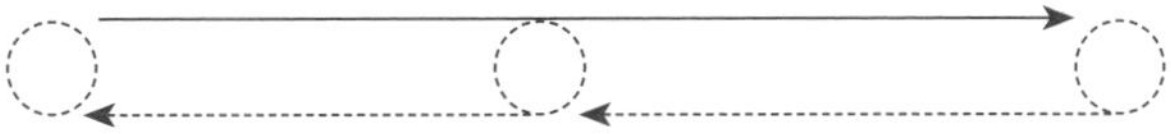

Figure 7.1 Composing as part of an academic writing process

In writing workshops and seminars, when I ask students which part of the overall writing process they find most challenging, typically slightly more than half say it is composing. This often applies irrespective of whether I am working with science, engineering, humanities, social science or arts students. It also seems to apply whether working with undergraduates or postgraduates. Reviewing and editing is usually chosen as most challenging by roughly one quarter to one third of students. Some students dislike reading and rereading their work, while others are unsure what to pay attention to in their writing, and just when to do so. For such students, Chapter 10 should be particularly helpful. Typically, about 10–20% of students opt for planning and researching as the most challenging. As considered in Chapter 4, this can be because they find it difficult to articulate exactly what they are looking for, and to narrow down the search for information accordingly, or because they find it difficult to know when to stop searching. Some find it difficult to create a plan, and wish to move swiftly on to composing without one.

## 7.1   Balancing the critical and the creative

According to Professor of English Peter Elbow (1981, p. 7), 'Writing calls on two skills that are so different that they usually conflict with each other: creating and criticizing.' Elbow recognised that composing creatively needs to be nurtured, and can be undermined by self-criticism. Often, the educational system we navigated through in order to reach university encouraged us to 'get it right first time' – at least in exams – because in a handwritten script, corrections are difficult to make and distracting for the reader.

Today, with the power of word-processing software to help us, when writing assignments there is no need to get it right first time. We can draft and redraft what we write. This works with the creative process.

Dorothea Brande, in her book *Becoming a Writer*, published in 1934 and still in print, recognised the importance of nurturing expression of the unconscious. I have sought to encapsulate the notion that writing involves both conscious (critical) processes and unconscious (creative) processes in Figure 7.2. In working with others, I have found this model helpful. It is simplistic, and I do not pretend that it is 'true' in the sense that processes can be neatly separated into conscious and unconscious, critical and creative. However, this model does highlight that in the writing process, some of the time you need to allow creative, unconscious processes to come to the fore (as in composing your first draft). At other times, critical, conscious processes should be at the forefront (such as when reviewing and editing). I spend much of my time encouraging students to write in such a way that they allow expression of both their creative and critical faculties when writing. Much of what follows in this chapter is about managing these two dimensions of the writing process.

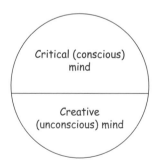

**Figure 7.2 Writing involves both conscious (critical) and unconscious (creative) processes. Both need to be encouraged**

## 7.2    Composing your first draft

Many writers – from university professors to fiction and non-fiction writers – do what I have also learnt to do. They gather everything they need to write the first draft – bringing together their plans, notes and any source material – and then they give themselves permission to 'go for it' in writing the first draft. For many, writing the first draft involves – to some extent – putting critical mind on hold, knowing that this will be engaged, again and again, when the draft is improved.

When I write a first draft, I give myself permission to 'go for it', knowing that I am 'getting my ideas down on paper' and that everything is open to change. I normally write in bursts of 50–90 minutes, then take a break, before returning to write for another block of 50–90 minutes. Like many professional writers, I prefer to write in the morning, getting my composing done by lunchtime. If I have chosen to spend the day on writing-related activities, in the afternoon I might review and edit a recent draft (although not normally what I'd composed that morning). Or I might carry out some literature searching or reading. Or planning. That way, I do not normally spend more than half of the day involved in one type of writing-related activity. This keeps me fresh. I do not become stale from spending too much time on any one activity. I find that many successful university staff and students do something similar. They break up their day with different activities. As we shall see later in this chapter, this contributes to managing the writing process effectively.

Here is an extract from the first draft of Chapter 1 of this book:

*Traditionally, most essays have a structure with a clear beginning (introduction), main body (development of an overall argument) and end (conclusion). This is based on the traditional notion of a lecture: tell the audience what you're going to talk about, talk about it, and then tell them what you've talked about. [Check: Is this based on a rhetorical tradition? How did it originate?]*

Notice that I have made notes to myself shown in square brackets […]. Normally, I do not let such issues or questions stop me composing. I set myself a target for composing a certain number of words, and then if I run into problems I make a note to myself rather than using the problem as an excuse for stopping composing. That said, I do need to make a judgement as to whether the issue is so important it is likely to undermine my whole argument. Usually, as here, problems are much less serious. In any case, many such problems cannot be resolved quickly. For example, to find out about the rhetorical tradition I did some more background reading and spoke to colleagues. Sometimes you may find that your argument is weak and that you have insufficient evidence to back up the claims you are making. This is not something you can quickly resolve by breaking off from your composing.

Here is another first draft extract from Chapter 1, where I marked up repeated words and then posed a question:

> *A major challenge for many students is to write assignments in an appropriate academic style, with a suitable structure, that develops an argument in an [appropriate] way. As we shall see later, there is no single kind of academic writing. Unless you are taking a generic, introductory course in writing at university, writing academically usually has a specific disciplinary context. Almost invariably you are writing for a particular audience with a specific purpose in mind and within a [particular] discipline. [Examples?]*

I could have chosen to stop composing there and then and make a decision about whether to include examples, and if so, which ones. As it was, I decided to carry on composing and delay the decision. That way, I could see which examples emerged later in the chapter, and I could then choose examples here to complement the later ones.

In writing a first draft, it is quite common to falter, trying to resolve an issue that is best left until later. Resolving the problem may require you to undertake more research, more thinking, or more writing (what you write further on in the document may help resolve the problem you are experiencing now). Often it is a case of returning to your work 'with fresh eyes'. Issues like these are not normally something that stops me composing unless they build up to a critical mass and I have to break off and resolve one or more of them.

There are several reasons why I propose it is helpful for most people, most of the time, to write a first draft fairly rapidly:

1 Perfecting sentences as you write your first draft may be an unnecessary expenditure of time and energy. It is only later – after you have written a few paragraphs or a whole section – that you know whether that perfect first sentence you crafted is doing its job. Or you may find that, after reviewing your written argument developed over several paragraphs, the sequence of logic needs to be changed.

2 The more time you invest in the first draft, the more reluctant you are likely to be to change what you have written. But making changes – perhaps substantial ones – is exactly what you may need to do. We return to this idea in more detail in Chapter 10.

3 Writing the first draft slowly, trying to resolve all the problems as you go, is effectively bringing together parts of the writing process – researching and planning, composing, and reviewing and editing – that might be better kept apart. If you are trying to complete all these actions as you compose, your composing could be slow and jerky. Writing quickly is more likely to clear mental space for ideas to flow.

## 7.3   Writing to a prompt

A common concern for some students is in starting to compose their first draft. Even though they have made their plans, compiled their notes and assembled their sources, they struggle to begin composing – the tyranny of the blank page. Or perhaps they begin writing the first sentence, and then adjust it, trying to perfect it. Composing grinds to a halt.

'Writing to a prompt' is a way to circumvent both problems: getting started and getting stuck on the first sentence. It involves writing the beginning of a sentence that prompts you to continue. I find one of the most useful prompts is simply to write down what the next section of your writing intends to do, and make this the prompt to continue writing. For example, if writing in the personal:

*In this section I will compare and contrast three models for … In doing so I propose …*

If writing in the impersonal:

*This section compares and contrasts the three models for … In doing so it proposes …*

In responding to such prompts, you begin writing. Later, you may well wish to rewrite the first sentence or two, but the prompt has served the purpose of getting you started. It is a useful strategy to employ when you feel uncertain about how to begin. There are other approaches that are helpful.

> **TIP**
>
> ### Write it like you say it
>
> If you find yourself writing your first draft in a formal manner, which is causing you to slow down or even grind to a halt, why not try writing like you speak? Often, when we have to explain something to someone else, we can do that best by talking out loud. Why not explain to a friend what you're trying to express in writing? You could make notes about what you've said or even audiorecord it, and use that as a basis for your writing. Remember, your first draft is just that. You can tidy it up and tighten the language, but you'll have breathed life into it at an early stage. With practice, you may find that writing the first draft becomes almost effortless.

## 7.4   Freewriting

Freewriting is the process of sitting down and writing in sentences for 5–15 minutes, without stopping, or at the very least, without pausing to analyse what you have written. The idea is to write in an uninhibited, uncensored way, and to just let your ideas flow. What comes out on paper can be anything between a stream of consciousness, a halting, repetitive outburst of emotion, or even a smooth, elegant argument. In freewriting you do not normally show your work to others (although you might discuss it). Conventionally, it works best when writing in longhand rather than typing on a keyboard.

Popularised by writing facilitators such as Peter Elbow (1973, 1981) and Linda Flower and John R. Hayes (1977) as a way of encouraging composing, its strength lies in it being rather different from the ways of writing normally encouraged on academic courses. It encourages expression of unconscious mind. It also tends to allay, at least temporarily, anxiety and self-criticism. In my work with students and staff, I tend to use freewriting as a way of getting people to write down what they think and feel – something that is often not encouraged in their formal academic writing within the discipline, except in certain forms of reflective writing (Chapter 6).

---

**ACTIVITY 7.1**

### Freewriting

Think of an assignment you are about to carry out. Spend 5–10 minutes writing down what you think and feel about writing this assignment. Keep going, writing in sentences, and don't stop to read what you have written. Keep pressing forward until you reach the end of the allocated time. Don't worry about whether what you have written is grammatically correct, elegantly punctuated or correctly spelt. Once you have finished, then read what you have written.

(a) How do you feel now that you have finished the freewriting? Have your feelings changed from before you started?

(b) How does what you have written differ from the way you normally write for academic purposes?

(c) Does what you have written reveal anything useful, unusual or surprising to you?

---

Here are three short extracts of freewriting from individuals given the opportunity to write down what they thought and felt about writing a dissertation. In all three cases, the experience was helpful to the person concerned, moving them on in the process of planning a dissertation:

*I like the lab work. The writing is a pain. Not done much writing except for lab reports and work placement reports. This is much bigger than anything I've done before! I'm going to need help. This session is a start.*

*[The dissertation] looks mighty big. John said it was hardest thing he did on the course. But really enjoyable. Felt like being a real academic engineer.*

*Even writing essays is difficult. This thing is much bigger. I've got a really interesting topic. I guess the thing is to really plan ahead and do the writing as I go, not leave it all to the end. And make the process enjoyable. After all, I chose the topic!*

> **TIP**
>
> **Other ways of using freewriting**
>
> Freewriting does not have to be used *before* you undertake an academic writing assignment. It can be used at any time as a way of unlocking ideas, emptying your mind, discovering what you think and feel about something, or simply exercising your writing 'muscles'. It can be used in quite a directive way to explore your thoughts and feelings, for example: 'What are my prejudices and biases about this topic?', 'Why am I bored with this topic?', 'What is holding me back about this assignment?', 'What is my biggest fear with this assignment?', 'What if I were [give a named person] writing this assignment? How would it change?'. Be creative about the questions you might ask yourself. It is engaging the unconscious mind that is the key, and shortening the distance between your thoughts and your writing. Freewriting is not academic writing, but it is an invaluable precursor or complement to academic writing.

People react very differently to freewriting. In my experience, mathematicians, scientists, engineers and those training to be lawyers are among those who find it most beneficial. There is much you can learn from freewriting. Here are some of the benefits of freewriting that students have identified on courses I have run:

> *It emptied my head of the buzz of thoughts so that I could think more clearly. It made me realise I knew much more than I thought I did.*
> *It's great for making room for ideas to emerge and then making connections between them.*
> *The problem became clear to me. I was avoiding seeing the Professor, but I needed to see him to get the section written.*
> *It really organised my thoughts. Something I wasn't expecting.*
> *Over time, I think it's loosened up my formal writing. I'm finding myself becoming more expressive, not so straitlaced … even with my technical writing.*
> *Freewriting helps reduce the distance between what I think and what I write. It was quite a release … and a relief!*

And one psychology lecturer:

> *I now use 10 minutes of freewriting routinely before I start a bout of writing for a journal article. It clears my head and gets my writing muscles working.*

In summary, freewriting can help by:

- encouraging you to start writing, rather than holding back
- 'brainstorming' – making and developing connections
- exploring a topic
- warming yourself up before a session of academic writing

- releasing writing blocks, both cognitive and emotional ones
- helping make your academic writing more expressive and fluent
- broadening your active vocabulary (the words you use in speech or writing)
- encouraging expression of 'unconscious mind', such as encouraging you to 'go for it' when writing your first draft
- benefiting your health and wellbeing. There is plentiful evidence for the value of writing down thoughts and feelings (see, for example, Lepore and Smyth, 2002).

As Elbow (1981, p.15) put it: '[Freewriting] doesn't always produce powerful writing itself, but it leads to powerful writing.' I recommend you give freewriting a chance. It only takes 5–15 minutes, and its benefits far outweigh the little time it takes. Even freewriting just once or twice a week, or when you get stuck, will reap benefits. But it has many more uses than that, and for some people at least, becomes an indispensible adjunct to their academic writing. I leave it to you to consider exactly how and when you might choose to use it.

---

**TIP**

**What do you do with freewriting afterwards?**

Once you have done some freewriting, what do you do with it? This rather depends on your purpose in doing it, what emerged from the process, and the kind of person you are. Some people I know keep their freewriting because they never know when it's going to prove useful. They might read what they have written weeks and months later to see how their thoughts have developed since. I know some who have analysed their writing to see how their sentence constructions and forms of expression have evolved. Many keep their freewriting if it informs something they're working on. Many others throw their freewriting away once it has served its purpose – clearing their head, releasing some pent up emotion, exploring their thoughts to help them organise their work. It is up to you what you do with your freewriting.

---

## 7.5   The 'no composing' approach

We have considered 'writing to a prompt' and freewriting as techniques for unlocking your composing. A third approach I call the 'no composing' technique because it involves reducing the process of composing to a minimum. It includes plenty of planning, and ample reviewing and editing, but comparatively little composing – bursts of writing fluently in sentences and paragraphs.

Imagine you have made notes for part of an essay. Those notes started out as a single bullet point for each paragraph and have now grown to several bullet points for each. However, when it comes to writing flowing prose, those paragraphs do not respond readily to your attention. You find you cannot move rapidly from bullet points to flowing text. You find yourself tinkering with what you have written, moving bullet points and phrases around, and you have trouble creating coherent sentences.

This tinkering process – which can be likened to fitting the pieces of a jigsaw together – is occasionally the only way to get something written. The pieces do not readily fall into place. This can occur for a variety of reasons. You may be trying to force the process of composing when you are not yet ready. Perhaps you have not thought deeply enough about the argument you are creating or you have not sufficiently absorbed the sense of the sources you have used. You may be in a poor state of mind to compose, and may need to break off and return refreshed. More often than not, it is because you need to do more thinking and information gathering to develop a coherent argument. This does not always happen through a flash of insight, but may require a gradual process of consolidation.

When I use the 'no composing' technique it tends to be towards the end of an article or book, when I am seeking to assemble information from many parts of the narrative in an interesting way. For some students, the approach is most likely to happen when writing the conclusion of an essay or the discussion of a practical report. A few students spend rather too much time using the 'no composing' approach. It is a slow process. For some students, assembling sentences a piece at a time by 'filling in the gaps' is a way of not having to take too large a step in one go. However, the process can be sluggish and laborious and, with practice, most students find they can move beyond it for all but some of the most difficult writing challenges. However, the tactic is there should you need it – part of your repertoire of approaches to writing.

## 7.6   Managing your composing

Commonly, when I ask a group of students what time of day they prefer to compose, most say in the morning, a sizeable group favour the evening, and only a few prefer the afternoon. Most students have preferences as to when and how they like to compose. I am strongly in favour of finding out what you prefer, and then making those preferences work for you. Location and state of mind make a big difference. At the end of this chapter there are suggestions for creating the right environment and nurturing an appropriate state of mind for composing.

Many students I work with respond well to setting themselves short-term writing goals and then reflecting on their practice. It helps them plan their writing, and stay focused and motivated. It also encourages them to learn swiftly about the process of writing and what they need to do to improve. A few students prefer to be more open-ended and adopt the philosophy of 'I'll see where I get to in a couple hours'. They prefer not to engage in systematic and regular goal setting and reflection. But for most students, these practices are beneficial and productive.

## Setting writing goals

A common approach to goal setting uses the mnemonic (memory aid) **SMART**. Applying goal-setting theory (e.g. Locke and Latham, 2002; Wade, 2009), effective goals are:

**S**pecific
**M**easurable
**A**chievable
**R**ealistic
**T**ime-scaled

For example, 'This morning, in three hours, I will write 750 words of first draft quality (with citations) on the literature review for my end-of-year project report.' Does this goal meet the SMART criteria?

The goal is specific insofar as it says what will be written, how much and to what standard. It is measurable – the student will know whether they have written 750 words or not, and to what extent they have included relevant citations.

Is the goal achievable? The ability to judge this well beforehand comes with practice. As you reflect on how well you complete a writing task (see below), this informs the goal setting for the next writing task. Even with practice, you will not always get it right. Writing is, after all, a creative process and how difficult a task proves to be may only become apparent after you have started. This is a good reason for beginning a task early, giving you the opportunity to adapt to unexpected challenges.

Is the goal realistic? There is, of course, a distinction between 'achievable' and 'realistic'. Suppose that, at 9 pm one evening, you were asked to write 1,500 words by 9 am the next morning. For most of us, doing this might be achievable, but would it be realistic? Would working through the night be an effective way to carry out the task? In most cases, when completing a writing task, you have choice about when and how to do it. Be realistic about what is possible. As with deciding what is achievable, the ability to set realistic goals comes with practice and wise reflection.

Lastly, is the goal time-scaled? Yes, it is. The student has given herself three hours. For most people it is more effective to work in two chunks of about 90 minutes or three chunks of about 60 minutes, with breaks in between.

Key to goal setting and then carrying out the task is reflecting on how it went, and learning from your practice. Systematically applied, goal setting in combination with wise reflection is a way to swiftly improve your academic writing and its management.

## Reflecting on your practice

Learning developers and theorists (e.g. Gibbs, 1988; Dennison and Kirk, 1990) propose that action-planning (including setting goals) and systematic reflection are key to learning from experience. Here is how you can apply this to your writing.

After a writing session, review how it went:

What went well?
What went less well?
What would I do differently next time?

For example, let us return to the student's goal: 'This morning, in three hours, I will write 750 words of first draft quality (with citations) on the literature review for my end-of-year project report.' She reflects on how it went. What went well included her writing 790 words in less than three hours, and the student feeling proud of what she had achieved. When she reads her work, she sees that there are gaps, and more literature searching and reading needs to be done, but she is satisfied that she has a reasonable working draft to develop further.

What went less well? She did not have all her paper sources to hand. And at one point, she lost wifi access to her online materials. This meant that she could not insert all the citations as she went. On one occasion she was unclear about the sources of evidence underpinning her argument. She also allowed herself to be distracted by arriving emails and a text message.

What might she do differently next time? All in all, she was fairly satisfied with her performance but realised that next time she could wait until a break to answer emails, texts or phone calls. If she had done so, she might have done a slightly better job and probably saved about half an hour. Breaking off from her composing in mid-flow, and then having to regain the right frame of mind, was disruptive. Next time, she would ignore emails and put her mobile phone on mute. Also, she would make sure she had good online access and had gathered all the source material she needed for her planned writing.

By reflecting in this manner, and making adjustments, one becomes a better writer. Managing the 'nuts and bolts' of writing, ensuring that you are in a supportive environment with everything you need, gives you the best opportunity to be creative rather than plagued by distractions.

TIP

**Nurturing your composing**

- Keep a notebook of ideas, questions and jottings.
- Try writing 'as if' you were a writer or researcher you admire.
- Analyse the work of writers or researchers you respect.
- Analyse your own work, but be constructively critical.
- Set yourself achievable, short-term goals.
- Gradually build your writing skills – start 'small chunk' and then aim larger.
- Gain feedback from those whose opinion you value. It helps to be specific about those aspects for which you want feedback (see Chapter 12).
- Give yourself a reward after a successful bout of composing!

## 7.7   Twelve ways to overcome writer's block

There are various definitions of writer's block. For professional writers – and especially those who are at their most creative as novelists, poets or playwrights – various psychological factors can cause them to abandon writing for weeks, months or years. Here, I am not talking about this rather grand kind of writer's block, but a more mundane one. Writer's block is the temporary inability to write, for psychological or organisational reasons. It is often associated with anxiety. Professional writers – and that includes academic writers – rarely have the luxury of this kind of writer's block. They have tight deadlines to meet and they have to keep their writing projects moving forward. There is always something practical they can do – whether it is planning, researching the subject matter, asking advice, thinking, composing small sections, or reviewing and editing. In other words, they can always find time somewhere to move the overall writing process forward. And there are various ways to reduce the anxiety associated with writing.

It is never too early to develop habits that help you overcome writing blocks. Here are twelve suggestions:

1   **Be aware of where you are in a writing process.** For a piece of writing, are you engaged in planning and researching, composing, or reviewing and editing? If you are finding it challenging to get started ask yourself: What is the best thing to do next? What am I avoiding? What needs to happen before I am ready to move forward?

2   **Plan the various activities in the writing process around your preferences.** When is the best time in the day for you to compose, review and edit, plan, or research and read the literature? If you can, match your daily activities to your preferences. Trying to engage in any one of these

activities for many hours in a single day may be counterproductive. You may become bored, inattentive and uncreative.

3    **Make sure you have understood the task.** Have you understood the requirements for the writing assignment? If not, the lack of clarity may well give rise to indecision. If necessary, seek help in order to gain clarity about the nature of the task (see, for example, Section 3.1 *Questions to ask your assessor*).

4    **Be realistic and plan ahead.** Panicking is a great way to induce writer's block. To avoid this happening, plan your writing task well ahead (see Chapters 1 and 6) and set yourself short-term writing goals. You can use SMART or a similar model. Reflect on your practice afterwards. With experience, you will become better at setting realistic goals and will more often reach them, giving yourself time to get the work done to a standard for which you can be proud.

5    **Practise.** It is a truism that you only get better at writing by writing. Thinking, on its own, is no substitute. So, get plenty of writing practice. This need only be in small chunks – writing daily notes or reflections. But the more you get used to starting writing, whether for yourself or for various readerships, the easier you will find it to get started in the future.

6    **Set up a place to write.** With practice, you can learn to write almost anywhere. But make it easy on yourself. Create an environment that supports your writing. For many of us, this includes an uncluttered writing surface where you can spread out your work, a computer with a high quality visual display, a chair that provides the right kind of support, lighting of high quality, and the absence of interruptions or distractions. Once you have established your writing environment, return to it or recreate it when you wish to compose, review or edit. Over time, you will come to associate the environment you have created with the act of writing, and sitting down in that place will act as a trigger to get you started.

7    **Freewrite.** Write for 5–15 minutes in an uncensored way without stopping, to develop the habit of composing and not holding back. If you are 'blocked' when composing, you could freewrite about the experience. Write down 'I'm stuck', and then respond to the statement in freewriting. More often than not, the act of freewriting will loosen up your writing, help you feel better and give insight about what you need to do to move forward.

8    **Use 'writing to a prompt'.** Rather than struggling with the blank page or trying to write the perfect first sentence, make what you are writing about the prompt to get you started; for example, 'In this introduction I will outline ...' or 'This introduction outlines ...'.

9    **Discuss your writing with someone you trust.** Any of the issues mentioned in this list can be helped by talking the matter over with someone else. Talking about writing issues with others helps at many levels. For example, you may gain greater clarity, and confidence in the process and content of writing, by

seeking to explain the problem to someone else, even before you benefit from their response.

10 **Take a break and get into the 'right state'.** Go off and do something else. Return rested, energised, or whatever for you is the right state to start writing. I've known students who've stood on their heads in yogic positions, gone for a run, meditated, played heavy metal or classical music, walked in the park, made coffee, or taken a nap, to shift themselves into the right state for writing. They tend to do one of these things, not all of them! But don't use taking a break as an excuse not to write. Rather, use it as a way to get into the right state to write – a combination of relaxed but alert.

11 **Do something completely different!** If your writing is becoming stale, break out of your normal patterns. Try going to a park bench and writing longhand, rather than sitting at a computer screen. And sometimes the best thing to do is take a day off.

12 **Recognise what you have achieved.** In those dark nights of the soul, when you find the going tough, remind yourself of what you have achieved so far. You've overcome writing challenges before and you will do so again.

## Key points in the chapter

1 The process of writing involves conscious and unconscious processes, both of which need to be nurtured.

2 The first draft is often best written swiftly, after thorough research and planning. This creates the opportunity for plenty of revision, without too much time being invested at an early stage.

3 Writing to a self-written prompt is a way of getting over the problem of slow starting.

4 Freewriting has many benefits, including encouraging self-expression, generating and connecting ideas, getting into the habit of writing quickly, clearing one's mind before writing more formally, or shedding light on a writing block.

5 The 'no composing' approach, in which text is gradually assembled in a series of small steps, is one strategy to use when composing does not flow smoothly.

6 Managing composing can be done holistically, taking into account factors such as environment, time of day and state of mind, and employs a wide range of strategies, including goal setting and wise reflection.

7 Writer's block, often linked to anxiety, can be countered successfully in many ways.

# Cited references

Brande, D. (1934, 1981). *Becoming a Writer*. London: Macmillan.

Dennison, B. and Kirk, R. (1990). *Do, Review, Learn, Apply: A Simple Guide to Experiential Learning*. Oxford: Blackwell.

Elbow, P. (1973). *Writing Without Teachers*. Oxford: Oxford University Press.

Elbow, P. (1981). *Writing with Power: Techniques for Mastering the Writing Process*. New York: Oxford University Press.

Flower, L. and Hayes, J. (1977). 'Problem Solving Strategies and the Writing Process'. *College English*, 39(4), pp. 449–461.

Gibbs, G. (1988). *Learning by Doing: A Guide to Teaching and Learning Methods*. London: Further Education Unit.

Lepore, S. J. and Smyth, J. (2002). *The Writing Cure*. Washington: American Psychological Association.

Locke, E. A. and Latham, G. P. (2002). 'Building a Practically Useful Theory of Goal Setting and Task Motivation: A 35-year Odyssey'. *American Psychologist*, 57(9), pp. 705–717.

Wade, D. T. (2009). 'Goal Setting in Rehabilitation: An Overview of What, Why and How'. *Clinical Rehabilitation*, 23(4), pp. 291–295.

## Further reading

Conrey, S. M. and Brizee, A. (2011). *Symptoms and Cures for Writer's Block*. West Lafayette: Purdue University, Purdue Online Writing Lab. Available from: https://owl.english.purdue.edu/owl/resource/567/1/ [accessed 10 August 2017].

# Chapter 8

# Words and Images

Although this book is about writing, it is also about images. There are at least 25 figures and 15 tables in this book, and the book's overall design and visual appearance adds to its interest and accessibility. And so it is with many of the documents you will produce during your time at university.

Increasingly in our digital age, words come with associated images. The online world is replete with images. In human history, drawn images came well before written words. Australian rock paintings, and French and Spanish cave art, pre-date Mesopotamian cuneiform writing by at least 30,000 years. Images can express more elegantly, more coherently and more completely what words may stumble to express. What can take thousands of words to describe inadequately, a single image may capture in an instant.

Many kinds of academic writing assignment, from posters and presentations to dissertations and research papers, have a strong visual component. This chapter considers how and when different visual devices – tables, graphs, charts and so on – can be integrated with text.

## 8.1   The role of visual elements

Writing is more or less linear. When you read, you follow the words across and down a page to capture meaning. Visual elements tend to be non-linear. In many cases, you capture meaning by comprehending the image overall. Even in the case of graphs and tables that present large volumes of data, they are rarely read downwards starting at the top-left, as is typically the case with written English prose. Visual elements are 'read' in a different way from normal written text.

Visual elements thus give the reader a distinctive experience. This difference can be used to engage the reader, inject variety and provide explanation that complements the text. As a general rule, visual elements should enhance the communication, not simply repeat, in a different form, what is already well explained in the text. The use of visual elements can be planned ahead, or may emerge naturally as text is written.

You need to check with an assessor whether visual elements are permissible for a given assignment. In a practical report they are often vital ingredients but in an essay an assessor might wish you to exclude them.

## 8.2   Content and design

When visual elements are incorporated with academic writing, there are conventions and good practice regarding **content** (how much and how clearly the element communicates) and **design** (how the element relates in appearance, size and position to text nearby). When interweaving visual elements with text, here are some of the most important points to consider:

- Does the visual element complement the text? Is it adding something that the text cannot provide?
- As with text, visuals are normally precisely targeted at a specific readership to meet an intended purpose.
- Does the visual adopt conventions that the reader will understand?
- The visual is normally referred to in the text so that the reader understands its relationship with the text.
- The visual should be close to where it is referred to in the text – ideally, on the same page.
- Normally, the visual should stand alone in meaning insofar as it can be interpreted without having to read large volumes of accompanying text.
- Visuals are usually numbered consecutively, either as tables or as figures ('figures' here refers to all kinds of formal visual element other than tables).
- Conventionally, tables have an explanatory title above, and figures a title (legend) below.
- Plan carefully the eventual size of the visual when it is printed, so that it has the appropriate degree of impact. Any text or other elements it contains should be clearly distinguishable.
- Leave plenty of white space around the visual so that it does not appear cramped on the page.
- The conventions on citing the source of a figure or table are strict. If the figure or table is copied from or is substantially similar to its source, a citation to the source should be given, e.g. 'Smith (2012)'. If the figure or table has been adapted from one or more sources, this should be stated and the sources cited, e.g. 'adapted from Smith (2012)'.

The following sections briefly consider the most common kinds of visual element, and where and how they should be used.

## 8.3   Using tables

Tables are usually used to compare and contrast numerical data (Table 8.1) although they can be used to compare discrete categories of written information (Table 8.2). A table is normally referred to in text nearby, as in the previous sentence.

In a written report, tables are usually used in the main body of the report to present summarised or processed data. If you need to present raw data to convince your assessor that you have carried out an experimental investigation appropriately, then such data can be placed in an appendix.

If you wish to reveal a clear pattern or trend in data, this is normally best done using a graph or chart rather than a table.

**Table 8.1   The world's five oceans: surface area, mean depth and volume (adapted from Day, 2008, p. 5)**

| Oceans | Surface area (million km²) | Mean depth (m) | Volume (km³) |
|---|---|---|---|
| Pacific Ocean* | 153 | 4,229 | 644 |
| Atlantic Ocean* | 82 | 3,777 | 308 |
| Indian Ocean* | 67 | 3,877 | 262 |
| Southern Ocean | 21 | 3,410 | 72 |
| Arctic Ocean | 9 | 1,935 | 17 |

*Excluding selected adjacent seas

**Table 8.2   Marine environments classified by salinity range**

| Environment | Examples | Terminology | Typical salinity range (ppt*) |
|---|---|---|---|
| Regions with high water loss by evaporation | Tidal pools, tropical or subtropical lagoons, Persian Gulf, Red Sea | Hypersaline | ≥39 |
| Open ocean | – | – | 32–37 |
| Shallow coastal areas near estuaries | – | Slightly hyposaline to hyposaline | 27–31 |
| Semi-enclosed seas that receive high levels of freshwater from rivers | Baltic Sea, Lake Bafa (Turkey) | Hyposaline (brackish) | <25 |
| Estuaries | Chesapeake Bay (USA), Severn estuary, Thames estuary (UK) | Hyposaline (brackish) | 1–30 |

*Parts per thousand. Dissolved solid (in grams) per 1,000 grams of seawater.

Refer to Tables 8.1 and 8.2 as you examine the various conventions used in constructing tables:

- If your document contains more than one table, assign each table a number in consecutive order and place the number before the title.
- The title is placed at the top and should clearly and concisely describe what the table contains.
- Plan the table so that it has an appropriate number of columns and rows to fit on the page (if it will not fit in portrait format, use landscape format).
- Typically, each column and each row has a brief heading. The heading may contain units and/or abbreviations that do not need to be explained if they

**ACTIVITY 8.1**

## Improving a table

Below is a table using data from page 37 of the United Nations Conference on Trade and Development (UNCTAD)'s *2016 Review of Maritime Transport*. Suggest three ways in which Table 8.3 could be improved.

**Table 8.3   The ten countries/territories with the largest owned fleets as of 1 January 2016**

| Country/territory of ownership | Number of national flag vessels | Number of foreign flag vessels | Total number of vessels | Total dead-weight tonnage (thousands of tonnes) |
|---|---|---|---|---|
| Bermuda | 14 | 404 | 418 | 48,453 |
| China | 3,405 | 1,915 | 4,960 | 158,884 |
| Germany | 240 | 3,121 | 3,361 | 119,181 |
| Greece | 728 | 3,408 | 4,136 | 293,087 |
| Hong Kong (China) | 854 | 594 | 1,448 | 87,375 |
| Japan | 835 | 3,134 | 3,969 | 228,980 |
| Republic of Korea | 795 | 839 | 1,634 | 78,834 |
| Singapore | 1,499 | 1,054 | 2,553 | 95,312 |
| United Kingdom | 332 | 997 | 1,329 | 48,453 |
| United States | 782 | 1,213 | 1,995 | 60,279 |

*Compare your answers with those at the end of the chapter.*

are likely to be familiar to the reader. If they are not familiar, or additional clarification is needed, further information can be given as footnotes beneath the table (see Tables 8.1 and 8.2).

- Columns and rows are arranged in a logical order. For example, in Table 8.1 the entries in rows are placed in order of decreasing size of ocean.
- Data in a column should be aligned consistently. Words are normally centred or aligned left. Numbers are typically centred or aligned right, with decimal points aligned.
- If the data or information in a table is not your own, the source should be cited (after the title or in a footnote just below the table).

## 8.4   Using graphs and charts

Graphs and charts are used to shows trends or patterns in numerical data. The most common types are line graphs, scatter plots, bar charts, histograms and pie charts (Figures 8.1–8.5). A graph or chart is normally referred to in text nearby, as in the preceding sentence.

Refer to Figures 8.1–8.5 as you examine the various conventions used in constructing graphs or charts:

- If your document contains more than one graph, chart or other kind of figure, assign each a number in consecutive order and place the number before the title.
- The title (legend) is placed below the chart or graph and should clearly and concisely describe what is being displayed.
- Plan the graph or chart so that it fits appropriately on the page, with all features being clearly visible.
- If the data or information used to create the graph or chart are not your own, the source should be cited (after the title or in a footnote just below the chart or graph).

### Line graphs

Use a line graph to display a relationship between two continuous variables (see Figure 8.1). The independent variable (the variable chosen by the investigator) is plotted in relation to the $x$ axis (the horizontal axis). The dependent variable (the variable that is dependent on the independent variable and for which values are not known before the investigation) is normally plotted in relation to the $y$ axis (the vertical axis). In a line graph, each plotted point is described by two numbers, its coordinates, which give its position with respect to the $x$ axis and $y$ axis respectively. Points are normally connected by a hand-drawn line or a statistically computed one. If more than one set of data are plotted on the same graph, the data sets should be clearly distinguished by using different symbols for plotted points and/or a different

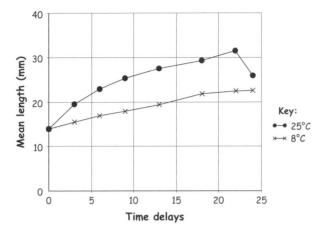

**Figure 8.1** The growth of tadpoles of the common British frog, *Rana temporaria*, at 8°C (*n* = 25) and 25°C (*n* = 25). Hypothetical data

form of line to connect them. A key is then needed to explain the symbols or forms of line, as in Figure 8.1. Full experimental detail would be included in the method section of the investigation, but might be summarised in the figure legend or in text accompanying the graph. Incidentally, the drop in mean length of the tadpoles at day 24 is due to them beginning metamorphosis from a tadpole into an adult frog, which is accompanied by the tail being absorbed.

The scales for graph axes normally start at zero. If a scale does not start at zero, this should be clearly indicated, and the start point clearly labelled. Each scale is labelled in writing that usually runs parallel to the axis, and any units of measurement are clearly stated. Figure 8.1 is a simple line graph. In your studies you may be plotting graphs from data generated from statistical analyses, in which case a vertical bar showing standard error may be included to indicate distribution about the mean.

## Scatter plots

Scatter plots are similar to line graphs (see above) in showing a relationship between two continuous variables. However, they plot individual data points, not aggregated ones, and they produce a scatter of points that are not joined by lines. A hand-drawn line of best fit (see Figure 8.2) or a statistically computed regression line may be drawn to highlight or reveal any trend in the data. A lecturer wishing to discover whether students' success in an exam-preparation module is associated with success in second-year exams might plot a scattergram of their results as in Figure 8.2. In this case, there appears to be a positive association between the two.

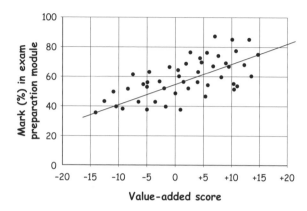

Figure 8.2 Marks (as percentages) for students' results in an exam-preparation module plotted against their value-added scores based on Year 2 exam results compared with Year 1 results. Hypothetical data

## Bar charts

Bar charts can be used to plot data where at least one variable is discrete (it falls into distinct categories rather than being on a continuum). In Figure 8.3 the discrete variable is the chemical fertiliser applied to the soil in

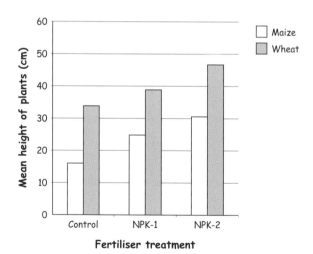

Figure 8.3 The effects of two types of NPK fertiliser on the growth of maize (*Zea mays*) and wheat (*Triticum aestivum*). Hypothetical data

which the plants are grown. To reflect this characteristic, when numbers of entries are plotted vertically as bars, the bars for different categories are kept separate. If there are two data sets within the same category, as in Figure 8.3, the bars need to be distinguished, often using shading or hatching. As usual, any use of shading or other notation needs to be indicated using a key. Summary details of the growth and treatment conditions could be added to the figure legend or given in the accompanying text.

Bar charts follow the usual conventions for graphs and charts that have axes: for example, the independent variable is plotted in relation to the horizontal (*x*) axis and the dependent variable in relation to the vertical (*y*) axis.

## Histograms

A histogram is similar to a bar chart but is used where variation in the data is continuous (data do not fall into distinct groups). Histograms are particularly useful for displaying large data sets, where the data are grouped into ranges (Figure 8.4). Like bar charts, histograms follow the normal conventions for graphs and charts that have axes.

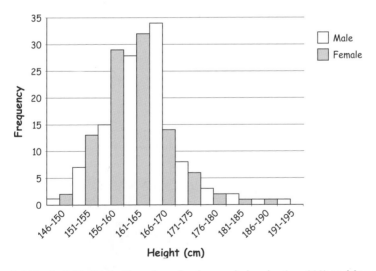

**Figure 8.4 The height distribution of randomly sampled males (*n* = 100) and females (*n* = 100) aged 18/19 in the Psychology Department at University X. Hypothetical data**

## Pie charts

A pie chart differs from the graphs and charts considered so far, because it does not employ axes. A pie chart is an impressionistic device for making comparison between several categories of data. It is most effective when used to display strong distinctions between just a few categories, such as population statistics or responses to a question that might be displayed in an essay, report or presentation (see Figure 8.5).

Pie charts can be readily drawn using computer software such as Microsoft Word or Microsoft Excel. If the charts are drawn by hand, percentages can be readily converted to degrees by multiplying by 3.6 (100% represents 360 degrees). The different 'slices' of a pie chart are called 'sectors' and they are commonly displayed anticlockwise in order of increasing size, or otherwise in a logical order (see Figure 8.5). It is difficult to distinguish sectors of similar size and so a pie chart is best used when the categories differ markedly in size. If they do not, a table or bar chart may be a better way to display differences between categories.

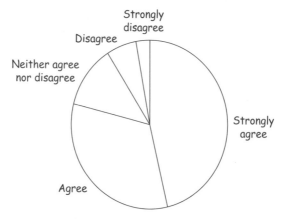

**Figure 8.5** Students' responses ($n = 90$) to the question 'Overall, do you consider the teaching on the exam-preparation module to have been effective?' Hypothetical data

**ACTIVITY 8.2**

## Improving a chart

Below is a simple bar chart comparing the exam marks of male ($n$ = 45) and female ($n$ = 48) students on a module from a History of Art course. Assuming further information about how the data was gathered is given in accompanying text, suggest two ways in which this bar chart could be improved.

*Compare your answers with those at the end of the chapter.*

**Figure 8.6  A comparison of the mean exam marks of male ($n$ = 45) and female ($n$ = 48) students on an Art and Protest module. Hypothetical data**

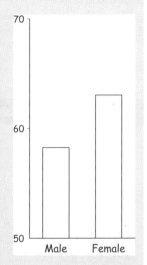

**TIP**

### Tufte's principles

American Edward R. Tufte is a visionary statistician and artist who wrote four classic books about the visual presentation of data, including his highly influential *The Visual Display of Quantitative Information*. Among Tufte's principles are:

- show the data
- tell the truth
- let the viewer think about the information rather than the design
- encourage the eye to compare data.

In other words, he was concerned with simplicity and elegance – how to show data in such a way that meaning and importance becomes clear. You would do well to do the same.

## 8.5   Other kinds of figure

Line graphs, scatter plots, bar charts, histograms and pie charts are just a few of the many ways of displaying information visually. Others include maps, Gantt charts (Section 1.3), mind maps, concept maps, flow charts (Section 5.7) and organisational charts. And then there are various kinds of line drawing, ranging from sketches and anatomical drawings to architectural plans and high-accuracy engineering and design drawings. Added to this are photographs and composite figures (figures that display information in more than one way, such as a map with histograms superimposed on it).

The various ways of depicting information visually cannot all be considered in this book, and the reader is referred to Tufte (2001), Nicol and Pexman (2010a, 2010b) and the Open University (2017) for further information. Advice on using software to generate figures is given in Section 11.4.

## Key points in the chapter

1 Visual elements, such as tables and figures, complement text in many kinds of assignment.

2 There are conventions for how visual elements are displayed and referred to in academic writing.

3 Tables can be effective for comparing and contrasting numerical and sometimes written information in a summary form.

4 Graphs and charts – such as line graphs, scatter plots, bar charts, histograms and pie charts – can be effective for displaying trends or patterns in numerical data.

5 Visual elements, such as tables and graphs, need to be integrated with the document's text. They should be referred to in the text, and complement rather than repeat information given in the text.

# Cited references

Day, T. (2008). *Oceans*. Revised edition. New York: Facts On File.

Nicol, A. A. M. and Pexman, P. M. (2010a). *Displaying Your Findings: A Practical Guide for Creating Tables*. 6th edn. Washington: American Psychological Association.

Nicol, A. A. M. and Pexman, P. M. (2010b). *Displaying Your Findings: A Practical Guide for Creating Figures, Posters and Presentations*. 6th edn. Washington: American Psychological Association.

The Open University (2017). *OpenLearn Online Unit: More Working with Charts, Graphs and Tables*. Milton Keynes: The Open University. Available from: www.open.edu/open learn/science-maths-technology/mathematics-and-statistics/mathematics-education/ more-working-charts-graphs-and-tables/content-section-0 [accessed 10 August 2017].

Tufte, E. R. (2001). *The Visual Display of Quantitative Information*. 2nd edn. Cheshire: Graphics Press.

UNCTAD (2016). *Review of Maritime Transport*. Geneva, Switzerland: United Nations Conference on Trade and Development (UNCTAD). Available from: http://unctad.org/en/pages/ PublicationWebflyer.aspx?publicationid=1650 [accessed 10 August 2017].

**Further reading**

Duarte, N. (2010). *Resonate: Present Visual Stories that Transform Audiences.* Hoboken: John Wiley & Sons.

# Answers for Chapter 8

## Activity 8.1: Improving a table

The table could be improved in these three ways:

- The source of the data is not cited. This could be done either at the end of the table title or in a footnote.
- Dead-weight tonnage is best defined. It is a measure of how much weight a ship can safely carry (carrying capacity), including cargo, fuel, ballast water, provisions, fresh water, passengers and crew.
- The countries/territories are ordered alphabetically. They would be more logically listed in order of fleet size or total dead-weight tonnage.

A revised table, incorporating these three features, is shown below:

Table 8.4   The ten countries/territories with the largest owned fleets as of 1 January 2016 (UNCTAD, 2016, p. 37)

| Country/territory of ownership | Number of national flag vessels | Number of foreign flag vessels | Total number of vessels | Total dead-weight* tonnage (thousands of tonnes) |
|---|---|---|---|---|
| Greece | 728 | 3,408 | 4,136 | 293,087 |
| Japan | 835 | 3,134 | 3,969 | 228,980 |
| China | 3,405 | 1,915 | 4,960 | 158,884 |
| Germany | 240 | 3,121 | 3,361 | 119,181 |
| Singapore | 1,499 | 1,054 | 2,553 | 95,312 |
| Hong Kong (China) | 854 | 594 | 1,448 | 87,375 |
| Republic of Korea | 795 | 839 | 1,634 | 78,834 |
| United States | 782 | 1,213 | 1,995 | 60,279 |
| Bermuda | 14 | 404 | 418 | 48,453 |
| United Kingdom | 332 | 997 | 1,329 | 48,453 |

*Dead-weight is a measure of how much weight a ship can safely carry (carrying capacity). It includes cargo, fuel, ballast water, provisions, fresh water, passengers and crew.

## Activity 8.2: Improving a chart

The bar chart could be improved in three ways:

- The vertical (*y* axis) scale does not begin at zero, giving an exaggerated impression of the difference in scores between males and females. Using a full scale would make the difference much less evident.
- The vertical (*y* axis) scale is unlabelled. Presumably it refers to the overall percentage marks obtained on the course.
- In addition, the chart would be more meaningful if standard errors were shown, indicating the distribution of marks for each category.

A revised chart, incorporating these three features, is shown in Figure 8.7:

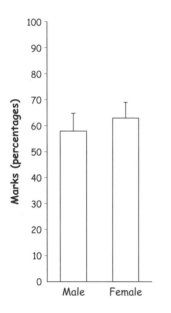

Figure 8.7 A comparison of the mean percentage score of male (*n* = 45) and female (*n* = 48) students on the Art and Protest module. The standard errors about the mean are indicated. Based on hypothetical data

# Citing, Referencing and Avoiding Plagiarism

The argument in this chapter is that citing and referencing are key to academic integrity (intellectual honesty). By full and correct acknowledgment of the sources of facts, ideas and arguments, the author's contribution and the contributions of others' work that has informed the author are made apparent to the reader.

You are a member of an academic community. By knowing the sources you have used in completing an assignment, and that you have used them appropriately, an assessor can determine the strength of your argument. He or she can also establish the extent of your contribution to that argument.

Academic integrity is also the starting point for considering plagiarism – the act of taking others' ideas, arguments, data, tables or figures and passing them off as your own in writing, whether accidentally or intentionally. Plagiarism, by a strict definition, is 'literary theft' but it can also apply to other elements integrated with the text.

Understanding plagiarism, and how to avoid it, can take weeks or months to fully appreciate. You do so by paying careful attention to the sources you use, deciding how you are going to weave them into your argument, and then paying scrupulous attention to tracking your use of that information, and acknowledging it correctly. Proficiency in these processes only comes with practice.

## 9.1 Citing and referencing

Citing is the use of a note in the text to refer the reader to the source of information (a fact, idea or argument). The note is called a citation. The citation refers to the source. The full publication details of the source are normally included as an entry, called a reference, in a list of references at the end of the document.

Two methods of citing and referencing are popular:

- Harvard style (author–date method)
- Numerical style (involving a numbering system)

## Harvard-style citing and referencing

When citing a source using the Harvard style (author–date method), the citation gives the surname(s) of the author(s) and the source's date of publication. For example: 'Pussycat and Dogmanger (2011) argue persuasively for giving students the opportunity to use plagiarism-detection software to help them improve their academic writing' or 'Enabling students to use plagiarism-detection software on their own work is a means of raising their awareness of the degree to which they must both acknowledge and adapt the work of others (Pussycat and Dogmanger, 2011).'

In Harvard style, references are listed in the references section alphabetically by author. For example:

Bandura, A. (1997). *Self-Efficacy: The Exercise of Control*. New York: Freeman.
Blakemore, S.-J. and Frith, U. (2005). *The Learning Brain*. Oxford: Blackwell Publishing.
Claxton, G. (2006). *Learning to Learn: The Fourth Generation – Making Sense of Personalised Learning*. Bristol: TLO.
Locke, E. A. and Latham, G. P. (2002). Building a practically useful theory of goal setting and task motivation: A 35-year odyssey. *American Psychologist*, 57(9): 705–717.
McNeil, F. (2009). *Learning with the Brain in Mind*. London: Sage.
Zimmerman, B. J. (2008). Goal setting: A key proactive source of academic self-regulation. In *Motivation and Self-Regulated Learning*, ed. D. H. Schunk and B. J. Zimmerman, 267–295. New York: Lawrence Erlbaum Associates.

The book you are reading right now uses a version of Harvard for citing and referencing.

## Numerical citing and referencing

In this system the citation is a number. The citation may be given in brackets:

*Aardvark and Womble [1] argue persuasively for giving students the opportunity to use plagiarism-detection software to help them improve their academic writing. Deer and Badger [2] suggest that this approach should come after a period of acclimatisation to academic writing, by which time the student will be aware of the need to avoid plagiarism, and the challenges in doing so.*

Alternatively, the citation can be given in superscript (raised above the normal line of text):

*Aardvark and Womble[1] argue persuasively for giving students the opportunity to use plagiarism-detection software to help them improve their academic writing. Deer and Badger[2] suggest that this approach should come after a period of acclimatisation to academic writing, by which time the student will be aware of the need to avoid plagiarism, and the challenges in doing so.*

In most numerical systems the references at the end of the piece of work are listed in the order in which they are cited in the text. For example:

1  Aardvark, T. and Womble, P. (2012). *Strategies for Avoiding Plagiarism.* Wonderland: Nowhere Press.
2  Deer, W. and Badger, C. (2013). *Academic Writing in the Round.* Atlantis: Over The Rainbow Press.

If a source is cited more than once, it uses the number from the first citation. So, if Deer and Badger (2013) were referred to several times in a document, the citation in each case would be [2] or [2].

---

**TIP**

**A reference list or a bibliography?**

Traditionally, a reference list and a bibliography are slightly different. In a reference list you give only the source documents you have cited in your text. A bibliography lists all the sources you have consulted in writing your document, including those you have not cited.

A bibliography can be useful because it shows the depth and breadth of your reading, which can provide useful information for an assessor. Items in the bibliography reveal key influences that might have shaped your thinking.

Sometimes the term 'reference list' and 'bibliography' are taken to mean the same thing. Check with your assessor whether he or she wants you to list all the sources you have consulted, or only those that you have cited.

---

## Styles of citing and referencing

Although two styles of citing and referencing have been referred to so far – Harvard-style and numerical – within these categories there are numerous styles of referencing. The Harvard-style (author–date) system is used by various versions of Harvard, including British Standard (Harvard). The American Psychological Association (APA) style, common in social science disciplines, uses an author–date citation system. Systems vary in detail as to exactly how citations are given, e.g. (Aardvark and Wombat, 2012) or (Aardvark & Wombat 2012), and exactly how punctuation and abbreviations are used in reference entries. For example:

Aardvark, A. and Wombat, T. (2012). Foraging strategies among burrowing mammalian herbivores. *Global Life Sciences*, Vol. 4, pp. 260–295.

or:

Aardvark, A. and Wombat, T. 2012, 'Foraging strategies among burrowing mammalian herbivores.' *Global Life Sciences*, 4: 260–295.

The Chicago referencing style is an author–date system in which the full reference entry is given in a footnote on the same page as the citation. The Modern Languages Association (MLA) system, popular in the arts and humanities, cites author and source page number or author and title rather than author–date.

There are many hundreds of versions of author–date referencing, and some universities have even developed their own version, e.g. the University of Bath has its own version of Harvard (http://www.bath.ac.uk/library/infoskills/referencing-plagiarism/harvard-bath-style.html). Whichever version you choose, and your department or institution will usually specify which one, use it with consistency within your document.

For numerical referencing there are several systems in common use. Three of the most prevalent are British Standard (Numeric), Vancouver (commonly used in life sciences, humanities and mathematics), and IEEE, Institute of Electrical and Electronics Engineers (in computer science and some engineering disciplines).

All citing and referencing systems have their strengths and weaknesses. They are often elegantly adapted for their specific discipline. For example, in certain contexts engineering and science disciplines use a numerical referencing system because it allows text to be compact. Numerical referencing is less likely to interrupt the flow of dense, fact- or data-rich sentences that refer to several sources. A disadvantage is that the reader has to turn to the reference list to locate the author(s) and date of a given source. Knowing the date and author for a citation, as you read text, can be invaluable in judging the quality of the account. For example, does it use the latest sources? Does it rely too much on only one or a few authors, and therefore might it be biased?

Useful guides to citing and referencing include Neville (2010) and Pears and Shields (2016), while Godfrey (2013) considers how to bring your researching, reading and writing together, to appropriately draw upon and acknowledge sources. The University of York Academic Integrity webpages (www.york.ac.uk/integrity/referencing.html) give style guides for several different referencing systems.

For a student, the key to using a referencing system is to find out what your tutor or department wishes you to employ for that assignment and similar ones. You need to be absolutely consistent in the way you cite and reference within that system, and develop confidence and expertise in using it.

## 9.2 Citing, referencing and academic integrity

Citing and referencing lie at the heart of what it means to be a scholar within your discipline. You are part of an academic community of students and professional academics who are developing written arguments using evidence and reasoning. It is extremely rare to write an assignment or academic paper that does not make reference to the work of others. Indeed, whether showing your understanding of your discipline, or as an academic pushing back the boundaries of knowledge, you do so by building on the work of others. As Sir Isaac Newton, the British physicist and mathematician, said so eloquently in his letter dated 5 February 1675 to his colleague Robert Hooke, 'If I have been able to see farther than others, it was because I stood on the shoulders of giants.'

When you write for academic purposes, it is only by citing and fully referencing the work of others that your reader can:

- Appreciate where your work is positioned within the discipline.
- Check the credibility of the sources you have used.
- Confirm that you have interpreted those sources correctly.
- Examine how you have assembled sources to provide a balanced account, or perhaps selected sources to promote a particular position or viewpoint.
- Assess the strength of the evidence and reasoning in support of your argument.
- Determine how you have critically analysed, synthesised and applied the work of others.
- Establish your contribution, in terms of what you have brought to the argument by thinking independently and perhaps gathering evidence of your own (for example, by observation, experiment or survey).

As a student, you are being 'trained' in your academic or vocational discipline. Academic research is challenging, time-consuming and often expensive. So too is the reporting of that research, in writing. Morally, it is right that an individual's contribution to the field should be acknowledged by others, by them properly citing and referencing his or her work. Beyond that, academic writing is intellectual property.

A person, group or organisation can 'own' an idea, or the form of its expression in the public domain. Form of expression in writing is linked to the concept of plagiarism. As a professional, being found committing plagiarism has financial implications. Apart from a person's professional integrity being challenged, which will impact upon their career, they may have to pay compensation (see, for example, Batty, 2008). For you as a student, it is comparatively easy for your assessor to find whether you have committed plagiarism. If you have, and you are at an early stage in your student career, it is an opportunity for you to develop correct academic practice. Later in your student career, being found committing plagiarism can result in you failing an assignment, a module, or your entire course.

Lastly, academic publications, each citing and referencing earlier publications, create an interconnected web of knowledge that stretches back in time (Neville, 2010). That network of connections can be followed, and through citing and referencing, the development of ideas, the gathering of facts and data, and their interpretation by successive generations, can be traced. This is vital for understanding the development of an academic discipline and for following the rise and fall of ideas within and between disciplines.

What I hope is emerging from the foregoing discussion is that acknowledging sources is much more than an annoying convention with which you have to comply. It underpins the very nature of your discipline. The body of knowledge, the practices of the discipline and the people who engage in them *are* the discipline. Undermine any of them and you threaten the integrity of the discipline itself.

---

**TIP**

**Latin abbreviations**

Scattered among academic text you might find Latin abbreviations such as 'et al.' and 'ibid.'; 'et al.' is short for *et alii*, meaning 'and others', and is commonly used where citations refer to three or more authors. Using 'et al.' avoids having to list in a citation all the authors of a source; for example, 'Smith, Jones, Curruthers and Sparkle (2017)' becomes 'Smith et al. (2017)'. It is, in most cases, the practice to list all the authors in the reference entry at the end of the document. The word 'ibid.' is short for *ibidem*, meaning 'in the same place'. It is used as a citation to indicate that the last named citation is being repeated. Strictly, 'et al.' and 'ibid.' should have a full stop after them, because they are abbreviations.

---

## 9.3   Using citations and quotes

Sources of information take many forms. They include documents, images, television or radio programmes, patent documents and statistics in databases. In Section 4.3 we defined 'primary literary sources' as publications in which facts or ideas are first communicated, and 'secondary literary sources', such as review articles and most books, as communications that report on, summarise or review other primary sources. In fact, the distinction between the two is not that clear-cut. Primary sources, such as articles in research journals, normally contain a substantial literature review component, which is reporting on other primary literature. And some review articles can contain new ideas and formulations, which could be regarded as a primary source of ideas.

As considered in Section 4.3, what is considered a primary or secondary source of literature does vary by discipline. For example, in history, a primary source can be a source material created by a person close in time or proximity reporting on an event, such as the diary of a World War II German soldier in a British prisoner of war camp. The book *World at War*, which accompanied the 26-part BBC television documentary series that screened in 1973–74, would be a secondary source. However, if a student were studying documentary narrative styles in the 1970s, the book and the television programmes could themselves be primary sources.

Returning to the more general definitions of primary and secondary literature sources, where possible, it is preferable to use primary sources for your writing, but in your first year or two at university it is likely that you will be referring to textbooks and review articles and less often consulting the primary sources to which they refer. If you cannot find a particular primary source, but are relying on an interpretation of what it says, which you have found in a secondary source, then you can cite the primary source but you should not list it in your references (see Tip below).

---

**TIP**

**Secondary referencing**

Where possible, it is preferable to find a primary source rather than rely on an interpretation of what it says as found in a secondary source. If you wish to cite a primary source, but you have not read it, you can refer to it through the secondary source: for example, 'Harland and Gross (2010, p. 12) agree with the views of Black (2009, cited in Harland and Gross, 2010, p. 12) that ...'. Harland and Gross (2010) would be included in the reference list, but Black (2009), the unread primary source, would not.

---

## Agree, disagree or qualify

The way you use sources in your argument is essentially by agreeing with the source you cite, disagreeing with it, or qualifying the facts or ideas of the source in some way. In fact, showing the extent with which you agree or disagree with a source can be a complex and subtle matter. Here are simple examples for each approach.

Agreement:

*Smith (2015) argues convincingly for ...*

Often, your agreement with a source is simply given by writing about it as though it were fact:

*Hitchcock (2013), Jones (2014) and Smith (2015) have determined the compound's properties.*

*Patel (2014) established ...*

Disagreement:

*Harcourt's (2015) conclusion is not warranted by the data presented because ...*

Qualification:

*Melbourne's (2016) findings apply in most cases, however, ...*

---

**TIP**

**Choose your verbs carefully**

You can write in such a way as to reveal the extent of your agreement with, or confidence in, a source you are citing. Using verb forms such as 'appears', 'seems', 'claims' or 'suggests' indicates to the reader that you are being tentative about any statements being made based on those sources. Using 'shows', 'reveals' or 'finds' suggest to the reader that you are more confident about what is being reported. By choosing your verbs carefully, you can give just the right amount of 'weight' to your statements.

---

## When to cite?

The extent to which you cite sources is likely to change (usually increase) as you work your way through your degree programme. Be guided by your assessor, but a good policy is to cite the source of all facts, ideas and opinions that relate to your argument, unless they are 'common knowledge'.

Common knowledge is information that a person living in your country at a similar educational level to yours is likely to know as a matter of course. That William Shakespeare was an English playwright, that Ludwig van Beethoven was a classical composer, and that the National Health Service provides many forms of free medical help at the point of need are examples of common knowledge for many people in the UK.

Disciplinary common knowledge is that which a person is likely to know having studied to a similar level in your discipline and in your country. Disciplinary common knowledge, if you were a chemistry student, would include the facts and principles you learnt before you joined university, or that were established soon after joining, such as the organisation of the periodic table, names of common elements and compounds, principles of ionic and covalent bonding, and so on. If you were an archaeologist, common knowledge might include the traditional methods for investigating an archaeological site. Other examples of disciplinary common knowledge include: for business studies students, the distinction between leadership and management; in chemical engineering, the distinction between laminar and turbulent flow; in film studies, the definition of a protagonist; in sociology, that many aspects of human behaviour are socially constructed.

There are occasions when terms that are frequently used within a discipline, and can be regarded as common knowledge, may nevertheless need to be defined and a citation used. For example, there is no single universally agreed definition for 'climate change', and if you were writing an essay about global warming you might wish to give a United Nations Development Program (UNDP) definition or one from the Intergovernmental Panel on Climate Change (IPCC), with an appropriate citation. This 'going back to basics' to carefully define terms that have become taken for granted can be a sign of rigorous academic practice. In writing academically it is important to define terms with reference to authoritative sources, particularly if those terms are controversial or have become misused or misinterpreted by others.

## Mentioning, summarising, paraphrasing or quoting

In weaving sources into your account, there are four main approaches to doing so, which operate at different levels of brevity and of correspondence to the original. When mentioning, you make brief reference to a source by pointing out a characteristic of that source. For example:

> *Several authors have reviewed this model in terms of application in the secondary school classroom (Bissell, 2015; Dyson, 2016; Procter, 2017).*

In **summarising**, you reduce a large volume of material to a much smaller volume, which captures the salient points that relate to your argument. At one extreme, you might be summarising a book, a book chapter or a journal article, and at the other extreme, you might be summarising a section from a chapter, a page or two of text from a journal article, or even just a paragraph or two.

The ability to summarise is highly valued by academics, because in doing so you have to take a large volume of material and adapt it to your own purposes. You have to be selective, and make critical choices. Summarising is also a way of demonstrating to an assessor your grasp of a wide range of sources. Rather than summarising being a process you do as part of an essay, report or other assignment, sometimes summarising a text is set as an assignment in itself, for you to practise and develop the craft.

The abstract of a journal paper (often somewhere between 100 and 300 words long) is a summary of the article's 1,500–5,000 words of main text. Examining the abstracts of journal articles – and noting their strengths and weaknesses as balanced, informative summaries of the whole document – is a valuable exercise. A well-written abstract of a research article, for example, usually contains the following elements in appropriate balance: background/context, aim, method, results and conclusion. If one or more of these elements dominate, the abstract might be poorly balanced.

**ACTIVITY 9.1**

### An abstract is a summary

In the hypothetical student's abstract below, identify those parts that relate to the background/context, aim, method, results and conclusion of the report. The sentences have been numbered to make this process easier.

**(a)** Which sentence(s) of the abstract relate(s) to:

(i) background/context

(ii) aim

(iii) method

(iv) results

(v) conclusion?

**(b)** Do you consider this abstract to be balanced?

*(1) Approaches to e-learning range from instructional (one-way) to collaborative and contested (two-way). (2) The existing literature is quite mixed as to the efficacy of the different approaches, with strong and distinct preferences between individuals in some studies. (3) The experience of students completing a life sciences e-learning module was investigated to reveal the extent to which different e-learning approaches were favoured by students. (4) A questionnaire census of all students (n = 85) was carried out immediately after students completed the module, with a stratified sample of students (n = 10) being interviewed within a week. (5) Analysis of questionnaire returns and interview themes reveals a complex pattern, with sizeable percentages of students favouring all approaches, but with strong preferences among a few students (n = 14). (6) The findings largely agree with the reviewed literature. (131 words)*

*Check your answers at the end of the chapter.*

The key to summarising well from source texts, as in so many other aspects of composing, is to have read the source(s) to meet your purpose, annotated the source text and/or taken notes appropriately, and considered what you are seeking to achieve. Once you know this, and how many words you are aiming to write, you can begin to plan your summary before drafting it. If you are summarising a page or less in a few lines you may be able to move swiftly to writing your draft without having to plan.

**Paraphrasing** involves restating what the author of a source is saying, but in your own words. Paraphrasing results in text that is closer to the length of the original than in summarising. Paraphrasing, with accompanying citation, shows that you have understood the source text, interpreted its meaning correctly in the context of your argument, and then captured the essence of that meaning in your own words. This is a high-level academic skill. As you paraphrase the words of others, you are integrating this contribution into your argument, critically evaluating it, and perhaps comparing and contrasting it with the work of others.

Here is an extract from Day and Tosey's (2011, p. 525) journal article about goal setting:

> Mental rehearsal has long been a key element employed by successful Olympic teams (Suin 1997). The benefits of mental rehearsal extend beyond physical skill and performance *per se*, but include qualities such as strengthening commitment, confidence and concentration, and enhancing the ability to control one's emotional state beneficially (Hale 1998; Hale et al. 2005). Such attributes clearly have relevance to learning in the classroom and elsewhere, not just applied to performance in sport.

And here is what a student might write in an assignment about students' goal setting in the classroom, paraphrasing the paragraph from Day and Tosey:

> *Day and Tosey (2011) draw comparison with the mental rehearsal athletes use to improve their performance in sport, and the mental rehearsal that students might employ in learning in the classroom to prepare for examinations. They argue that using mental rehearsal to develop better concentration, commitment and confidence, along with an improved ability to control emotional state, can apply to both the sports field and the exam room.*

The fourth approach is **using quotations (quoting)**. It is permissible to quote, word for word, from a source, but in most disciplines, this should be done sparingly. Relying too much on quotations reduces your ability to formulate your own argument and will not convince your assessor that you have understood the sources you are quoting. In most disciplines, quotes are likely to make up less than 5% of any assignment. Literary, language and historical disciplines (where close analysis of text is common) are among the few where extensive quoting is permissible.

In general, there are five situations where using a quotation is appropriate:

1  Where a source author has expressed a point so well that you can't (or don't think you can) improve on it. Such quotes are likely to be short. For example:

> *According to Hartley (2008, p. 3), the language commonly used in the text of scientific journal articles is 'precise, impersonal and objective. It typically uses the third person, the passive tense, complex terminology, and various footnoting and referencing systems.'*

2  Where you are referring to an authoritative definition. For example:

> *According to the Intergovernmental Panel on Climate Change (IPCC, 2007, Section 1.1) climate change refers to 'a change in the state of the climate that can be identified (e.g. using statistical tests) by changes in the mean*

*and/or the variability of its properties, and that persists for an extended period, typically decades or longer. It refers to any change in climate over time, whether due to natural variability or as a result of human activity.'*

3 Where a passage of source text is highly technical, difficult or dense, and requires it to be shown in its original form for the reader to comprehend its significance within the context of your analysis.

4 Where you are disagreeing with a source or making an unusual claim about it. To convince the reader that doing so is valid, you may need to quote the source sufficiently to reveal the original context and meaning and that you have not misinterpreted it.

5 At the beginning of an essay, or a chapter in a dissertation, to capture the sense of what the essay or chapter is about, perhaps in a provocative or amusing manner.

## Rules for quoting

If you have chosen to include a quotation, make sure it performs one of the five functions above. Do not simply insert it as 'padding' or to impress your assessor or to save you having to paraphrase what the source said.

Here are seven rules for quoting:

1 Quote just enough source text to do the job.

2 Quote word for word, even if the original contains unusual spelling, punctuation or grammar. There are two ways of modifying the text slightly, as we will see below.

3 If the quotation is short, it can be woven into a sentence and enclosed in quotation marks, like so:

> *Armadillo and Koala (2010, p. 46) claim that 'without close attention to the starting conditions, the end point will always be in doubt'.*

If a quotation is more than four lines of prose, it is normally indented from normal text. For example:

> *According to Day et al.'s (2010) investigation of undergraduate dissertation writing on a Civil Engineering programme, the course was:*

> *... rich in learning and assessed assignments, including individual and group work, which encouraged several types of discourse for different purposes and audiences. However, there were missed opportunities for providing timely developmental feedback and to scaffold learning experiences to develop students' abilities and confidence in writing. (p. 20)*

4 Use verbs carefully to introduce the quotation with just the right amount of emphasis.

5 When using a quotation, its accompanying citation should refer to page number(s) so that the reader can go straight to the exact location of the quotation in the

source material. If the quoted material is on a webpage, you may wish to cite the section name or number so that the quote can be readily located.

6  Rarely, you might wish to omit words from a quote that would distract the reader and weaken the power of the quotation for the purpose you have in mind. This is done using an ellipsis (…) to show where words have been cut. The original:

> *Tiger and Mongoose (2015, p. 97) argue that 'failing to acknowledge a client's distress at the outset of a counselling session, and so avoiding what is "on the surface" for the client, is not only disrespectful but is likely to undermine the value of the session.'*

becomes:

> *Tiger and Mongoose (2015, p. 97) argue that 'failing to acknowledge a client's distress at the outset of a counselling session … is not only disrespectful but is likely to undermine the value of the session.'*

7  Very occasionally, the original sentence or phrase might need to be modified in order to make sense in its new context (for example, the subject of the sentence may not be clear in the original). Any new text is normally placed in square brackets to add to or replace what was in the original text.
For example, the original:

> *It was apparent that 'with the Trade Union backing them, they were not impressed by the management's attempts at persuasion' (Lion and Hyena, 2014, p. 12).*

becomes:

> *It was apparent that 'with the Trade Union backing them, [the employees] were not impressed by the management's attempts at persuasion' (Lion and Hyena, 2014, p. 12).*

---

**TIP**

### Three principles for using sources

Harvey (2008, pp. 18–19) recommends three principles for drawing upon sources in your written arguments. The first is to do so in as concise a manner as possible, so as to leave room for your own argument and voice to shine through. The second is to ensure you distinguish between what is attributable to your sources and what is attributable to you. This can be achieved by citing early on when you are drawing upon the material of others, rather than leaving the reader guessing. If you are drawing substantially on the work of a source, cite the source at the beginning, and then remind the reader, either through further citation or by mentioning the source author in the text, that you are still referring to that source. The third principle is to ensure, for example by appropriate choice of verbs, how each source contributes to your argument.

## 9.4 Plagiarism

Plagiarism is using other people's words or ideas in writing without giving the source(s) due credit. It is literary theft. According to Rozakis (2007, p. 117), and quoting directly, plagiarism is:

1 Using someone else's ideas without acknowledging the source.
2 Paraphrasing someone else's argument as your own.
3 Presenting someone else's line of thinking in the development of an idea as if it were your own.
4 Presenting an entire paper or a major part of it developed exactly as someone else's line of thinking.
5 Arranging your ideas exactly as someone else did – even though you acknowledge the source(s) in parentheses.

In essence, plagiarism involves passing off someone else's ideas as though they are your own. As argued earlier in this chapter, committing plagiarism strikes at the very heart of academic practice. Avoiding plagiarism is not something that can be learnt overnight since it involves understanding and applying a range of practices.

Different higher education institutions define plagiarism in slightly different ways (and have various penalties for students committing plagiarism). Some universities distinguish, or seek to distinguish, between plagiarism done with the student's awareness and that done by ignorance or accident, and the university imposes penalties accordingly. Plagiarism is plagiarism, however, whether it is done intentionally or by accident. The end result is the same in terms of the effect on the reader and not properly attributing the work of others.

In your first few weeks and months of an undergraduate degree programme you will learn about plagiarism and how to avoid it. Your first few steps to avoid plagiarism may not be entirely successful, but you will be expected (at least by the second year) to be able to complete assignments without committing plagiarism.

To give a concrete example of plagiarism, here is an original extract from Day and Tosey (2011, p. 515):

> In the secondary and 16–19 education sectors in England and Wales some form of action planning, in which a teacher or tutor sits down with a student and discusses their progress and negotiates learning targets with plans to achieve them, has emerged to become a recognisable feature of teaching practice within the last 25 years.

A student could be committing plagiarism if they had read and drew upon parts of this statement in their essay, without referring to the original source. The student would also be committing plagiarism if they did refer to the original source, but their wording was too close to that of the original (underlined words are the same as in the original):

> *In secondary and further education, action planning has become a recognisable feature of teaching practice within the last 25 years (Day and Tosey, 2011, p. 515).*

The student would have avoided plagiarism if he or she had paraphrased the original and cited the source:

> *Day and Tosey (2011, p. 515) contend that staff and students engaging in action planning towards negotiated learning targets has become common practice in 11–19 education.*

An alternative approach would be to quote part of the original source exactly. As explained earlier, quoting word for word is normally done only sparingly:

> *According to Day and Tosey (2011, p. 515), 'action planning … has emerged to become a recognisable feature of teaching practice within the last 25 years'.*

## Detecting plagiarism

It is comparatively easy for a staff member to determine that a student has committed plagiarism. They can notice changes in writing style in a student's work and, from their own knowledge of the subject, know whether the student has cited sources appropriately or has tried to pass off the evidence and reasoning of others as their own.

The staff member can also submit a student's work to plagiarism detection software such as Turnitin (www.turnitinuk.com). This compares the student's work with sources held in a database. A staff member can also use Turnitin to create their own database, to which students submit their current assignment. The database contains work submitted by other students in this and previous years, to reveal whether the student has copied the work of others.

## Using Turnitin

In some universities, before submitting an assignment, students are encouraged to submit their work to Turnitin and receive an analysis. This is seen as a checking process, to ensure that students are aware if they are commiting plagiarism, and can do something about it before they submit an assignment. This is fine assuming students understand the feedback Turnitin is giving them, that they see Turnitin as part of their learning process to understand plagiarism and avoid it, and that they do not come to rely on Turnitin as a lazy way for checking their work. If a student has learnt and is applying the principles of academic integrity, they will come to see Turnitin as an additional tool rather than something on which they rely.

Some university staff are using Turnitin's functions in a more comprehensive way, as a vehicle to give students feedback on work in development, not just about plagiarism but about other aspects, such as structure and argumentation. Turnitin's use for such purposes may well grow in the next decade.

### TIP

#### Self-plagiarism

Can you plagiarise yourself? Yes. Normally, you cannot submit the same work for different parts of your degree programme. If you simply copy work from one assignment and submit it in another, then this is self-plagiarism. If you are drawing upon previous work you have submitted you would normally reword the original text or quote an extract directly, and cite the source, just as you would for any other source.

## Why do students plagiarise?

There are several common reasons why students plagiarise, whether accidentally or with awareness:

- Not understanding what plagiarism is.
- Not having practised sufficiently the skills of summarising, paraphrasing and quoting.
- Not knowing how to cite and reference appropriately.
- Lacking confidence to explain the work of others in their own words.
- Lacking the confidence or capability, as yet, to develop their own argument.
- Not giving themselves enough time to read and understand sources and weave them into their own argument.

To avoid plagiarism clearly requires a wide range of skills, from the general (managing your time) to the specific (summarising, paraphrasing and quoting appropriately, with accompanying citations and references).

> **TIP**
>
> **Collusion or collaboration?**
>
> Collaborating with other students is a common and accepted way of learning and of completing some assignments. In writing up work collaboratively, the contributions of all group members should be specified and appropriately acknowledged. For many group tasks, however, when it comes to writing up, the submitted assignment is expected to be written up individually. Any assistance from other students should be specified and acknowledged. If you have submitted work as your own which has benefited greatly from the work of someone else (with or without their permission), and this has not been acknowledged, then this is collusion – a form of cheating – and is unacceptable academic practice.

## 9.5    Avoiding plagiarism

You can avoid committing plagiarism by:

- Reminding yourself exactly what plagiarism is, and why it is important.
- Writing an assignment that is your own argument.
- Organising your research, note-taking, planning, drafting, reviewing and editing so that you have enough time to do them well, without taking shortcuts.
- Weaving the facts and ideas of others into your argument by mentioning, summarising, paraphrasing and quoting, and using the appropriate conventions to cite and reference.
- Keeping careful track of your sources and how you have used them to inform your argument.

Managing information from sources is a case of keeping a sound 'audit trail':

1  Keep a full bibliographic record for each source you wish to use (authors, date, publication title, publisher, and so on). If you don't, it is very annoying and time-consuming to gather this information later. It is also helpful to make a short note of how you tracked down the source (see Chapters 4 and 11).

2  Keep your bibliographic records in an electronic database (perhaps using reference management software such as Endnote or Mendeley), or in a card index, along with any notes you have made about the reference source.

3 Never copy and paste chunks of source text into your plan or draft for an assignment, thinking that you can later 'tweak it' and make it your own.

4 If you ever copy and paste material from a source, and decide to add it to your background notes for an assignment, put quotation marks around the copied material along with a full citation that includes the page number. This way you will know that the words are not your own and you can locate, and if necessary report, exactly where they came from. If you have copied and pasted from a web resource, record full details including the webpage's address (URL), the relevant section name, number, or both, and the date you accessed the resource.

5 If a source is key to an assignment (and you are not infringing copyright by keeping a personal copy), photocopy it or print it out. You can now interact with your paper copy, underlining or highlighting key parts, adding notes or questions in the margins, using numbers, letters or some other system to cross-reference between parts of the original and your notes. Alternatively, you could perform similar actions with an electronic copy of the source and makes notes in database entries within reference management software such as Endnote or Mendeley (see Section 11.3).

6 When making notes from sources, and then planning an assignment, devise a system to distinguish your own ideas from those of others. You can do this by writing your original ideas in a different colour, or highlighting or distinguishing them in some other way.

---

**TIP**

**Avoid using the wrong kind of shortcut**

Some students, lacking confidence in their own writing, think that the quickest way to write well is to copy and paste from sources, and then tweak the copy, by changing verbs and moving parts of the sentence around. This is not the way to improve your writing. Not only is it plagiarism, but you are not improving your writing 'from the ground up'. Instead, seek to understand what the source material is saying in relation to your argument, jot down key words and ideas *in your own words*, then put the source material away and write down what you want to say *in your own words*. Your writing may not be as well expressed as the source material, but it will be your own writing, which you can improve through checking and editing. As you progress through your degree, your writing will develop and your confidence will grow, along with knowing that what you write is a unique expression of you – your own voice.

## 9.6 Remember, your writing is an argument – your argument

Mentioning, summarising, paraphrasing and quoting, while citing and referencing appropriately, are all ways of bringing the work of others into your argument and duly acknowledging them. It is helpful to remind yourself that the context in which a source was written is very unlikely to be the same as the document you are writing. The source you are using was written for a different purpose, and probably for a different audience, than the assignment you are writing. Seeing it this way, you are less likely to lapse into simply saying what a source said, in the same or a similar way. Instead, you are taking the essence of what the author(s) said and shaping it to apply to your own argument. While duly acknowledging the author(s), you are nevertheless making their contribution to your argument your own.

### Key points in the chapter

1 Rigorous conventions for citing and referencing are used in academic writing in order to acknowledge appropriately the work of others.

2 Harvard style (author–date) and numerical style are the two major systems of citing and referencing, each with many variants.

3 Unless information or ideas are common knowledge, the source of material should be cited and referenced.

4 Mentioning, summarising, paraphrasing and quoting are ways in which sources are brought into, and referred to in, academic writing.

5 Plagiarism concerns using information and ideas from other people's work, in writing, without appropriately acknowledging the source.

6 Plagiarism is unacceptable practice in academic writing. It is avoided by employing a wide range of strategies, from developing confidence in your own words, carefully tracking information gathered from sources, knowing how to adapt source material for use, to citing and referencing appropriately.

## Cited references

Batty, D. (2008). 'GMC Suspends Raj Persaud for Plagiarism'. *Guardian Online*, 20 June 2008. Available from: www.theguardian.com/society/2008/jun/16/mentalhealth.health [accessed 11 August 2017].

Day, T., Pritchard, J. and Heath, A. (2010). 'Sowing the Seeds of Enhanced Academic Writing Support in a Research-intensive University'. *Educational Developments*, 11(3), pp. 18–21.

Day, T. and Tosey, P. (2011). 'Beyond SMART? A New Framework for Goal Setting'. *The Curriculum Journal*, 22(4), pp. 515–534.

Godfrey, J. (2013). *How to Use Your Reading in Your Essays*. 2nd edn. Basingstoke: Palgrave Macmillan.

Hartley, J. (2008). *Academic Writing and Publishing*. Abingdon: Routledge.

Harvey, G. (2008). *Writing with Sources: A Guide for Students*. 2nd edn. Indianapolis: Hackett Publishing.

IPCC (2007). *IPCC Fourth Assessment Report. Climate Change 2007: Synthesis Report. Section 1.1. Observations of Climate Change*. Geneva: Intergovernmental Panel on Climate Change (IPCC). Available from: http://ipcc.ch/report/ar4/syr/ [accessed 11 August 2017].

Neville, C. (2010). *The Complete Guide to Referencing and Avoiding Plagiarism*. 2nd edn. Maidenhead: Open University Press.

Pears, R. and Shields, G. (2016). *Cite Them Right: The Essential Referencing Guide*. 10th edn. London: Palgrave Macmillan.

Rozakis, L. (2007). *Schaum's Quick Guide to Writing Great Research Papers*. 2nd edn. New York: McGraw-Hill.

Turnitin (2017). *Turnitin Home Page*. Newcastle: Turnitin. Available from: www.turnitinuk.com/ [accessed 11 August 2017].

University of York (2011). *Referencing Styles*. York: University of York. Available from: www.york.ac.uk/students/studying/develop-your-skills/study-skills/study/integrity/ [accessed 11 August 2017].

# Answer for Chapter 9

## Activity 9.1: An abstract is a summary

(a) (i) Background/context lies in sentences 1–2.

   (ii) Aim, sentence 3.

   (iii) Method, sentence 4.

   (iv) Results, sentence 5.

   (v) Conclusion, sentence 6.

(b) The abstract is balanced. However, if the word count limit were 150 words, then more detail could have been provided about the results.

# Reviewing and Editing Your Work

For most of us, reviewing and editing our work is essential, and greatly improves the final result. Many professional writers review and edit their work three times, often more, at different stages in the writing process. So should you.

In book publishing, reviewing and editing occurs in three phases and it is useful to check your own work in a similar manner. This involves moving from the general to the specific. This is logical. It means that you are less likely to spend time working on fine detail only to discover later that the effort has been wasted as you remove this material because it no longer serves your purpose.

As we have seen in Chapter 1, it is common to consider the process of revising your work in three stages: developmental editing, copy-editing and proofreading (Figure 10.1). These steps may not be as distinct as Figure 10.1 suggests, although there is clear progression from the general to the specific. Changing one aspect of the work, e.g. moving a table or figure, has 'knock on' effects on other aspects, which will need checking.

---

**TIP**

**Read your work out loud**

At proofreading stage (if not before), you should read your work out loud. When you do, you will discover improvements you can make that you would not have discovered otherwise.

When we read our own work 'in our heads', without speaking, it is easy to 'fill in the gaps' and assume our writing is actually saying what we think it is saying. Reading the work out loud reveals the naked truth. We may have missed a word or used an incorrect word. Our elegant sentences are not as elegant as we thought. We stumble over reading them, discovering that our punctuation is not as effective as we thought, or that a sentence construction is clumsy or overlong. If your work is important, read it out loud. The time taken will more than repay itself.

---

| 1 Developmental editing (early stages of drafting) | 2 Copy-editing (later stages of drafting) | 3 Proofreading (final checks) |
|---|---|---|
| Large-scale changes to the work, such as:<br><br>• adding new paragraphs<br>• changing the sequence of paragraphs<br>• removing paragraphs<br>• substantially editing paragraphs<br>• reorganising sections and subsections<br>• adding, removing or editing tables and figures<br><br>Have you clearly conveyed the important steps in your logic to enable the reader to follow your argument?<br><br>Is there a clear beginning, middle and end?<br><br>Check: Is your writing meeting the brief? | Fine-tuning paragraphs and checking other elements, such as:<br><br>• sentence constructions. Do sentences flow well? Are they varied and interesting? Are they readable?<br>• grammar, punctuation and spelling<br>• improving the strength of your argument<br>• removing any repetition and unnecessary words<br>• checking that you have included appropriate sections, subsections, tables, figures, citations and references<br>• checking factual accuracy<br>• editing citations and references<br><br>Check: Have you kept to the word limit? | The three Cs. Checking for completeness, consistency and correctness in:<br><br>• content lists<br>• sections and subsections<br>• citations and references<br>• figures and tables<br>• layout<br>• grammar, spelling and punctuation<br>• font size and type<br><br>Double check: Have you met the brief and kept to the word limit? |

Figure 10.1 **Reviewing and editing in stages**

## 10.1   Fulfilling the brief

Chapters 1 and 2 explored the nature of fulfilling a writing brief – meeting the assignment guidelines – from a variety of perspectives. Section 3.1 suggested some questions you might ask your assessor. Here, I propose some questions you might ask yourself, and actions you could take, when you come to review your work. When a draft of your work is complete or nearly complete:

1  Go back to the assignment guidelines, and check that you have interpreted them correctly. In broad outline, have you met them? The detail, you can check later – citing and referencing, word count, use of graphic elements, and so on – but have you met the broad intent of the assignment? Now is the time to check that, while you still have time to steer your work in the right direction.
2  Ask yourself: Have you expressed your identity as you wished? Are you writing from a particular viewpoint? And is that viewpoint appropriate?

3  Weigh up: Have you met the purpose of the assignment from your reader's perspective? What should your reader have gained from reading your completed assignment?

4  Consider: Have you correctly interpreted the nature of the audience (readership) for your assignment? Have you taken into account what your reader is bringing to their reading, which will influence how they interpret your writing? If your assessor is adopting a particular persona – for example, as an employer to whom you are submitting a report, or a member of the public who does not have specialist knowledge of the subject – have you responded appropriately to that persona?

5  Decide: Have you adopted an appropriate code (format, structure and writing style) in your assignment? Have you misinterpreted any of the requirements or overlooked them?

Now is the time to consider these broad matters, along with a more detailed consideration of the organisation of your document and the clarity and strength of its overall argument.

## 10.2   Structure and argument

Consider the following:

1  Does your account have a well-balanced and signposted beginning, middle and end? If sections and subsections are required, or would be appropriate, are they present?

2  If front matter (title page, abstract, table of contents, and so on) and end matter (references, appendices) are required, are they in place or in the process of being created?

3  Is your argument logical and does it move forward in small, incremental steps? Are there any gaps in the logical flow? Have you used transitional words or phrases to signpost to the reader the nature of the argument at that point?

4  Is there sufficient evidence and reasoning at all stages in your argument? Are any generalisations justified?

5  Is everything in your account relevant? Have you included some material simply because you have researched it and found it interesting, but which is a distraction from your argument overall?

6  Is your account balanced or biased? If you are employing a thesis statement, and are arguing for a particular position, have you nevertheless acknowledged and effectively countered alternative arguments and explanations?

7  Have you helped the reader through long, involved trains of thought by periodically reminding them where they are in the journey, and where they are heading?

8 Does your introduction to the assignment appropriately set up what is to follow in the body of the assignment? Does the conclusion satisfactorily bring your account to a close?

9 Have you checked your facts? Does the evidence and reasoning come from good sources, or is it your own?

10 Have you clearly distinguished what is your own contribution to the overall argument, and what is that of others? Have you summarised, paraphrased or quoted the work of others and given due credit by citing appropriately?

Having considered such wider-scale issues, now let us drop down to a smaller scale, to consider matters at the level of the paragraph and sentence.

## 10.3 Paragraphs

Paragraphs are the building blocks of a piece of extended prose writing. They organise what would otherwise be a single block of writing into bite-sized, manageable chunks, each representing a thought or topic – part of your argument. Paragraphs are also the stepping stones in your argument. And well-written paragraphs enable the reader to navigate their way through your writing, ideally with comparative ease.

### Paragraph structure

In capturing a thought or topic, a paragraph often does so in a recognisable way:

- A paragraph normally develops **one main idea**.
- The idea is often expressed in one or two sentences – the **topic sentences** – that are often the first sentences of a paragraph, but need not be. For example, topic sentences can follow an introductory sentence that links the paragraph with the previous one(s).
- Sentences in the middle of the paragraph **develop the topic** sentence(s). They do so, for example, by giving definitions, offering explanation, providing examples, going into further detail, offering evidence and interpreting and evaluating it, considering causes and effects, and so on. There are many ways in which topic sentences can be developed.
- Sometimes a paragraph will have a **concluding sentence**, which considers how the topic sentence has been developed and/or provides a link to the next paragraph.

A paragraph has at least two sentences, with many assessors favouring paragraphs that are at least four sentences long (a topic sentence and at least three supporting sentences). Most paragraphs in many kinds of assignment contain between 50 and 300 words. A paragraph of more than 300 words is a long one and may be seeking to cover too much ground. In many cases, such a paragraph can be split into two or more, to consider at least two topics rather than one larger one. Note that this paragraph contains 92 words.

Notice, in the following short paragraph, that the student begins with the topic sentence. This is followed by a statement of the importance of the medical condition and a brief explanation of its cause. The link with lifestyle is developed, with three factors introduced.

> *Coronary heart disease (CHD) is a problem that is increasing in many countries as a result of changes in modern lifestyle. In the United States, for example, CHD now causes more than half of human deaths[1]. Many factors increase the risk of CHD, all with a common outcome – the build up of fatty deposits within coronary arteries, known as atherosclerosis[2]. Atherosclerosis is one of the effects created by cholesterol building up on artery walls, suggesting diet is likely to be a contributory factor in CHD[1]. Other lifestyle choices, such as smoking and lack of exercise, are also predisposing factors[3].*

---

**ACTIVITY 10.1**

### Paragraph structure

In the following paragraph modified from a student's essay:

(a) Which sentence(s) introduce(s) the topic of the paragraph?

(b) In your own words, summarise the ways the paragraph develops the topic sentence(s).

(c) Does the paragraph contain a concluding sentence, which summarises how the one or two topic sentences have been developed and/or introduces a link to the next paragraph?

> *As discussed earlier, as a result of excessive prescribing of penicillins, Gram-positive and Gram-negative bacteria have developed penicillin-resistance. Such resistance has arisen through natural selection in three main ways. Firstly, changes in the conformation of the pores (porins) in the outer membrane of Gram-negative bacteria can exclude penicillin[3]. Secondly, in Gram-positive bacteria, changes in the DNA in the penicillin target site can confer resistance[4]. Lastly, both Gram-positive and Gram-negative bacteria can produce the enzyme penicillinase, which destroys the drug[5]. The three routes to resistance have required pharmacologists to stay 'one step ahead' of the bacteria, by finding new natural antibiotics or developing synthetic ones.*

*Check your answers at the end of the chapter.*

## Linking within and between paragraphs

We have considered how academic writing, in most cases, concerns developing an argument. But how can that argument be sustained and developed across many paragraphs? There are two literary devices commonly used: transitional words or phrases; and repeating key points, words, phrases or sentence constructions.

### Transitional words or phrases

One way of helping the reader follow your line of thought is by using transitions, also called connectors, which are single words or short phrases that draw the reader's attention to relationships within and between paragraphs.

As we have seen earlier (Section 3.3), transitions point out to the reader where the current text lies within the developing argument. For example:

- Beginning or introducing, e.g. 'To begin, …', 'At the outset, …'
- Building or reinforcing, e.g. 'Similarly, …', 'Likewise, …'
- Limiting or qualifying, e.g. 'However, there are exceptions. …'
- Countering, contrasting or giving alternatives, e.g. 'Alternatively, …', 'By contrast, …', 'Conversely, …'
- Consequences, evaluations or associations, e.g. 'As a result, …', 'Consequently, …', 'It follows, …', 'Therefore, …', This indicates …', 'This suggests …', 'Thus …'
- Drawing conclusions or summarising, e.g. 'In conclusion, …', 'In summary, …'.

Finally, not all paragraphs need transitions to show connections between them. If your argument is logical and coherent, the sequence of topics in paragraphs may fall out naturally, without the need to signpost them in each and every case.

> **TIP**
>
> **Transitions cannot or should not disguise a lack of connection**
>
> Do not use transitions to force artificial connections between sentences or paragraphs. Transitions should signpost *real* connections. Your assessor will soon notice if you are using transitions to compensate for a poorly structured argument.

**ACTIVITY 10.2**

### Spot the transitions

In the following paragraph, underline the words or phrases that are key transitions – that connect one sentence with another.

*Many public health specialists consider knowledge of hepatitis C, and how its causative agent the hepatitis C virus (HCV) is transmitted, to be poor among young adults in the UK[1,2]. This situation is unlike that of AIDS (acquired immune deficiency syndrome) and its causative agent HIV (the human immunodeficiency virus), which have been the subject of widespread public health campaigns in recent years[3,4]. However, current public awareness of hepatitis C infection can be compared with that of AIDS and HIV in the late-1980s[5]. Moreover, exaggerated fears about routes of transmission and the likelihood of infection may be similar for hepatitis C now as they were for AIDS and HIV more than 25 years ago.*

*Check your answer at the end of the chapter.*

### Returning to main points and repeating key words or sentence constructions

This offers an alternative approach for emphasising connections within and between paragraphs. For example, here key words and phrases (shown in bold) are restated, to develop the argument in a punchy manner:

*University lecturers are often keen to say that they teach in a student-centred manner. However, when observed by staff developers, **those same lecturers** often reveal very different traits. **They** take centre stage rather than give a voice to the students in their classes. **They** control rather than empower.*

Here, sentence constructions are repeated, to add emphasis and to highlight contrasts:

*Getting the balance right in devolving power to students is difficult. **Too much, and the teacher** is put on the back foot, responding to unreasonable demands from determined students with self-centred aims. **Too little, and the teacher** is in danger of holding students back from expressing themselves and developing as flexible, independent learners. Nevertheless, ...*

Repetition should be used sparingly. Too much and, like many any other literary devices, it becomes boring or irritating.

## 10.4   Sentences

Sentences, of course, are the building blocks of paragraphs. A sentence normally makes sense on its own, without the need to read surrounding sentences. To be a proper sentence, a cluster of words must also contain a **subject** and a **finite verb**.

The subject is what the sentence is about – its focus. In most sentences, it is the answer to the question, 'In this sentence, who or what is performing the action?' In the following sentences, the subjects are shown in bold in each case:

*The nucleus of the cell contains the chromosomes.*

*Nevertheless, the ancient Egyptians had sophisticated ways of marking the progress of time by tracking objects in the night sky.*

*The political stance of most UK farmers is conservative, perhaps reflecting their deep connection with the land and traditional social structures.*

*Abstract art seeks to express features of the visual world but without resorting to conventional representations or notions of objectivity.*

The finite verb in a sentence tells us what the subject is doing or expressing. It is called 'finite' because the verb is limited by the subject, with which it must agree. The finite verb agrees with its subject in terms of number (singular or plural), and person (I/you/she/he/it/we/they), and displays tense (past/present/future). Here, the finite verbs are emboldened in each case:

*The nucleus of the cell **contains** the chromosomes.*

*Nevertheless, the ancient Egyptians **had** sophisticated ways of marking the progress of time by tracking objects in the night sky.*

*The political stance of most UK farmers **is** conservative, perhaps reflecting their deep connection with the land and traditional social structures.*

*Abstract art **seeks** to express features of the visual world but without resorting to conventional representations or notions of objectivity.*

---

**TIP**

**Non-finite verbs**

There are three other verb forms found in sentences. Unlike finite verbs, they remain the same in form and are not shaped by the subject:

- infinitives, such as 'to go', 'to feel' and 'to analyse'
- present participles, ending in 'ing', such as 'going', 'feeling' and 'analysing'
- past participles, such as 'went', 'felt' and 'analysed'

Non-finite verbs may or may not be present in a sentence, but at least one finite verb should be.

---

## Writing clear sentences

Having confirmed that your sentences really are sentences, you can make them short or long, or something in between. Short sentences have impact. Longer sentences can gradually develop a train of thought, with one clause building on another, pulling the reader along. In prose writing, a more enjoyable reading experience often comes about through the writer employing sentences of varying length, so changing the rhythm of the prose.

Medium to long sentences can fall down in several ways and become difficult to interpret. Fortunately, there are various devices to counter such problems, including:

- Getting to the point (introducing the subject early).
- Keeping a sentence's subject and finite verb close together.
- Considering whether to change 'ing' verb forms.
- Checking whether pronouns are used appropriately.

### Getting to the point

As we have seen, the subject of the sentence is the person or thing on which the sentence hangs. Choosing not to reveal to the reader the subject of the sentence early on can be akin to teasing, and while sometimes it works, more often than not it is annoying. The reader is having to process many words before knowing the subject to which they refer. Here is an example:

*By interpreting the colour of seawater, the depth and direction of currents, and the patterns of waves, wind and clouds, ancient Polynesians could navigate hundreds of miles beyond sight of land.*

This sentence would be clearer if the subject were brought towards the beginning:

*Ancient Polynesians could navigate hundreds of miles beyond sight of land by interpreting the colour of seawater, the depth and direction of currents, and the patterns of waves, wind and clouds.*

Of course, transitional words or phrases can be put at the beginning of a sentence to link it to other sentences. But even here, the subject follows as soon as possible. The transitional word or phrase is marked off from the rest of the sentence by a comma:

*In comparison to the coast-hugging, medieval seafarers of Europe, Ancient Polynesians could navigate hundreds of miles beyond sight of land by interpreting the colour of seawater, the depth and direction of currents, and the patterns of waves, wind and clouds.*

### Keep the sentence's subject and finite verb close together

Sometimes, through a wish to sound authoritative or to pack large amounts of material into a sentence, the subject can become separated from a finite verb. This can make the sentence difficult to decipher, often requiring the reader to read the sentence more than once. For example:

*In rugby, two important factors that contribute to robust performance in running, kicking and tackling are muscular strength and power.*

To avoid this, bring the subject and main verb closer:

> *In rugby, muscular strength and power are two important factors that contribute to robust performance in running, kicking and tackling.*

---

### Move closer

Consider the sentence below. Find the subject and main finite verb, and bring the two closer to make the sentence easier to read.

> *Male drivers aged 18–21, because they are more likely to be involved in car accidents for which they are responsible, pay much higher car insurance premiums than their 45–55-year-old counterparts.*

*Compare your answer with the suggestions given at the end of the chapter.*

---

**In longer sentences, check whether 'ing' verb forms are appropriate**

In a long sentence, present participles (verb forms with an 'ing' ending) may be used to connect clauses to extend a sentence. This can work well for shorter sentences. For longer sentences, 'energy' may be lost at the point where a present participle is used, and the sentence may also become harder to interpret. In such cases, it is often better to remove the present participle and split the sentence into two or more. For example:

> *According to commentators writing in the 1940s, Charles Darwin took many years to write* The Origin of Species, *apparently troubling over how the book would be received by his religious wife, clergymen and the general public, but finally being prompted to publish by hearing from Alfred Russell Wallace, who had arrived independently at similar conclusions about evolution and natural selection.*

This long sentence is improved if the present participles are removed so that one sentence becomes three:

> *According to commentators writing in the 1940s, Charles Darwin took many years to write* The Origin of Species. *Apparently, he was troubled over how the book would be received by his religious wife, clergymen and the general public. He was finally prompted to publish by hearing from Alfred Russell Wallace, who had arrived independently at similar conclusions about evolution and natural selection.*

**ACTIVITY 10.4**

### Shortening sentences 1

Consider the two sentences below. In both cases, find the present participles and split the sentence into two or more to improve readability.

(a) *In a normal person, when a blood vessel is breached, platelets at the site of the injury release clotting factors, triggering a 'coagulation cascade', resulting in a blood protein called fibrinogen being converted into fibrin, creating a tangled mesh that traps blood cells, so forming a clot.*

(b) *A shipboard navigation system receiving continuous signals from several overhead global positioning system (GPS) satellites can process them, establishing the identity, locations and time signals of the satellites, and electronically triangulating the ship's location to within a few metres.*

*Compare your answers with those given at the end of the chapter.*

### Check whether overuse of pronouns (such as 'that', 'which' and 'who') is causing confusion

Longer sentences can become very convoluted when they are scattered with several pronouns (words used in place of nouns). It is often better to dismantle the sentence at one or more of the pronouns. For example, this sentence shows the pronouns in bold:

> *In his 1609 work,* Mare Liberum, *Hugo Grotius promoted the concept of 'freedom of the seas',* **which** *considered the ocean as an open resource available to all nations,* **which** *suited the purposes of European seafaring nations* **who** *wished to have access to resources in distance seas, and especially in the Far East.*

This sentence reads better when it is split into three, and specific nouns (shown in bold) are introduced to replace the pronoun 'which':

> *In his 1609 work,* Mare Liberum, *Hugo Grotius promoted the concept of 'freedom of the seas'.* **This book** *considered the ocean as an open resource available to all nations.* **This principle** *suited the purposes of European seafaring nations who wished to have access to resources in distance seas, and especially in the Far East.*

**ACTIVITY 10.5**

### Shortening sentences 2

Consider the two sentences below. In both cases, find pronouns that could be replaced with nouns to split the sentence to improve readability.

(a) *Discovered in 1985, the wreck of the RMS Titanic has since been rusting rapidly by a process involving the action of microbes, and it has also been visited by numerous expeditions, which have stripped the wreck of thousands of its artefacts and damaged its superstructure.*

(b) *Proteins are made up of one or more polypeptide chains, each containing repeating units called amino acids, which exist in several forms, the precise sequences of which give the protein its specific properties.*

In this case, decide how this sentence could be better split into two or three sentences to improve readability:

(c) *Near the end of King William III's reign, between the years 1695 and 1701, English copper coinage reached its nadir, with former employees of the Royal Mint being contracted to produce official coinage independently without close supervision with the result that they manufactured coins by employing cheap labour and using substandard copper, improperly processed, with farthings and halfpennies minted using poorly engraved dies so that the resulting coins often had blemishes, omissions and even spelling mistakes.*

*Compare your answers with those given at the end of the chapter.*

This short section cannot do justice to the complexities of sentence construction. We have not, for example, considered where you might wish to place emphasis or weight within a sentence. In the following example it could be argued that the subject and main finite verb are widely apart and ought to be brought together:

*In our study many teachers, even though they lacked personal experience of work in industry or commerce, were willing to include business-relevant examples in their subject disciplines.*

However, bringing the subject and main finite verb together does change the emphasis within the sentence, and not necessarily for the better:

*In our study many teachers were willing to include business-relevant examples in their subject disciplines, even though they lacked personal experience of work in industry or commerce.*

For advice about writing clear and powerful sentences, refer to Peck and Coyle (2012a, 2012b) or Copus (2009).

## 10.5 Grammar

It is possible to write a whole book about grammar, and many people have. Numerous books pitched at university-level students devote large sections to grammar and punctuation (see, for example, Peck and Coyle, 2012a, 2012b).

Grammar is a system of rules. It operates at two levels. At one level it describes individual words and their functions. At another level it concerns how words are combined to form meaningful phrases, clauses and sentences. This second aspect of grammar is sometimes called syntax.

Words in the English language belong to one of seven or eight common categories according to their function (Table 10.1). Knowing the names for different categories of word is useful when it comes to reviewing and editing, and when discussing work with others. Each category of word has several forms, although to keep the table to a manageable size, Table 10.1 shows only the various forms for nouns.

## Common grammatical errors

Three grammatical errors are common among university students, and especially among those for whom English is not their first language.

### Lack of subject–verb agreement

As we know, a sentence contains a subject and a finite verb. The verb needs to agree with the subject in terms of number, person and tense. When it does not, there is said to be 'lack of subject–verb agreement'. It is particularly easy to have a lack of agreement when a clause and/or infinitives are inserted between the subject and the finite verb, as in this case. Here the subject 'need' is singular but the finite verb form 'were' is plural:

*The need for groups of students to meet, to agree ways of working, were established early in the project.*

For the subject and finite verb to be in agreement, the sentence should read:

*The need for groups of students to meet, to agree ways of working, was established early in the project.*

### Appropriate use of the definite or indefinite article

Correctly using the definite article ('the') or the indefinite article ('a' or 'an') can be a minefield. Reading a sentence out loud can reveal missed articles. For example:

*Although helicopters are viable means of swiftly taking a film crew to remote location, their use is expensive, carries higher-than-usual risk, and extensive technical backup may be required.*

The sentence should read (with the missing articles shown bold):

*Although helicopters are a viable means of swiftly taking a film crew to a remote location …*

Usually, but not always, 'the' refers to a specific item but 'a' or 'an' refers to any example of that item. For example, articles (shown bold) are correctly used in this sentence:

*The tiger is a member of the genus Panthera.*

| Table 10.1 | Common categories of word in the English language | |
|---|---|---|
| **Category of word** | **Function** | **Examples** |
| Noun | A word used to name a person, living organism, inanimate object, idea, state or quality. | **Common noun** (name common to members of a large category): friend, human, dog, pineapple, car, chair, word, sentence.<br>**Proper noun** (capitalised name specific to a particular person, place, item or thing): Abdullah, Eiffel Tower, Ferrari, Manhattan, Monday.<br>**Collective noun** (refers to a collection or group of people, living organisms or other things): gathering, government, herd, team, women.<br>**Abstract noun** (refers to a quality, idea or action that cannot be physically touched): analysis, belief, bias, intelligence. |
| Pronoun | A word that stands in place of a noun. | I, he, she, it, they, we, you.<br>This, that, these, those.<br>Myself, yourself, herself, ourselves, themselves.<br>Anybody, somebody, all. |
| Adjective/ Determiner | A word that describes or qualifies a noun or pronoun. | *This* book. *Every* car. *My* shoulder. A *warm* welcome. An *exciting* journey.<br>**Definite article**: the.<br>**Indefinite article**: a, an. |
| Verb | Most verbs are 'doing words'; they express action. Verbs can also refer to expression of feelings and mental or physical states. | Harry Potter *killed* Voldemort.<br>Hermione *wished* she could help.<br>Dumbledore *felt* powerless. |
| Adverb | An adverb modifies other categories of word except nouns and pronouns. Adverbs can also modify other adverbs. | A *very* expensive suit.<br>A *fairly* attractive dress.<br>She *never* seems bothered.<br>He gave the order *quite* clearly. |
| Preposition | A preposition is a short word or phrase that indicates a relationship between a noun, pronoun or phrase, and other words in a sentence. | Above, across, at, below, beside, by, down to, in, near, on, to, with. |
| Conjunction | A conjunction is a 'joining word'. It links words, phrases or clauses. Conjunctions sometimes come in pairs. | After, and, because, both, but, even, so, then.<br>Either ... or, neither ... nor, whether ... or. |

There are other members of the genus *Panthera*, such as lions, so it is appropriate to say 'a' member. There is only one genus *Panthera*, so 'the' is appropriate. The complexity of using articles is shown by 'The tiger ...'. Here the definite article refers to both a unique species and all the members of it. In the context of this sentence it is not referring to an individual tiger.

For advice and examples on the use of articles, and other grammatical topics, go to Education First (www.ef.com/english-resources/english-grammar/) for UK English, or the Purdue Online Writing Lab (https://owl.english.purdue.edu/owl/section/1/5/) for US English.

### Tenses

It is easy to write a paragraph containing tenses that drift back and forth in time, causing confusion for the reader. Normally, consistency is needed.

> *Smith and Jones (2010)* **reported** *on the problem of juvenile delinquency in rural communities but* **fail** *to address the issue of the teenagers' family backgrounds.*

The inconsistent use of tenses in the sentence above could be addressed in two ways. By making both verbs take the present tense (shown in bold):

> *Smith and Jones (2010)* **report** *on the problem of juvenile delinquency in rural communities but* **fail** *to address the issue of the teenagers' family backgrounds.*

Or writing both verbs in the past tense:

> *Smith and Jones (2010)* **reported** *on the problem of juvenile delinquency in rural communities but* **failed** *to address the issue of teenagers' family backgrounds.*

There is a subtle difference between these two choices. Using the present tense suggests that the source cited is still current. Using the past tense pushes the citation back in time. If you refer to an old source in the present tense, it suggests that the point you are making (even if the source is old) is still valid. For example:

> *Sharp and Blunt (1995) conclude that strength of gender identity is a key issue in the association between self-esteem and body image in teenagers.*

## 10.6   Punctuation

Punctuation is the use of marks in the text that serve to group or separate words to give them specific meaning. In non-fiction writing, good punctuation makes a text much easier to read, helping the reader to 'get the meaning right first time'. For example, this sentence is ambiguous:

> *Doctors who are so concerned about being right don't last long.*

It could mean more than one thing. The statement could apply to all doctors, or only those who are so concerned about being right. The careful use of punctuation makes the meaning clearer. This version is a generalisation about all doctors:

*Doctors, who are so concerned about being right, don't last long.*

While this version refers to only a subset of doctors:

*Doctors who are so concerned about being right, don't last long.*

English punctuation has evolved over many centuries and continues to evolve. The punctuation in Charles Dickens' novel *A Tale of Two Cities* – such as the use of dashes – is rather different from the way we punctuate today. Punctuation for UK English is slightly different from that for US English.

If academic writing depends on formulating a convincing argument, and that in turn depends on making meaning clear, then good punctuation is vital to getting your message across. Like many other aspects of writing, it is something you can improve with diligent attention and practice.

The punctuation marks that students find most challenging are shown in Table 10.2, along with their most common uses. For more guidance about the use of punctuation marks, refer to Chapters 2, 5 and 8 in Peck and Coyle (2012a) or to Copus (2009).

| Table 10.2   Five punctuation marks that students find challenging | |
| --- | --- |
| Punctuation mark | Common uses |
| Full stop (.) | At the end of a sentence, e.g. *Sentences end in a full stop.*<br>In some abbreviations, e.g. *incl.* in place of 'including'. |
| Comma (,) | A comma has numerous uses. Only four are shown here:<br>• Separating items (words, phrases or clauses) in a list, e.g. *The chaplain ordered egg, bacon, sausage, scrambled egg, baked beans and mushrooms for breakfast.* Note: In UK English a comma is normally omitted after the second to last item in a simple list – the item before the 'and'.<br>• Setting off an introductory element from the rest of the sentence, e.g. *Nevertheless, many modern-day surgeons do have a good bedside manner.*<br>• To mark off an inserted phrase or clause (dashes or brackets/parentheses can also be used for this purpose), e.g. *Numerous surveys, systematically carried out by birdwatchers over several decades, testify to the declining numbers of sparrowhawks.*<br>• When a clause is added at the end of a sentence, e.g. *A large majority of managing directors in the retail sector are men, although this situation is gradually changing.* |

| Colon (:) | A colon comes after a statement and introduces what follows. Of its many functions, here are four:<br>• Introducing a list that is preceded by a sentence, e.g. *There are several factors to consider: the depth of water, seawater temperature, the diver's experience and their physical fitness.*<br>• Introducing a quotation that is a few lines long, or a bullet point or numbered list, as has been done on numerous occasions in this book.<br>• Reinforcing, explaining or illustrating a statement, with emphasis, e.g. *Each year we find a few students who are very reluctant to work with those from other cultures: a challenge for us to address.*<br>• Within a sentence to give strong emphasis between two contrasting statements, e.g. *Smith proposed the motion: Jones rejected it.* Here, the colon replaces 'whereas'. |
|---|---|
| Semicolon (;) | Semicolons potentially have numerous uses. Two common ones are:<br>• To separate items where a comma is already being used in one or more items, e.g. *There are several concerns with this approach. It does not take account of individual preferences; Panad and Jones, for example, are against it; and Schmidt will be on holiday at that time.*<br>• To connect two closely related sentences, e.g. *There were technical problems with the space mission that were finally resolved by the engineering team; we should involve them at an earlier stage next time.*<br>For further examples, see Copus (2009). |
| Apostrophe (') | Apostrophes have two uses:<br>• To indicate possession, e.g. *Christina's book. The women's game. The doctors' grievances.*<br>• To denote contraction (missing letters), e.g. *Let's* (short for 'let us'). *Rock'n'roll* (short for 'rock and roll').<br>A guide to using apostrophes is downloadable from https://reading-writing-results.com/top-tips/, or see Chapter 2 of Peck and Coyle (2012a). |

**TIP**

Avoid exclamation marks!

Academic writing tends to be understated, relying on carefully constructed argument to win over the reader. As a general rule, exclamation marks should be avoided, except when quoting speech or using dialogue.

Punctuation is not always an exact science. For example, in the use of commas, dashes and parentheses (round brackets) there is room for personal preference:

*Some people, and especially those who have studied the English language or literature at an advanced level, may have strong preferences about how a sentence like this should be punctuated.*

*Some people (and especially those who have studied the English language or literature at an advanced level) may have strong preferences about how a sentence like this should be punctuated.*

*Some people – and especially those who have studied the English language or literature at an advanced level – may have strong preferences about how a sentence like this should be punctuated.*

Assessors sometimes have deep-seated preferences about punctuation, some favouring the liberal use of commas, while others think they should be used sparingly. You can probably detect my love of commas, dashes and parentheses in the pages of this book.

**ACTIVITY 10.6**

### Applying punctuation to create meaningful sentences

This is an extract adapted and simplified from Day (2008, p. 89). Punctuation has been removed except for apostrophes and two full stops. Without removing words or changing their order, break up this paragraph into ten meaningful sentences by adding eight full stops and at least seven commas, and changing eight lower case letters to capitals.

*It is the unequal heating of Earth's surface by the Sun that powers the circulation of the atmosphere the equator and the Tropics receive a much higher intensity of sunlight than the poles this is a consequence of several factors first the Sun is overhead or nearly overhead at the equator and the Tropics so the Sun's rays are directed almost directly downward. At the poles however the Sun's rays strike Earth's surface much more obliquely and have travelled farther through the atmosphere to reach Earth's surface this means that each spot on the polar surface receives more diffuse light than an equivalent area at the equator added to this is an effect known as albedo a measure of reflectiveness. At the poles the pale ice and snow reflect light well so reducing light absorption in equatorial regions by contrast the green or yellow landscape and the clear oceans reflect less light the sum total of these effects is that the equator and Tropics heat up more than the poles*

*Compare your answer with that given at the end of the chapter.*

## 10.7 Spelling

Modern English spelling is challenging because English is such a hybrid language. It has grown over more than 1,500 years from many roots, including Anglo-Saxon, Norse, French, Latin and Greek. As a result, the spelling of English words can be cussedly unpredictable, with the sound of a word not necessarily being a reliable guide to how it is spelt. Many words that sound the same have different spellings as well as different meanings, for example: to, too and two; their and there; compliment and complement; practice and practise; principle and principal; and wait and weight.

If you have difficulties with spelling, consider fine-tuning a visual spelling strategy. This involves linking the sound and meaning of a word with an internal image of the correctly spelt word in your mind's eye. Dilts and DeLozier (2000, pp. 1285–1290) describe a visual spelling technique that works for at least some people. Chapter 3 of Peck and Coyle (2012a) includes a helpful guide to some of the rules of English spelling. Betteridge (2011) is an adult learner's guide to spelling with a refreshingly accessible and visual approach, also appropriate for those with dyslexia.

## 10.8   Presentation

Presentation matters. Even if the content of your text is superb, if your work is carelessly laid out, with inconsistent use of fonts, bold, italics, spacing and other features, this will create a poor impression. It will lead your assessor to assume that if your presentation is poor, other features of your work will be wanting. Consistency is important, and in many cases you will be required to present your work in a typewritten, word-processed form, perhaps with many presentational features defined by your assessor. Such features can include:

- Whether the assignment is to be submitted as a hard copy (printed out), as an electronic file of a specified type (e.g. .rtf or .docx), or both.
- Title page (with a specified layout and with key information, e.g. student's name and number).
- Page size (in the UK usually A4).
- Font type (sans serif, e.g. Arial, or serif, e.g. Times New Roman).
- Font size (e.g. body text, 11 pt; title, headings and subheadings, 12 pt).
- Page margins of specified width (top, bottom, right and left margins may be of the same width, or not).
- Text justification (whether the right hand edge of text should be aligned or ragged).
- Line spacing (whether single or 1.5 line spaced).
- Headers or footers (whether one or other should be used, e.g. to show page numbers).

Using word-processing software such as Microsoft Word, styles can greatly help you create an attractive layout presented consistently. In an essay it is quite common to use six to ten different styles (Essay title, Normal text, Section heading, Page number, Quotation, Reference style, and so on). In a report containing tables and graphs, using 10–20 styles is not uncommon.

As with many aspects of academic writing, leave yourself enough time to ensure that your presentation matches or surpasses the quality of the rest of your work. Reviewing and editing the presentational features of an essay or short report may take much less than an hour, but for a dissertation could take several hours.

Figure 10.1 can serve as a checklist to ensure that you have completed all stages of reviewing and editing appropriately.

### Key points in the chapter

1 Reviewing and editing normally proceeds in stages, from large scale to small, from developmental editing through copy-editing to proofreading.

2 Paragraphs have recognisable structures, and transitional words and phrases help connect them in developing a coherent narrative.

3 Sentences have a subject and at least one finite verb. Engaging prose contains sentences of variable length.

4 Clearly written sentences, which are not overlong, may employ devices such as introducing the sentence's subject early on, keeping subject and finite verb close together, the sparing use of present participles, and replacing pronouns with nouns.

5 Knowing the terminology for words with different functions can be useful in discussing writing.

6 Common grammatical errors include: lack of subject–verb agreement, inappropriate use of articles, and inconsistent use of tenses.

7 Punctuation marks are used to group or separate words and letters to convey particular meanings.

8 Most good spellers employ a visual spelling strategy.

9 Checking your work before submission involves checking for completeness, consistency and correctness. Effective visual presentation is important, as this is the first impression the assessor has of your work.

## Cited references

Betteridge, A. (2011). *Chambers Adult Learners' Guide to Spelling*. 2nd edn. London: Hodder Education.
Copus, J. (2009). *Brilliant Writing Tips for Students*. Basingstoke: Palgrave Macmillan.

Day, T. (2008). *Oceans*. Revised edition. New York: Facts On File.

Dilts, R. and DeLozier, J. (2000). 'Spelling Strategy', pp. 1285–1290. *Encyclopedia of Systemic NLP and NLP New Coding*. Scotts Valley: NLP University Press. Available from: http://nlpuniversity press.com/html3/SoSto31.html. [accessed 14 August 2017].

Peck, J. and Coyle, M. (2012a). *The Student's Guide to Writing: Grammar, Punctuation and Spelling*. 3rd edn. Basingstoke: Palgrave Macmillan.

Peck, J. and Coyle, M. (2012b). *Write it Right: The Secrets of Effective Writing*. 2nd edn. Basingstoke: Palgrave Macmillan.

---

### Further reading

Greetham, B. (2018). *How to Write Better Essays*. 4th edn. London: Palgrave Macmillan.

Morley, J. (2017). *The Academic Phrasebank*. Manchester: University of Manchester. Available from: www.phrasebank.manchester.ac.uk/ [accessed 29 August 2017].

Sayce, K. (2010). *What Not to Write*. Revised edition. Singapore: Talisman.

Truss, L. (2009). *Eats, Shoots and Leaves*. London: Fourth Estate.

---

## Answers for Chapter 10

### Activity 10.1: Paragraph structure

Two sentences introduce the topic of the paragraph: 'As discussed earlier, as a result of excessive prescribing of penicillins, Gram-positive and Gram-negative bacteria have developed penicillin-resistance. Such resistance has arisen through natural selection in three main ways.' The first sentence also refers back to earlier paragraphs.

The paragraph's third to fifth sentences explain the three mechanisms by which bacteria develop penicillin resistance.

The paragraph's final sentence is a concluding one.

### Activity 10.2: Spot the transitions

*Many public health specialists consider knowledge of hepatitis C, and how its causative agent the hepatitis C virus (HCV) is transmitted, to be poor among young adults in the UK[1,2]. This situation is unlike that of AIDS (autoimmune deficiency syndrome) and its causative agent HIV (the human immunodeficiency virus), which have been the subject of widespread public health campaigns in recent years[3,4]. However, current public awareness of hepatitis C infection can be compared with that of AIDS and HIV in the late-1980s[5]. Moreover, exaggerated fears about routes of transmission and the likelihood of infection may be similar for hepatitis C now as they were for AIDS and HIV more than 20 years ago.*

## Activity 10.3: Move closer

A suitable answer: Male drivers aged 18–21 pay much higher car insurance premiums than their 45–55-year-old counterparts because young drivers are more likely to be involved in car accidents for which they are responsible.

Or the sentence could be recast: In comparison with middle-aged drivers, young drivers are more likely to be involved in car accidents for which they are responsible. As a result, male drivers aged 18–21 pay much higher car insurance premiums than their 45–55-year-old counterparts.

## Activity 10.4: Shortening sentences 1

(a) One possible answer: In a normal person, when a blood vessel is breached, platelets at the site of the injury release clotting factors. They trigger a 'coagulation cascade', resulting in a blood protein called fibrinogen being converted into fibrin. The fibrin creates a tangled mesh that traps blood cells, so forming a clot.

(b) One possible answer: A shipboard navigation system can process signals received continuously from several overhead global positioning system (GPS) satellites. By establishing the identity, locations and time signals of the satellites, a navigation system can electronically triangulate the ship's location to within a few metres.

## Activity 10.5: Shortening sentences 2

(a) One possible answer: Since the discovery of the wreck of the RMS Titanic in 1985, it has been rusting rapidly by a process involving the action of microbes. The wreck has also been visited by numerous expeditions, which have stripped the wreck of thousands of its artefacts and damaged its superstructure.

(b) One possible answer: Proteins are made up of one or more polypeptide chains. Each chain contains repeating units called amino acids, which exist in several forms. The precise sequences of amino acids give the protein its specific properties.

(c) One answer: Near the end of King William III's reign, between the years 1695 and 1701, English copper coinage reached its nadir, with former employees of the Royal Mint being contracted to produce official coinage independently without close supervision. The contractors chose to manufacture coins by employing cheap labour and using substandard copper, improperly processed, with farthings and halfpennies minted using poorly engraved dies. The resulting coins often had blemishes, omissions and even spelling mistakes.

## Activity 10.6: Applying punctuation to create meaningful sentences

A possible answer (yours may contain fewer or more commas and might incorporate dashes and parentheses):

*It is the unequal heating of Earth's surface by the Sun that powers the circulation of the atmosphere. The equator and the Tropics receive a much higher intensity of sunlight than the poles. This is a consequence of several factors. First, the Sun is overhead or nearly overhead at the equator and the Tropics so the Sun's rays are directed almost directly downward. At the poles, however, the Sun's rays strike Earth's surface much more obliquely and have travelled farther through the atmosphere to reach Earth's surface. This means that each spot on the polar surface receives more diffuse light than an equivalent area at the equator. Added to this is an effect known as albedo, a measure of reflectiveness. At the poles the pale ice and snow reflect light well, so reducing light absorption. In equatorial regions, by contrast, the green or yellow landscape and the clear oceans reflect less light. The sum total of these effects is that the equator and Tropics heat up more than the poles.*

# Using Technology to Help You

Technology (usually in the form of computer software) can be used at all stages of the writing process; from generating ideas, to planning, literature searching, through composing, and on to reviewing and editing, and then preparing the final communication. Technologies to assist in these processes are rapidly changing. Smartphones and tablets have revolutionised access to the kinds of software applications only previously available on larger computers. Nevertheless, most students still complete their university assignments using a desktop or laptop computer, and that is what I assume in this chapter.

A danger lies in this chapter rapidly becoming out of date. To avoid this, I discuss general strategies rather than focusing on specific software applications in detail. Using computer software and online technologies can help you better manage the various stages of the writing process, but their use needs to be tempered with caution. Learning to use them can be a distraction from the creative process of writing. On the other hand, they can save a great deal of time and effort once mastered.

---

**TIP**

### Which operating system?

An operating system (OS) is the suite of software that manages your computer hardware to allow application programs to run. On desktop and laptop computers used by students, the commonest operating systems are Microsoft Windows, Mac OS and Linux. Your choice of operating system is best guided by the application programs you intend to use. It is helpful, therefore, to find out from your university department which application programs they advise you to use during your degree. This might help determine, for example, whether you purchase a computer that operates Microsoft Windows, Mac OS, or both. Proprietary software, such as Microsoft Office (and its components including Excel, Powerpoint and Word) are available in Windows and Mac versions. Microsoft Office documents saved in Windows can normally be read appropriately by the Mac OS version of Microsoft Office, and vice versa, with few exceptions. Occasionally, formatting can change in moving between Windows and Mac versions, and not all fonts are available for both Mac and  Windows. One way of avoiding formatting problems in moving between Windows and Mac versions is to save your final file as an Adobe Portable Document Format (PDF) document. Check with university staff that this is an acceptable form in which to submit an assignment.

## 11.1   Using your word processor's functions (but critically)

Word-processing software has revolutionised the processes of planning, composing, reviewing, editing, and publishing. Software makes it easier to draft and redraft text, compared with writing longhand, and electronic files can be readily shared, with reviewers' comments and changes incorporated and tracked. Images, spreadsheets and other digital elements can be inserted into word-processed files and the whole document then exported to publishing software such as Adobe InDesign or Microsoft Publisher for professional presentation.

Used effectively, word-processing software can save you time and help ensure consistency of text and layout. But there are, of course, dangers. Using the technology needs to be moderated with critical awareness. In seeking to automate functions, word-processing software can 'get it wrong', and only you know what you are seeking to convey in your writing. In this section, I will briefly review some of the ways word-processing software can be best utilised.

Microsoft Word®, the commonest commercial word-processing software, has many helpful features, including:

- spelling check
- grammar check
- dictionary
- thesaurus
- readability score

> **TIP**
>
> **Using LaTeX**
>
> If you are a maths or computing student, or working in a discipline with a strong mathematical emphasis, you may well be used to writing within the document preparation system LaTeX (usually pronounced as in the Greek, LAY-tekh). This system handles mathematical expressions better than word-processing software. If using LaTeX, you can still benefit from the functions of word-processing software by importing text into Microsoft Word®, or another word-processing system, for checking.

## Spell checker

A spell checker in your word-processing software will underline or highlight spelling mistakes according to the form of English you are using. It will also pick up occasions when you have joined two words by accident. It will not, however, be able to determine whether a correctly spelt word is the right word for you to use in a given context. It will not suggest which of the two in each of these pairs is the correct one to use in a specific situation: 'practise' or 'practice'; 'its' or 'it's'; 'from' or 'form'; 'not' or 'now'. The grammar checker (see below) may, however, suggest the best form to use in some cases.

You can 'educate' your software and add new technical words to its dictionary, against which it can check spelling. You can also 'teach it' to accept unconventional spellings common to your discipline, or those from another language or another form of English. For example, using Word 2016 (for Windows), the English (UK) spell checker accepts both 'programme' and 'program', while the English (US) spell checker rejects 'programme' but could be 'taught' to accept it.

## Grammar checker

A grammar checker suggests stylistic changes (such as changing the passive voice to active) as well as pointing out grammatical errors. Given the sophistication (and quirkiness) of English grammar, the rules that a grammar checker employs are comparatively simple. It will fairly reliably catch errors in subject–verb agreement; for example, 'The use of acidic chemical reagents, many of which can be damaging on short-term contact with skin, are gradually being phased out.' The plural verb form 'are' is incorrectly matched with a singular subject 'use of acidic chemical reagents'. The verb form should be 'is'. The grammar checker will also detect misuse of 'that' or 'which'. Grammar checking, as with other automated functions of word-processing software, should be used as a guide, which you may choose to override.

You can customise how the software checks your document for correct spelling and grammar. For example, by consulting the 'Help' menu for Microsoft Word, you can switch on the readability function so that the software automatically provides a Flesch-Kincaid Grade Level readability score (see below) at the end of a spelling and grammar check.

> **TIP**
>
> **Using Grammarly**
>
> Some students have taken to using the online grammar checker Grammarly (www. grammarly.com) to check their spelling, grammar and punctuation. As in using such functions within word-processing software, it is no substitute for knowing and applying the rules yourself. If you choose to use Grammarly, do so critically, checking any suggestions it makes.

## Dictionary and thesaurus

The dictionary and thesaurus provided as part of your word-processing software are comparatively simple. When you choose a specific form of English (for example, UK English or US English) the appropriate dictionary and thesaurus are accessed. The dictionary gives meanings. The thesaurus offers alternative words that have the same meaning, such as 'think about' or 'reflect on' as alternatives to the verb 'consider'. The closest matches in meaning are usually given at the top of the software's list of suggestions, with less close matches further down. At the end of the list is sometimes given the word with the opposite meaning (the antonym); for example, 'retreat' as the antonym of 'approach'.

Given the limitations of the generic dictionary and thesaurus that come with your software, it can be helpful to access more sophisticated dictionaries and thesauruses; perhaps, those specifically relevant to your discipline. Some of these are available online free or by subscription through your institution (for example, the Oxford Reference suite of dictionaries available at www. oxfordreference.com). Some specialist dictionaries can be downloaded, usually for a fee.

## Readability

Microsoft Word can be set to calculate a Flesch-Kincaid Grade Level readability score when making a spelling or grammar check. It is a simple, automated calculation based on average sentence length and the average number of syllables per word. The Flesch-Kincaid score equates to the number of years' education a typical reader needs, to read and comprehend the text (the system was originally based on the US education system). So, a score of 12 equates to 12 years' schooling (an age of 17 for most young people in Western education). For many forms of undergraduate academic writing I recommend a target Flesch-Kincaid Grade Level in the range 12–18. Scores of 19 and above are high and tend to be associated with disciplines such as philosophy or sociology, where complex sentence constructions might be favoured. In most disciplines, it is appropriate to aim for scores in the region of 15. But this, of course, depends on the purpose of, and audience for, your writing. It might be appropriate to write your assignment with a lower readability score if the assignment brief makes clear it should be aimed at a general audience.

A useful learning exercise is to cut and paste an extract from a paper by an author whose writing style you admire. Running a readability check on such a document often yields a score in the region of 15 – proof that elegant writing does not have to be inordinately complex.

Although the Flesch-Kincaid Grade Level score is a simple tool, it offers an additional source of information about your sentence constructions. In calculating the score, Microsoft Word software also gives the percentage of passive sentences in the extract. This is useful information if you are seeking to improve your ability to write engaging prose.

---

**TIP**

**Save your file regularly**

As soon as you create your file for a word-processed document, save it to your computer's hard drive or local server using a logical file name, e.g. AnneBernsteinaccountessaydr1.docx, or that specified for you for your module and assignment, e.g. AnneBernsteinAccountMod1adr1.docx. Then continue to save the file manually after every few minutes of work (do this even if your software saves work automatically). This way, should your computer crash you will have a recently saved version of your file and will not have to waste valuable time recreating work you have lost. Every two to three hours, back up your work-in-progress file onto other forms of memory, such as a USB memory stick, a portable hard drive, a remote server and/or 'in the cloud'. Change the name of your document file as you work on it so that you have a saved 'electronic trail' of revisions. Such strategies are designed to ensure that you do not lose valuable work and that, should you need to, you can retrace your steps to recover earlier work.

> **TIP**
>
> **Use 'styles'**
>
> When using Microsoft Word, or similar word-processing software, use 'styles' to specify the various kinds of text in your document. Using styles will help you organise the visual appearance and specifications of your document in a systematic and consistent manner. Each style specifies numerous qualities (either automatically, or selected by you). For example, within your document, for main headings you could use a Heading 1 style (Arial, bold, 12 pt, left aligned, and so on). When writing an essay or report, it is not unusual to use ten or more styles, especially if you include elements such as tables and figures. Once you start using styles systematically, it will save you time and avoid unnecessary complication. In Microsoft Word, for example, it will be an easy matter for you to change the font size of all your headings in one go, or to generate a contents list incorporating page numbers by using the 'Table of Contents' function.

## 11.2   Using bibliographic databases

In Chapter 4, we considered how to find and evaluate source material, especially that gathered online. As you progress through your degree course you will increasingly use peer-reviewed literature as your sources, and especially articles from academic journals and conference proceedings. To search through these sources is an unreasonable task unless you have a powerful search facility to help you; this is where bibliographic databases come into their own. A bibliographic database holds digital bibliographic records (author, date, title and other information) for journal articles and other information sources, often with accompanying abstracts. A database contains thousands or millions of such records that are searchable using keywords. Increasingly, databases include some full-text documents or will provide links to providers of full-text documents.

The scope of a particular database varies, from specific to general. Web of Science and ScienceDirect, for example, are wide-ranging databases spanning science, technology and the social sciences. Engineering Village incorporates Compendex and other key engineering databases, whereas ProQuest databases cover a wide range of disciplines in arts, humanities and social sciences, while Business Source Premier focuses on business studies and economics. Each discipline has its own most relevant searchable databases. Library or resource centre staff are invaluable sources of guidance on the best databases to use for your particular needs; for example, if you are undertaking assignments that straddle the disciplines.

## The benefits of using bibliographic databases

There are numerous benefits to using bibliographic databases, and employing them effectively is a key aspect of being a successful student:

- Bibliographic databases are regularly updated, giving you access to recent research.
- You can search rapidly across thousands of journals and other publications using keywords to target those documents in which you are most interested.
- You can combine keywords in various ways, using operators such as AND, OR or NOT to precisely target relevant documents.
- Publications listed in such databases have normally undergone a 'quality control' peer-review process.
- The bibliographic records provide information (keywords and abstracts) that can help you assess the likely relevance of a particular document, as well as referring you to ways of locating the document.
- Some databases include the full text of selected documents.
- If you are involved in a long-term project you can store your literature searches, allowing them to be repeated automatically so that you are informed of any new sources (search alerts).
- You may be able to automate the tracking of citations so that you are contacted if new articles cite key papers in which you are interested (citation alerts).

## A search strategy

Let us imagine you have been asked to write a 1,500-word essay on 'Discuss how arsenic contamination in groundwater arises. With particular reference to Bangladesh, consider how effective attempts have been to mitigate the effects of arsenic in drinking water.' This essay is really in two parts. The first tests your knowledge and understanding of the geological, physical and chemical processes by which arsenic enters groundwater. The second considers the specific case of Bangladesh, and the attempts made to deal with possible contamination of drinking water. Some of the information for the first part of the essay is available in textbooks and obtainable in review articles searchable on the World Wide Web using, for example, Google Scholar. However, if you wanted to be sure that you'd obtained up-to-date information from the most reputable sources, you might search for review articles using a bibliographic database such as Web of Science.

The search terms for finding sources for the first part of the essay are straightforward: arsenic, contamination, groundwater. You want all three terms to be present, not just one or two, otherwise you are likely to be swamped with responses. So, within your chosen database you would search for 'arsenic AND contamination AND groundwater'. Even then, you are likely to be inundated with many hundreds of responses. How can you narrow the search?

### Finding too many sources

Depending on the type of bibliographic database you are using, and what you are seeking to achieve, there are numerous ways to narrow your search. You can often specify the type of document you are searching for, such as review articles as opposed to research articles. You could ask for only the most recent sources (perhaps those published in the last five years). You could also narrow your search by geographic region. In this case, you might be particularly interested in articles that include or focus on Asian countries, so you might include 'asia*' in your search string. Here, the * is a wildcard symbol (some databases use ? or # instead of *). The * allows various endings to the word, so your search will also capture 'Asian', not just 'Asia'. You could use the NOT operator to exclude, for example, articles referring to the 'United States', e.g. 'arsenic AND contamination AND groundwater AND Asia* NOT United States'. In this case, be aware that you might reject some useful sources that mention both Asia and the United States. Other ways of narrowing your choices are by selecting for certain journals or authors or, if you are using a wide-ranging database such as Web of Science, restricting your search to certain disciplines.

### Finding too few sources

The second part of the essay question concerns mitigation of arsenic contamination, with particular reference to Bangladesh. Initial search terms are likely to be 'Bangladesh AND arsenic AND contamination AND 'drinking water' AND mitigat*' (the last term would pick up 'mitigating', 'mitigate' or 'mitigation'). If you found only a few sources you could look for ways of expanding the search. One way would be to find alternative words with meanings the same as or similar to the words you are already using: for example, 'treat' or 'treatment'. This could be added to the search string, which would become 'Bangladesh AND arsenic AND contamination AND 'drinking water' AND (mitigat* OR treat*)'. Some databases will search automatically for synonyms of a base word you have used; checking for mentions of 'better' and 'desirable', for example, when you have entered 'good'.

Another way to widen the search would be to use similar search terms but in a different database or in a search engine. For example, Google Scholar searches the World Wide Web and might capture sources that are not included in a bibliographic database. These might include published journal articles linked to scientists' homepages or university course websites, or reports by intergovernmental organisations such as the United Nations Development Programme (UNDP).

### Following the trail

Once you have found a journal article or other source that meets RABT requirements (relevant, authoritative, balanced and timely) it becomes a rich source of information that will lead you to other documents. Its reference list will cite earlier documents, while many bibliographic databases include a 'cited by' option, which will allow you to find more recent articles that have cited the one you are viewing. You might also search for other publications by the same author(s) or research group.

All the above suggestions are tempered, of course, by the time you have available to carry out the search, how efficient you are at determining what is most useful for your task (Chapter 4) and how you extract and use information from your sources (Chapters 5 and 9). Once you become adept at using bibliographic databases, you begin to develop confidence that you are carrying out effective searches. This will stand you in good stead for any final-year projects and should you wish to continue in postgraduate study or employment within your discipline.

## 11.3   Using reference management software

If you are writing a long document that cites many references, it can be worthwhile to use reference management software such as BibTeX, EndNote, Endnote Web, Mendeley, Procite, Reference Manager, RefWorks or Zotero to organise your citing and referencing. Such software creates a personal bibliographic database, to which you can add notes about each source. The software allows you to choose a specific name–date referencing system, such as that of the American Psychological Association (APA), or a numeric system, such as Vancouver. You can change from one referencing system to another, almost at the click of a mouse button. When using word-processing packages such as Microsoft Word or Corel WordPerfect, the software will routinely insert citations in your text in the correct format for your referencing system. Increasingly, library-accessible databases such as Web of Knowledge, SciDirect and ProQuest allow you to download reference details directly into your reference management database.

A word of warning: I suggest you only use reference management software after you have mastered how to cite and reference manually. You need to appreciate the great precision you must employ – both in citation and in referencing. You also need to develop confidence in knowing how to cite to best effect, to underpin the elements of your argument. Using automated software such as EndNote, before you have fully appreciated the power and precision of correct citing, may encourage shallow thinking and taking shortcuts. Most importantly, without having appreciated what it takes to create a bibliography or reference list manually, you are much more likely to overlook errors and inconsistencies. Not all sources you find may have a bibliographic reference that you can download or copy and paste into the reference management software. So, at some point you are likely to have to type in information manually. In any case, reference management software, like any other software, is not foolproof. You need to be aware of its limitations, and correct for them, which is only possible if you have learnt the rules of citing and referencing, starting with the basics.

## 11.4   Creating tables and figures

Several proprietary software programs are available to help you create tables and figures. Some of the most common are shown in Table 11.1. Your department or your tutor is likely to have their own preferences for software programs they recommend for particular purposes.

| Table 11.1    Some software programs commonly used for creating tables and figures | |
|---|---|
| Items to be created | Examples of suitable software |
| Tables | Microsoft Excel, Microsoft Word |
| Line graphs, scatter plots, bar charts, histograms, pie charts | Microsoft Excel, IBM SPSS Statistics |
| Flow charts, concept maps, Gantt charts | Microsoft PowerPoint, Microsoft Word, Mindmanager, iMindQ |
| Mind maps | Freemind, iMindMap, MindManager, iMindQ, Mindomo, XMind |
| Line drawings | Adobe Illustrator, CorelDraw |
| Photographs | Adobe Photoshop, Corel Photo-Paint, Corel Paintshop Pro |

**Table 11.2**  Common formats for image files

| File type | File extension | Pluses | Minuses | Applications |
|---|---|---|---|---|
| EPS (Encapsulated Postscript) | .eps | Files in this format can be imported into software programs for manipulation, e.g. for cropping, scaling or saving in other file formats that use less memory. | Large file sizes. | A wide range of images. Often converted into this format before professional publication. |
| GIF (Graphic Interchange Format) | .gif | Smaller file sizes. Can be compressed without reduction in image quality. | For comparatively simple images. Limited colour palette (256 colours). | Simple images and line drawings. |
| JPEG (Joint Photographic Experts Group) | .jpeg or .jpg | Small file sizes. In widespread use and almost universally accessible. | Not suitable for saving an image that requires manipulation. High compression or repeated saving can produce visual distortion. | Good choice for saving photographic images in a final form, e.g. for word-processed documents, slides or webpages. |
| PNG (Portable Network Graphics) | .png | Compression does not necessarily reduce image quality. | In less widespread use than other formats. | Suitable for line drawings and photographic images in slides or word-processed documents. |
| TIFF (Tagged Image File Format) | .tif or .tiff | Suitable for original or manipulated images. Can be compressed without reduction in image quality. | Large file sizes. | Suitable for a wide range of images, including photographs and line drawings. |

Your institution is likely to offer guidance notes and staffed or online courses to help you develop expertise in particular software programs. Most software has an accompanying instruction manual and many manufacturers' websites offer tuition or advice in using their software. Independently published hardcopy books or ebooks exist for the most widely used software packages. For most software programs there is a flourishing online community that discusses particular problems and offers solutions.

Depending on your course (and mathematics-rich, computing, and art and design courses are possible exceptions) you are likely to submit written assignments with any tables or figures embedded in a word-processed document. Excel and Powerpoint software within the Microsoft Office suite can create image files that can be readily imported or pasted into a Microsoft Word document. Images can be saved in a variety of file formats, and some are more suited for specific purposes. Encapsulated Postscript (EPS) and Adobe Portable Document Format (PDF) files can contain so-called vector graphics, meaning that the shapes and lines are generated by algorithms that may allow the image to be readily enlarged without distortion or loss of quality. Photographs are more suited to saving as bitmap files, for which various formats exist (GIF, JPEG, PNG and TIFF). Each format has particular strengths and weaknesses (Table 11.2).

Whatever format a graphics file is saved in, two major considerations are the final file size of the document into which it is placed and the resolution (readability) of the final image. An original image, however generated, should be saved in its original file format, so that it can always be returned to should any subsequent manipulation cause problems. Large TIFF files can be reduced in size and saved in one of several formats that use less memory.

Whenever creating a table or image, bear in mind the final form in which it will appear in a printed document or other type of communication. You want to be sure that the image or text is readable. As a general rule of thumb, simple serif or sans serif fonts printed out at a size of 9 point or larger are likely to be readable on white paper. Images with a resolution of 300 dots per inch (dpi) will normally show good detail on paper, whereas for material presented online a resolution of 72 or 96 dpi may be acceptable.

## 11.5   Handling large documents

If you are going to write a large document – perhaps a dissertation of 15,000 words or more that contains memory-hungry graphics – you may wish to use your word-processing software's more advanced functions. Among these is the ability to link files or create master documents.

If your document is large and memory-hungry, you may find that the word-processing software's functions slow down as a result. Large files are also more likely to crash your software, which can involve you losing precious work and wasting your time. One way to solve such problems is to divide your large file into several smaller ones that are linked. That way, you can work on one of the smaller files, quickly and efficiently, knowing that you can save any changes, and your file will be automatically linked to the other files. In Microsoft Word, one elegant way of doing this is using the master document function. You can, for example, make a document's title page, contents list and so on (the front matter) the master document, and link to it the various sections of your dissertation as sub-documents. The power of doing so is that the master document can automatically store all the styles you use in your sub-documents. It can also automatically compile the contents list, list of tables, figures and so on, without you having to do so manually. This can save a great deal of time if your document is large. As with using any software, you need to make a decision whether spending time learning its more advanced functions will save you time in the long term. If you are intending to have an academic career after completing your first degree, it might be time well spent.

### TIP

#### Back up regularly

Every year I hear about students who have lost valuable work because they did not back up their electronic files regularly to a safe place. Back up your work-in-progress files every 2–3 hours in at least two places. One of these should be geographically separate in case of fire, flood or other rare catastrophic events. These days, electronic memory is cheap and so there is little excuse for not having an electronic 'trail' of revisions to your work-in-progress, saved under different file names. I also find it useful, when working on an assignment, to keep a file with the abbreviated assignment name and the suffix 'offcuts'. When I am editing my work, this is where I put all the paragraphs or phrases I have rejected. Should I change my mind, it is easy to find material I had earlier discarded.

### TIP

#### On group projects, use 'track changes'

If you are compiling a document as a group, it can be helpful to use the 'track changes' function in Microsoft Word. This highlights who made which changes to the document, and when, and all changes can be agreed and accepted in a systematic manner. When changes are made, make sure you alter the name of the document using an agreed system to ensure that there is no confusion and that you are all working with the latest version.

**TIP**

## Staying up to date with apps

The software applications available for computers, smartphones and tablets – and which are the best for particular tasks – can change swiftly. One way of keeping up to date with latest developments is to visit websites that keep track of the best ones. At the time of writing, www.dnamatters.co.uk/resources/ was a useful first place to look.

## Key points in the chapter

1  Using the functions of word-processing and other kinds of software can enhance your writing efficiency, but should not become a distraction from the process of writing.

2  Word-processing software's functions – such as the dictionary, thesaurus, readability, spelling and grammar checks, styles and tracking changes – should be used with critical awareness.

3  How to search bibliographic databases efficiently is a key skill to master. This includes learning how to expand or narrow your search based on the material you find.

4  Reference management software can automate citing and referencing, but should not be used until you have mastered manual citing and referencing. With that experience you will then be able to identify and correct errors, omissions and inconsistencies.

5  A wide range of software is available to help create visual elements such as figures and tables. Choose the format of your graphics files with awareness so that you can manipulate images, but create a final output of appropriate file size and image quality.

6 If you need to create a large written document, such as a final-year dissertation, it is probably worth learning to use some of your word-processing software's more advanced functions.

7 Safeguard your work by saving work-in-progress every few minutes and backing up onto other storage media every few hours.

**Further reading**

Hacker, D. and Fister, B. (2015). *Research and Documentation in the Electronic Age*. 6th edn. Boston: Bedford/St Martin's.
Thomas, G. (2017). *Doing Research*. 2nd edn. London: Palgrave Macmillan.

# Building on Success

This final chapter pulls together threads from previous chapters and introduces ideas and activities that will help you develop your writing within your learning overall. Every assignment represents a turn of a cycle of learning (sometimes several turns) and is an opportunity – often the best opportunity – to improve.

## 12.1 Cycles of learning

For several decades now, those with a particular interest in the processes of learning have developed various models for how people learn from experience. Many are variations on a theme based on the work of Kolb (1984), who likened learning from experience to the way scientists learn when they carry out experiments. Seen this way, each assignment you write is an experiment. Indeed, each assignment can be a series of smaller experiments.

At several points in this book I have suggested that you reflect on how well you have carried out a task. I offered three prompt questions:

1 What went well?
2 What went less well?
3 What might you do differently next time?

In the wider scheme, such questions fit in well with an experiential cycle of learning (Figure 12.1).

Imagine that you have been set an essay. You check that you've understood the task and (hopefully) you plan what you need to do to complete it (step 1). You carry out a literature search, do the required reading, plan a structure for your essay, write a draft, gradually improving it through reviewing and editing, and then you finalise your work and submit it (step 2). However, what have you done along the way to consciously improve your practice? If you are very results-focused you may be driven to produce the best work you can in the time you have, but how much have you learnt from the experience that you can apply next time?

Each time you carry out a task for your degree programme, it is an opportunity not only to complete the task well and gain good grades but to maximise your learning from the experience, which you can apply in the future.

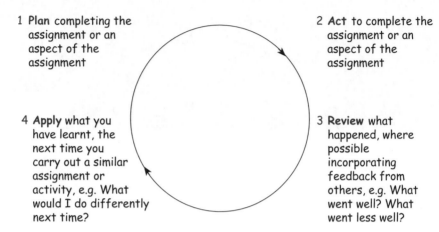

1 **Plan** completing the assignment or an aspect of the assignment

2 **Act** to complete the assignment or an aspect of the assignment

4 **Apply** what you have learnt, the next time you carry out a similar assignment or activity, e.g. What would I do differently next time?

3 **Review** what happened, where possible incorporating feedback from others, e.g. What went well? What went less well?

**Figure 12.1 A model for learning from experience (developed from Kolb, 1984, and Gibbs, 1988)**

This is not so difficult to do, but it does require awareness at times when you might rather be getting on with something else. For example, having just finished your assignment you might wish to watch a streamed movie on your tablet, or go out and do some shopping. If you're just about to start a task, you might want to just get on with it. However, the point at which you start or finish a task is an excellent place to reflect on your practice (step 3), to help apply your learning next time (step 4). And it only takes a few minutes. You can maximise your learning by applying this model to the different stages in completing a task, as well as to the task overall.

**TIP**

A learning log

In some disciplines, students are expected to keep a logbook in which they write notes recording details about practical investigations. They might jot down observations about any difficulties they encountered (and what they did in response). They might record experimental conditions and the raw data they gathered, or their reaction to a piece of art or an historical artefact, along with any questions that sprang to mind about what they were doing. Such information is invaluable for their development within the discipline.

You too can create a log – whether in a notebook or in an electronic form – about what you have learnt, what you might need to do to improve, and any questions that spring to mind. Each time you submit an assignment, or receive feedback on one, you can reflect and make a note of:

1   What went well?
2   What went less well?
3   What might I do differently next time?

By applying what you have learnt to future assignments, you will be maximising your opportunities to learn and develop within your discipline.

---

**TIP**

**Becoming a better writer in your discipline**

The horror writer Stephen King famously said, 'If you want to be a writer, you must do two things above all others: read a lot and write a lot' (King, 2000, 2012, p. 164). In relation to academic writing I would add, 'get quality feedback'.

---

## 12.2   Making the most of feedback

Feedback takes many forms. Here, I am talking about feedback that you gain from staff and other students about your work, but also that you give to staff and other students to help them improve. Feedback is, or should be, a two-way process.

Some students seem to regard feedback as essentially the comments and marks they receive on their completed work. However, spoken feedback and feedback given to you before work is finally completed and submitted (called *formative* feedback) can be at least as useful to your learning as final (*summative*) feedback.

### Feedback from staff and other students

It is all too easy, when you receive your marked work, to glance at it, note any marks and accompanying comments, and then breathe a sigh of relief as you file your work away. But stop for a moment. Now is a great time to consider what you are doing right and what you can do to improve. Written feedback on marked work ideally should:

- Indicate how well you are progressing in terms of meeting the standards and assessment criteria for your degree programme.
- Suggest ways you can improve that you can apply to future assignments (tackling any weaknesses).
- Reinforce those things you are doing right and should continue to do (building on your strengths).

### Staff feedback on a recent assignment

Find a writing assignment that you recently completed and has been marked and returned:

**(a)** From the marks you have been awarded, are you aware how well you are doing in relation to other students and to the standards expected on your course?

**(b)** Is it clear what you need to do to improve for next time?

**(c)** Do you know what you are doing right and should continue doing?

**(d)** Was feedback on the assignment discussed in a lecture, seminar, tutorial, practical or other session? If so, did you make notes on those points most relevant to you?

**(e)** If you are not sure about any of the answers to (a)–(d) you may not be making the most of feedback. What could you do to find out what you have missed? What could you do next time to make the most of feedback?

Reflecting in this way, and making notes about what you have discovered, will only be of value, of course, if you actually take action to apply what you have learnt. This is one reason why keeping a learning notebook or logbook is so useful.

You may be on a degree programme where hundreds of students are taking a particular module. Written feedback on assessed work may be minimal. General comments may be given at the end of your work or on an accompanying cover sheet. Specific comments may be written on the work itself. Examine each and every comment and make sure you understand it and know what you can do about it for the future. If you do not understand any comments, you might be able to raise the issue with the person who set the assignment or the assessor. Other factors aside, they are normally the best people to approach. Or you might discuss the work with your tutor and other students at a tutorial, or more informally at other times. Comparing the feedback you received with the feedback other students received can help you clarify your understanding of particular writing issues. There may be other forms of learning support available in your university, such as writing tutors or learning advisors, who you can approach. But do follow up. Not taking action about something you do not understand is an opportunity wasted, which may come back to haunt you later.

Here is an example of how interpreting feedback is translated into action and is applied to your practice. Consider the following comments made at the end of an essay you might have submitted:

*Mark 58%. The essay is well organized and you have developed your overall argument in a clear manner. There are a few minor factual errors and your writing sometimes jumps from one topic to the next, lacking coherence. You have drawn substantially upon the lecture notes and recommended textbooks but there is little evidence of you exploring the relevant literature further. Your citations and references show some inconsistency. Overall, however, a reasonable effort.*

Reviewing these comments, the student's notes for follow-up actions might be:

1  *Find out how to write more 'coherently'. Review comments on work and check with Dr Patel and/or friend Geoff.*
2  *Check the factual errors and correct them. Cross-reference to revision notes.*
3  *Get advice from subject librarian about literature searching next time I write an essay.*
4  *Consult citing and referencing guide to check where I have been inconsistent.*

If asking for advice from staff or students, it helps to be specific. Getting comment while you are drafting a piece of work is one of the best times to learn and improve, and it may influence your grade for that assignment. However, in asking for feedback about your writing, be specific. You might wish to give your work-in-progress to different people, drawing upon their individual strengths. One friend might be really strong on grammar and punctuation, another very effective in guiding you in formulating a convincing argument, and so on. As you are now well aware, there are many matters to comment on about a piece of writing, from fine-scale to broad (see Chapter 10).

Rather than asking someone to read your work and comment on everything, it helps to draw their attention to what you are most concerned about or where you think they can best help. For example:

*In the introduction, have I set up my thesis statement correctly?*

*Are you convinced by my evidence and reasoning overall?*

*Have I cited and referenced correctly?*

*Is my conclusion doing its job?*

By being specific you are more likely to gain useful feedback that you can apply to improve your work. When giving or receiving feedback, I suggest there are six levels of analysis on which you can focus (see Tip). Whether reviewing your own work, asking for feedback on your work from others, or giving feedback on the work of others, I recommend focusing on only two or three levels at a time.

TIP

## Six levels of analysis

| Level | Detail |
|---|---|
| Structure | Is the overall structure (beginning, middle and end) appropriate and well-balanced? Is each part doing its job? Do sections or subsections have appropriate headings, which reflect well the progression of the argument? |
| Argument | Does the argument flow logically within and between paragraphs? |
| | Does the argument lead logically to a conclusion? |
| | Is the argument clearly signposted using connectors? |
| | Are there any omissions, distractions, misinterpretations or over-generalisations? |
| | Is there plentiful evidence of critical evaluation of the assignment writer's own work and that of others? |
| Writing style | Is the writing style and vocabulary used appropriate for this assignment and the intended readership? |
| | Is the writing clear, precise and accurate? |
| | Is the viewpoint, e.g. personal or objective, appropriate? |
| | Are the sentence and paragraph constructions repetitive, or is there appropriate variety? |
| | Do you suspect any plagiarism? |
| Citing and referencing | Has citing and referencing been used elegantly, with precision and consistency, to support the paper's overall argument? |
| | Does the citing and referencing appear to be balanced or biased? |
| | If quotations are used, have they followed appropriate conventions? |
| Grammar, punctuation and spelling | Are tenses used consistently? |
| | Do subjects and verbs agree? |
| | Is punctuation complete, accurate and consistent? |
| | Are spellings correct and consistent, e.g. UK or US spelling? |
| Visual and other elements | Are these clear, complete and correct? Are they appropriately labelled? Do they meet the assignment's requirements? |
| | Do visual elements, e.g. graphs and tables, complement the text and are they referred to appropriately in the text? |
| | Is there any undue repetition? |

> **TIP**
>
> Turning feedback into feed-forward
>
> There is always a danger that feedback is seen as something that relates to work that has been completed. Feedback becomes useful when it is a spur to action. This involves turning feedback into feed-forward; reflecting on feedback and responding with specific points of action that you can apply in order to improve. For example, if your work had received this comment from your assessor:
>
> *About 15% of the words in your essay are quotations. This is far too much.*
>
> you could turn this into feed-forward:
>
> *In the future, I will paraphrase more and use quotations sparingly, reserving them to make a particularly strong point or for key definitions.*

## Feedback to staff and other students

The tutors and lecturers who set and mark your assignments are the best people to speak to about understanding the feedback you have been given and how this can translate into action on your part. Asking for such guidance is not just of benefit to you. It is part of the staff member's job to provide effective feedback to students. If you are having problems in translating their feedback, it is likely that other students are too. Your feedback to staff can help them improve, which will be of benefit to students in the future.

Working with other students should also be a two-way process. Unless you are doing a group assignment, any submitted work should, of course, be your own. However, that does not prevent you from asking for guidance from other students along the way, discussing work with them, or offering them guidance. Giving advice is often as helpful as receiving it. Evaluating the work of others helps clarify your own thoughts about writing and encourages you to express them. Doing so often informs and improves your own writing. There is plenty of evidence from educational research that working with another student – whether they are more capable or less capable than you about the issue you are discussing – is likely to be of benefit to both (see, for example, Falchikov, 2001).

> **ACTIVITY 12.2**
>
> ## Making the most of feedback
>
> Think about the assignments you have done over the last few months:
>
> (a) Do you discuss your work with other students or ask their advice? Often/ sometimes/never

(b) Do you ask the staff member who marked the work to clarify any feedback they have given? Often/sometimes/never

(c) Have you spoken with another staff member, perhaps the person who set the assignment or a personal tutor, to clarify any feedback you have been given? Often/sometimes/never

(d) Do you check through the comments you have received for a piece of work and translate them into action that can help you improve for future assignments? Often/sometimes/never

(e) Do you keep a learning log or journal, or something similar? Yes/no

(f) What do you do with your completed and marked assignments? Where do you file them? Do you refer to them later?

(g) Review your answers to (a)–(f). What could you be doing to improve your opportunities to learn from feedback?

## 12.3   Where to get help

This book, and the further reading referred to in it (some of which is online), are good starting points. In addition, there are many people and services at your university to help:

- The lecturers, tutors and other staff on your degree programme, and especially those who set or mark your assignments, are perhaps the first port of call.
- Learning development staff and writing tutors.
- Library or resource centre staff.
- If English is not your first language, your university may have an English language centre, international student centre or similar, with staff who can help you.
- If you have a specific learning challenge, such as dyslexia, there are learning skills advisors who come from services with titles such as 'widening participation', or 'learning support'.
- There are likely to be various kinds of online learning support, whether provided by a centralised learning or study skills centre, your university library, your faculty or your department.
- Finally, other students may be among your best sources of help.

## 12.4   Be inspired by what you read

Earlier in this chapter we considered what it takes to become a better writer – read a lot, write a lot, and get quality feedback on what you write. Part of learning from what you read is looking for what makes that writing so persuasive. What is it about the writing that you find so powerful and engaging?

To become a better writer in your discipline it helps to look wider and deeper than your degree course. If you only read bite-sized news items on social media, and then focus on the technical material for your degree, you are missing out on a wealth of inspiring writing from which you can learn – consciously and unconsciously. If you read high-quality writing beyond your discipline, you will be enriching your vocabulary and finding forms of expression that can enliven your writing within the discipline. There are numerous sources of fine writing, and reading them can become a truly life-enhancing habit. Many newspapers and news and features magazines – *The Economist, Harvard Business Review, The New York Times, i, The Times, The Guardian, The Telegraph, Prospect, The Spectator, New Scientist, Scientific American, The Times Literary Supplement* – will have articles that will be of interest, many of which will be available online. And websites have recently emerged that have articles that are both scholarly and engaging – among them *Aeon* (https://aeon.co/) and *The Conversation* (https://theconversation.com/uk). Whether within your discipline, or beyond, one of the elements you can look for in the writing you read is the use of techniques of persuasion.

## Rhetoric: the art of persuasion

Rhetoric is the art of speaking or writing in a form that's intended to persuade the listener or reader. In classical Greek times orators used three approaches to rhetoric to persuade listeners to their point of view: *ethos*, *logos* and *pathos*. These approaches still have great relevance today. *Ethos* refers to the ethical standing of the orator. How do you know that this person has authority? That they are a person to be trusted? Some of that originates from their position in the community. But it also comes from the language they use and how they use it. Translated to modern academic writing, what is it about the writing that convinces you that the writer knows what they're doing? That they carry authority? *Logos* refers to logic. The use of logic – including using evidence and reasoning to draw conclusions – is, of course, prevalent in academic writing. The third approach, *pathos*, concerns evoking emotional responses and feelings from the reader or listener. Although the use of pathos is seemingly frowned upon in many branches of academia, it is nevertheless quite common.

Recently, I was running a workshop with a group of academic writing specialists and we were examining the title and introduction of a scientific paper (Lavers and Bond, 2017) for signs of rhetoric. The title of the paper included the phrase 'pristine islands' and the introduction contained the verb 'littered' (Lavers and Bond, 2017, p. 6052). Among several of the 16 people in the group, those words were enough to cause emotional responses as they pictured pristine beaches becoming littered with debris. Whenever you use statistics to convey how many people are affected by illness or misfortune, or you are encouraging your reader to picture a scene of devastation, or you are inspiring them to appreciate the beauty in a painting or the design of a building, you are likely to be using pathos.

As you will see in Activity 12.3, one of the ways of learning what is acceptable in writing in your discipline is to examine how rhetoric is used. There are disciplinary differences. What can you be doing to show ethos, logos and pathos wisely in your writing in the chosen discipline?

**ACTIVITY 12.3**

### The use of rhetoric in your discipline

Find a research article or essay written by an author in your discipline that you admire. Read the first 500–600 words at the beginning of the item. To what extent does the author use the different strands of rhetoric – ethos, logos and pathos – in their account? Would it be appropriate for you to do so in a similar manner in an assignment you are writing?

**TIP**

### Notice yourself improving

In being self-critical, it is easy to focus on what you are doing wrong (or could do better) to the exclusion of what you are doing right. In terms of academic writing, it is helpful to reflect on what you are doing now that you could not do a few weeks or months ago. Noticing the progress you have made so far should reassure you about making progress in the future.

## 12.5 Final word

Near the beginning of this book we considered how writing helps you to think. Writing, of course, is but one way to express your thoughts. Nevertheless, doing so changes your relationship with those thoughts, whether you choose to share your writing with others or not. When you write and see your thoughts expressed 'outside of yourself', your relationship with those ideas shifts, encouraging reflection and reappraisal. Your ideas transform, advance, and become shaped, refined and clarified. The process of academic writing encourages higher-level thinking – analysing, synthesising, evaluating and applying – that is an integral part of your academic development. Beyond this, the qualities you develop as a skilful writer – even patience and diligence – will be of immense benefit to you in your later life, whatever path you take. In your writing, be guided by others, but open yourself up to the possibility of stepping beyond the guidance you have been given. Be prepared to be inspired.

**Key points in the chapter**

1 Each assignment you carry out represents one or more turns of the experiential learning cycle: planning, taking action, reviewing and applying.

2 You can maximize your learning by reflecting on your learning process for each assignment; especially when starting, finishing, and after gaining feedback.

3 At its best, feedback is a two-way process in which you receive guidance and opinion from staff and perhaps other students, and also offer it.

4 During an assignment, and after you have completed it and received marks, is where you can ask for specific feedback to clarify your understanding. Reflect on the feedback and take planned action where appropriate.

5 In offering thoughtful feedback and guidance to another student you will probably gain as much as you give.

6 There are many people and resources to help you develop your writing and your learning more generally. Some are formal, others informal. Make good use of them.

7 Each academic discipline has its own acceptable practices. This includes how rhetoric – ethos, logos and pathos – is used to persuade readers. One way to raise the power of your own writing is to learn how good writers in your discipline – and beyond – use rhetoric wisely.

8 Remind yourself of the importance of clear and compelling writing. Through writing you have the power to express, influence and impress.

## Cited references

Falchikov, N. (2001). *Learning Together: Peer Tutoring in Higher Education*. London: Routledge.

Gibbs, G. (1988). *Learning by Doing: A Guide to Teaching and Learning Methods*. London: Further Education Unit.

King, S. (2000, 2012). *On Writing: A Memoir of the Craft*. Revised edn. London: Hodder & Stoughton.

Kolb, D. A. (1984). *Experiential Learning: Experience as a Source of Learning and Development*. Englewood Cliffs, NJ: Prentice Hall.

Lavers, J. L. and Bond, A. L. (2017). 'Exceptional and Rapid Accumulation of Anthropogenic Debris on One of the World's Most Remote and Pristine Islands'. *PNAS*, 114(23), pp. 6052–6055.

**Further reading**

Pinker, S. (2014). *The Thinking Person's Guide to Writing in the 21st Century.* London: Penguin.

Sword, H. (2012). *Stylish Academic Writing.* Cambridge: Harvard University Press.

# Glossary

**Academic writing** Writing that is usually formal and follows certain conventions, such as specific document structures, writing styles, and citing and referencing.

**Active voice** Refers to the construction of a sentence in which the subject performs action.

**Adjective** A word that describes and modifies the meaning of a noun or pronoun.

**Adverb** A word that modifies a verb, an adjective or another adverb.

**Article** In grammar, a type of determiner. There are two articles: the definite article (the) and the indefinite article (a or an).

**Audience (readership)** The people who will read and might assess a piece of written work. An assessor may take on a particular *persona* when assessing your work.

**Authoritative** Refers to a publication that has high credibility based on its authors' backgrounds, qualifications, experience and/or associations with academic or professional organisations. Such publications normally cite and list their sources.

**Balanced** Refers to a source, or your own work, seeking to present an unbiased view of a topic.

**Bar chart** A bar chart plots discrete data where numerical values are shown by the height of bars of equal width.

**Biased** Refers to a source you are using, or your own argument, seeking to promote one or more sides of an argument at the expense of other sides.

**Bibliographic database** An electronic database holding bibliographic information about journal articles and conference proceedings within specified disciplines. Such databases are searchable using keywords and may provide an abstract (summary) of the document plus links to providers of the document's full text.

**Bibliography** A list of all the sources consulted in the process of writing a document. It is different from a list of references, which lists only sources that have been cited within the main body of a document.

**Citation** A short note within a document, e.g. '(Jones, 2013)', which refers to a source. Full details of the source are normally given as an entry in the list of references at the end of the document.

**Cite** In text, to refer to a source using a citation.

**Clause** In traditional grammar, a simple sentence or a group of words in a sentence that contains a subject and a predicate (words, including a verb, that give further information about the subject). For example, 'They voted for the president.' and 'If they voted for the president …' are both clauses.

**Code** In the IPACE model, 'code' refers to format, structure and writing style. Code is shaped by the writer's identity and the purpose and audience for a given piece of writing.

**Collusion** Collaborating with another person to produce a piece of work that you submit as your own without crediting the other person. It may also involve copying from another person's work (with or without their permission) or having them produce work for you.

**Common knowledge** Within a discipline this refers to facts, arguments or opinions that are so well known that when used in written work, citing a reference is not normally required.

**Composing** For non-fiction writing, the act of writing flowing prose.

**Concept map** A form of note-taking and planning in which information is organised in a logical hierarchy from top to bottom, with an appearance similar to a family tree. A line between one idea and the next is usually accompanied by words explaining the connection between the two.

**Conjunction** A 'joining word' that links words, phrases or clauses.

**Determiner** A category of adjective. It includes the definite and indefinite article.

**Dissertation** An extended piece of academic writing on a specialist topic, normally in the form of a report, which is submitted towards the end of a degree programme.

**Editing** Implementing changes to text to better match it to its intended purpose and audience.

**Essay** A piece of prose writing several hundred to several thousand words long. It normally has a recognisable introduction, body and conclusion. It may be a balanced account or promote a particular point of view.

**et al.** Abbreviated form of the Latin *et alii* meaning 'and others'. It is used in in-text, author–date citations that refer to a source which has more than two authors. It is normally placed after the first author's surname.

**Experience** In the IPACE model, experience concerns what a writer is bringing to a writing task in terms of their knowledge, skills and attitudes in relation to the content of the writing and the process of creating it.

**Feedback** Information given to a person – in writing, verbally or by other means – that gives that person information about how well they have carried out, or are carrying out, a task.

**Figure** In relation to visual elements accompanying text it refers to a chart, graph, drawing or photograph.

**Finite verbs** A verb form that changes to agree with a subject of a sentence. All proper sentences contain at least one finite verb.

**Flow diagram (flow chart)** A visual device employing arrows together with squares, circles, and other geometric shapes to show relationships between items. Flow diagrams are particularly effective at depicting cyclic and step-by-step processes.

**Formative feedback** Feedback given before a task is completed and before work is submitted for final assessment.

**Freewriting** Writing in an unfettered, unselfconscious fashion, usually for 5–15 minutes, without stopping.

**Glossary** An alphabetical list of words, abbreviations and/or symbols with their accompanying definitions. A glossary may be found near the beginning of a report or dissertation, or at the end of a book.

**Grammar** Grammar concerns the system of rules to describe words and their use in constructing meaningful phrases, clauses and sentences.

**Grey literature** Published or unpublished material of potential academic significance that may not be easy to catalogue because it does not carry full bibliographic information. Grey literature includes patents, newspaper articles and editorials, personal letters and diaries, and some technical reports from government agencies or research groups.

**Histogram** A histogram plots continuous data where numerical values are shown by the height of bars of equal width.

**ibid.** Abbreviated form of the Latin *ibidem* meaning 'in the same place'. It is occasionally used in in-text, author–date citations to indicate that the last given citation is being repeated.

**Identity** The *persona* that an individual uses, or aspires to use, in writing an assignment and that shapes his or her writing to meet its purpose and audience.

**Learning journal (log)** A diary of reflections about learning, completed regularly. It may be for personal use only or viewable by a supervisor.

**Line graph** This type of graph displays a relationship between two continuous variables. It shows plotted points, usually connected by a line joining all the points.

**List of references** This lists full details of all the references cited within the main body of a document. It is different from a bibliography, which lists all sources that have been consulted in the writing of a document.

**Logbook** In experimental and highly observational disciplines, such as science, engineering and archaeology, it is a diary recording briefly, often in note form, what has taken place. It may include experimental or other observations, measurements and results. Reflections and questions encourage learning from current investigations and planning for future ones.

**Matrix (pl. matrices)** A matrix is a table in which items or themes are identified in the headings of rows and columns. Information is placed in the cells where columns and rows intersect. Matrices are particularly useful for summarising and comparing data or themes from different viewpoints or sources.

**Mind map** A visual means of presenting information that encourages creative and associative thinking. It involves drawing or writing a topic in the middle of a landscape sheet of paper and connecting it by lines to linked ideas that radiate out from the centre. A similar mind map can also be drawn using mind-mapping software.

**Narrative** When applied to writing, refers to elements being organised into a coherent story, whether in fiction or non-fiction.

**Non-finite verb** A verb form that does not change to agree with a subject of a sentence.

**Noun** The name of a person or thing, whether concrete or abstract.

**Object** Where present in a sentence, it is the person or thing that is the recipient of action as determined by a verb.

**Operating system** The suite of software that manages a computer's hardware to run application programs. Common operating systems for desktop and laptop computers are Microsoft Windows, Mac OS and Linux.

**Paragraph** Sentences grouped together in a single block of text on a particular topic.

**Paraphrase** To restate someone else's information or ideas but in your own words. It is standard academic practice and is normally accompanied by a citation to the original source.

**Passive voice** Refers to the construction of a sentence in which the subject is the recipient of action (is acted upon).

**Peer review**  The process of a document being checked and commented on by other scholars before the document is rejected, passed for publication, or considered for acceptance subject to specific changes being made.

**Phrase**  A group of words in a sentence, which adds information but does not contain a finite verb.

**Pie chart**  A pie chart is a circular (pie-shaped) chart. It is divided into sectors to show the relative contributions of different categories of data.

**Plagiarism**  Presenting someone else's information, ideas or words as your own without citing or otherwise acknowledging the source. It is unacceptable practice whether it occurs by accident or on purpose to gain an advantage.

**Practical report**  A written account of a practical investigation, reporting on what has happened. Typically, it has a structure based on: introduction, method, results, discussion and conclusion. Writing style and structure are normally modelled on scientific research papers in peer-reviewed journals.

**Preposition**  A short word or phrase that indicates a relationship between a noun, pronoun or phrase, and other words in a sentence.

**Presentation**  Making a visual presentation to a group, usually with a spoken narrative. It also refers to the final visual form of a document or other communication.

**Primary source**  In many disciplines this refers to a publication in which original information or ideas are first communicated.

**Pronoun**  A word that stands in place of a noun.

**Punctuation**  The use of marks in the text that serve to group or separate words and letters to give them specific meaning.

**Purpose**  In the IPACE model, purpose concerns the intention of an assessor in setting a written assignment, the student's intention in terms of what the intended reader will gain from the writing, and the potential benefits for the student in completing the assignment.

**Qualifier**  A term or expression that narrows a literature search based on key words or phrases when using a search engine on the World Wide Web or within a bibliographic database.

**Quote (quotation)**  Text taken from a source that is quoted word for word. Quotations are normally used sparingly and must adhere to certain conventions to be acceptable in academic writing.

**Readability**  The ease with which text can be read and comprehended by a target reader.

**Reference**  The full publication details about a source document. A reference for a book, for example, includes: author(s), date of publication, title of the publication, edition (if not first), place of publication, and publisher. References are normally placed in a list of references or a bibliography at the end of the document.

**Reference management software**  Computer software that gathers and organises bibliographic information and manages its use for citing and referencing within a document.

**Reflective writing**  Involves documenting a personal view, focusing on recent experience. It usually involves moving beyond mere description, to explaining and justifying what has taken place. It may include critical reflection in which a systematic attempt is made to learn from the experience, often by referring to relevant theory or good practice recommendations.

**Reviewing**  Checking written work. Reviewing can occur at various levels of detail, from developmental editing, to copy-editing, to final proofreading.

**Scan**  To speedily read written material, searching for specific words, phrases or other items, e.g. names, dates, definitions, quotations.

**Scatter plot**  This type of graph displays a relationship between two continuous variables, but unlike a line graph, it plots individual data points, not aggregated ones. A line of best fit may be drawn through the scatter by hand or using appropriate software.

**Secondary source**  In many disciplines this refers to a publication that reports on, summarises, or otherwise reviews one or more primary sources.

**Sentence**  A group of words that has complete meaning in itself and contains a subject and a finite verb. It starts with a capital letter and usually ends with a full stop.

**Skim**  To speedily read written material to gain an overview. It involves paying attention to summaries, headings and subheadings, visual elements, and beginning and endings at different scales, from paragraphs to the whole document.

**Subject**  In a sentence, a person or thing that is performing or expressing the action of a verb.

**Summarise**  To sum up someone else's information or ideas in your own words. Summarising is shorter than paraphrasing. Like paraphrasing, summarising should be accompanied by a citation to the original source.

**Summative feedback**  Feedback given after a task is completed and after work has been submitted for final assessment.

**Thesis statement**  A sentence or two at or near the end of an assignment's introduction that summarises a student's argument and their point of view on the topic they are considering. It is a common feature of essays in social sciences, arts and the humanities but is less common in STEM (science, technology, engineering and maths) disciplines.

**Verb**  A 'doing or being word' that expresses action, feelings or state.

# Cited References and Further Reading

Barker, A. (2017). *Alex Essay Writing Tool*. London: Royal Literary Fund/Middlesborough: Teesside University. Available from: https://alexessaytool.com [accessed 29 August 2017].

Baron, N. (2016). 'Do Students Lose Depth in Digital Reading?' *The Conversation*, 20 July 2016. Available from: https://theconversation.com/do-students-lose-depth-in-digital-reading-61897 [accessed 8 August 2017].

Barrass, R. (2002). *Scientists Must Write: A Guide to Better Writing for Scientists, Engineers and Students*. 2nd edn. London: Routledge.

Barrass, R. (2007). *Students Must Write*. 3rd edn. London: Routledge.

Batty, D. (2008). 'GMC Suspends Raj Persaud for Plagiarism'. *Guardian Online*, 20 June 2008. Available from: www.theguardian.com/society/2008/jun/16/mentalhealth.health [accessed 11 August 2017].

Betteridge, A. (2011). *Chambers Adult Learners' Guide to Spelling*. 2nd edn. London: Hodder Education.

Boud, K., Keogh, R. and Walker, D. (1985). *Reflection: Turning Experience into Learning*. London: Kogan Page.

Brande, D. (1934, 1981). *Becoming a Writer*. London: Macmillan.

Bullock, K. and Wikely, F. (1999). 'Improving Learning in Year 9: Making Use of Personal Learning Plans'. *Educational Studies*, 25(1), pp. 19–33.

Buzan, T. (2010). *The Speed Reading Book*. Revised edn. Harlow: BBC Active.

Buzan, T. and Buzan, B. (2010). *The Mind Map Book*. Revised edn. Harlow: BBC Active.

Cañas, A. J., Carff, R. and Marcon, M. (2012). 'Knowledge Model Viewers for the iPad and the Web.' In A. J. Cañas, J. D. Novak and J. Vanhear eds., *Concept Maps: Theory, Methodology, Technology – Proceedings of the Fifth International Conference on Concept Mapping*. Malta: University of Malta. Available from: http://cmc.ihmc.us/cmc2012papers/cmc2012-p193.pdf [accessed 8 August 2017].

Cardiff University Information Services (2006). *Evaluating Information Flowchart*. Cardiff: University of Cardiff. Available from: https://ilrb.cf.ac.uk/evalinfo/evalinfo.html [accessed 7 August 2017].

CBI (2016). *The Right Combination. Education and Skills Survey 2016*. London: Confederation of British Industry/Pearson. Available from: www.cbi.org.uk/cbi-prod/assets/File/pdf/cbi-education-and-skills-survey2016.pdf [accessed 2 August 2017].

Chivers, B. and Shoolbred, M. (2007). *A Student's Guide to Presentations: Making Your Presentations Count*. London: Sage.

Conrey, S. M. and Brizee, A. (2011). *Symptoms and Cures for Writer's Block*. West Lafayette: Purdue University, Purdue Online Writing Lab. Available from: https://owl.english.purdue.edu/owl/resource/567/1/ [accessed 10 August 2017].

Copus, J. (2009). *Brilliant Writing Tips for Students*. Basingstoke: Palgrave Macmillan.

Cottrell, S. (2017). *Critical Thinking* Skills. 3rd edn. London: Palgrave Macmillan.

Creme, P. and Lea, M. R. (2008). *Writing at University: A Guide for Students*. 3rd edn. Maidenhead: Open University Press.

Day, T. (2008). *Oceans*. Revised edition. New York: Facts On File.

Day, T. and Tosey, P. (2011). 'Beyond SMART? A New Framework for Goal Setting'. *The Curriculum Journal*, 22(4), pp. 515–534.

Day, T., Pritchard, J. and Heath, A. (2010). 'Sowing the Seeds of Enhanced Academic Writing Support in a Research-intensive University'. *Educational Developments*, 11(3), pp. 18–21.

Deane, M. (2010). *Academic Research, Writing and Referencing*. Harlow: Pearson Education.

Dennison, B. and Kirk, R. (1990). *Do, Review, Learn, Apply: A Simple Guide to Experiential Learning*. Oxford: Blackwell.

Dewey, J. (1938). *Experience and Education*. New York: Collier.

Dilts, R. and DeLozier, J. (2000). 'Spelling Strategy', pp. 1285–1290. *Encyclopedia of Systemic NLP and NLP New Coding*. Scotts Valley: NLP University Press. Available from: http://nlpuniversitypress.com/html3/SoSto31.html [accessed 14 August 2017].

Dochartaigh, N. O. (2012). *Internet Research Skills*. 3rd edn. London: Sage.

Duarte, N. (2010). *Resonate: Present Visual Stories that Transform Audiences*. Hoboken: John Wiley & Sons.

Elbow, P. (1973). *Writing Without Teachers*. Oxford: Oxford University Press.

Elbow, P. (1981). *Writing with Power: Techniques for Mastering the Writing Process*. New York: Oxford University Press.

Elbow, P. (1998). *Writing with Power: Techniques for Mastering the Writing Process*. New edition. Oxford: Oxford University Press.

Fairbairn, G. J. and Winch, C. (2011). *Reading, Writing and Reasoning: A Guide for Students*. 3rd edn. Maidenhead: Open University Press.

Falchikov, N. (2001). *Learning Together: Peer Tutoring in Higher Education*. London: Routledge.

Flower, L. and Hayes, J. (1977). 'Problem Solving Strategies and the Writing Process'. *College English*, 39(4), pp. 449–461.

Forsyth, P. (2016). *How to Write Reports and Proposals*. 4th edn. London: Kogan Page.

Gibbs, G. (1988). *Learning by Doing: A Guide to Teaching and Learning Methods*. London: Further Education Unit.

Godfrey, J. (2013). *How to Use Your Reading in Your Essays*. 2nd edn. Basingstoke: Palgrave Macmillan.

Godwin, J. (2014). *Planning Your Essay*. 2nd edn. Basingstoke: Palgrave Macmillan.

Greetham, B. (2018). *How to Write Better Essays*. 4th edn. London: Palgrave Macmillan.

Hacker, D. and Fister, B. (2015). *Research and Documentation in the Electronic Age*. 6th edn. Boston: Bedford/St Martin's.

Hartley, J. (2008). *Academic Writing and Publishing*. Abingdon: Routledge.

Harvey, G. (2008). *Writing with Sources: A Guide for Students*. 2nd edn. Indianapolis: Hackett Publishing.

Hickman, D. E. and Jacobson, S. (1997). *The POWER Process: An NLP Approach to Writing.* Carmarthen: Crown House Publishing.

Hyland, K. (2016). *Teaching and Researching Writing.* 3rd edn. Abingdon: Routledge.

Illumine Training (2017). *The Mind Mapping Site.* Windsor: Illumine. Available from: www.mind-mapping.co.uk/ [accessed 8 August 2017].

Institute for Human & Machine Cognition (2017). *CMAP.* Florida: Institute for Human and Machine Cognition (IHMC), University of West Florida. Available from: http://cmap.ihmc.us/ [accessed 8 August 2017].

IPCC (2007). *IPCC Fourth Assessment Report. Climate Change 2007: Synthesis Report. Section 1.1. Observations of Climate Change.* Geneva: Intergovernmental Panel on Climate Change (IPCC). Available from: http://ipcc.ch/report/ar4/syr/ [accessed 11 August 2017].

Jabr, F. (2013). 'The Reading Brain in the Digital Age: The Science of Paper versus Screens.' *Scientific American,* 11 April 2013. Available from: www.scientificamerican.com/article/reading-paper-screens/ [accessed 8 August 2017].

King, S. (2000, 2012). *On Writing: A Memoir of the Craft.* Revised edn. London: Hodder & Stoughton.

Kolb, D. A. (1984). *Experiential Learning: Experience as a Source of Learning and Development.* Englewood Cliffs: Prentice Hall.

Lavers, J. L. and Bond, A. L. (2017). 'Exceptional and Rapid Accumulation of Anthropogenic Debris on One of the World's Most Remote and Pristine Islands'. *PNAS,* 114(23), pp. 6052–6055.

LearnHigher (–). *Report Writing.* LearnHigher/Association for Learning Development in Higher Education. Available from: www.learnhigher.ac.uk/writing-for-university/report-writing/ [accessed 16 August 2017].

LearnHigher (2007). *Oral Communication.* Liverpool: Liverpool Hope University/London: Brunel University. Available at: www.brunel.ac.uk/learnhigher/giving-oral-presentations/delivering-your-presentation.shtml [accessed 16 August 2017].

Lepore, S. J. and Smyth, J. (2002). *The Writing Cure.* Washington: American Psychological Association.

Levin, P. (2011). *Excellent Dissertations!* 2nd edn. Maidenhead: Open University Press.

Levin, P. and Topping, G. (2006). *Perfect Presentations!* Maidenhead: Open University Press.

Lewin, K. (1946). 'Action Research and Minority Problems'. *Journal of Social Issues,* 2(4), pp. 34–46.

Locke, E. A. and Latham, G. P. (2002). 'Building a Practically Useful Theory of Goal Setting and Task Motivation: A 35-year Odyssey'. *American Psychologist,* 57(9), pp. 705–717.

Marsen, S. (2013). *Professional Writing.* 3rd edn. Basingstoke: Palgrave Macmillan.

McMillan, K. and Weyers, J. (2011). *How to Write Dissertations and Project Reports.* 2nd edn. Harlow: Prentice Hall.

McMillan, K. and Weyers, J. (2012). *The Smarter Study Skills Companion.* 3rd edn. Harlow: Pearson.

Morley, J. (2017). *The Academic Phrasebank.* Manchester: University of Manchester. Available from: www.phrasebank.manchester.ac.uk/ [accessed 29 August 2017].

Murray, R. (2008). 'Writer's Retreat: Reshaping Academic Writing Practices'. *Educational Developments,* 9(2), pp. 14–16. Available from: www.seda.ac.uk/?p=5_4_1&pID=9.2 [accessed 8 August 2017].

Narduzzo, A. and Day, T. (2012). 'Less is More in Physics: A Small-scale Writing in the Disciplines (WiD) Intervention'. *Journal of Learning Development in Higher Education,* 4, Case Study 5.

Neville, C. (2010). *The Complete Guide to Referencing and Avoiding Plagiarism.* 2nd ed. Maidenhead: Open University Press.

Nicol, A. A. M. and Pexman, P. M. (2010a). *Displaying Your Findings: A Practical Guide for Creating Tables.* 6th edn. Washington: American Psychological Association.

Nicol, A. A. M. and Pexman, P. M. (2010b). *Displaying Your Findings: A Practical Guide for Creating Figures, Posters and Presentations.* 6th edn. Washington: American Psychological Association.

Orna, E. and Stevens, G. (2009). *Managing Information for Research: Practical Help in Researching, Writing and Designing Dissertations.* 2nd edn. Maidenhead: Open University Press.

Paton, G. (2014). 'OECD: UK Graduates "Lacking High-Level Literacy Skills"'. *Telegraph newspaper,* 9 September 2014. Available from: www.telegraph.co.uk/education/ educationnews/11082842/OECD-UK-graduates-lacking-high-level-literacy-skills.html [accessed 2 August 2017].

Pears, R. and Shields, G. (2016). *Cite Them Right: The Essential Referencing Guide.* 10th edn. London: Palgrave Macmillan.

Peck, J. and Coyle, M. (2012a). *The Student's Guide to Writing: Grammar, Punctuation and Spelling.* 3rd edn. Basingstoke: Palgrave Macmillan.

Peck, J. and Coyle, M. (2012b). *Write it Right: The Secrets of Effective Writing.* 2nd edn. Basingstoke: Palgrave Macmillan.

Pinker, S. (2014). *The Thinking Person's Guide to Writing in the 21st Century.* London: Penguin.

Reid, M. (2012). *Report Writing.* Basingstoke: Palgrave Macmillan.

Ridley, D. (2012). *The Literature Review: A Step-By-Step Guide For Students.* 2nd edn. London: Sage.

Rowntree, D. (1998). *Learn How to Study: A Realistic Approach.* London: TimeWarner.

Rozakis, L. (2007). *Schaum's Quick Guide to Writing Great Research Papers.* 2nd edn. New York: McGraw-Hill.

Ryan, R. M. and Deci, E. L. (2000). 'Intrinsic and Extrinsic Motivations: Classic Definitions and New Directions'. *Contemporary Educational Psychology,* 25, pp. 54–67.

Sayce, K. (2010). *What Not to Write.* Revised edition. Singapore: Talisman.

Schön, D. (1983). *The Reflective Practitioner: How Professionals Think in Action.* London: Temple Smith.

Schön, D. (1987). *Educating the Reflective Practitioner.* San Francisco: Josey-Bass.

Smith, F. (2004). *Understanding Reading: A Psycholinguistic Analysis of Reading and Learning to Read.* 6th edn. London: Routledge.

Swatridge, C. (2014). *Effective Argument and Critical Thinking.* Oxford: Oxford University Press.

Sword, H. (2012). *Stylish Academic Writing.* Cambridge: Harvard University Press.

Taylor, G. (2009). *A Student's Writing Guide: How to Plan and Write Successful Essays.* Cambridge: Cambridge University Press.

The Open University (2013). *Skills for OU Study: Note-taking Techniques.* Milton Keynes: The Open University. Available from: www2.open.ac.uk/students/skillsforstudy/notetaking-techniques.php [accessed 8 August 2017].

The Open University (2017). *OpenLearn Online Unit: More Working with Charts, Graphs and Tables*. Milton Keynes: The Open University. Available from: www.open.edu/openlearn/science-maths-technology/mathematics-and-statistics/mathematics-education/more-working-charts-graphs-and-tables/content-section-0 [accessed 10 August 2017].

Thomas, G. (2017). *Doing Research*. 2nd edn. London: Palgrave Macmillan.

Truss, L. (2009). *Eats, Shoots and Leaves*. London: Fourth Estate.

Tufte, E. R. (2001). *The Visual Display of Quantitative Information*. 2nd edn. Cheshire: Graphics Press.

UNCTAD (2016). *Review of Maritime Transport*. Geneva: United Nations Conference on Trade and Development (UNCTAD). Available from: http://unctad.org/en/pages/Publication Webflyer.aspx?publicationid=1650 [accessed 10 August 2017].

University of New South Wales (2016). *Reflective Writing*. New South Wales: University of New South Wales. Available from: https://student.unsw.edu.au/reflective-writing and links [accessed 16 August 2017].

University of Southampton (2017). *Introduction to Research Skills*. Southampton: University of Southampton. Available from: http://library.soton.ac.uk/sash/introduction-to-research-skills [accessed 7 August 2017].

University of York (2011). *Referencing Styles*. York: University of York. Available from: www.york.ac.uk/students/studying/develop-your-skills/study-skills/study/integrity/ [accessed 11 August 2017].

Wade, D. T. (2009). 'Goal Setting in Rehabilitation: An Overview of What, Why and How'. *Clinical Rehabilitation*, 23(4), pp. 291–295.

Walliman, N. (2014). *Your Undergraduate Dissertation: The Essential Guide for Success*. 2nd edn. London: Sage.

Watson, J. D. and Crick, F. H. C. (1953). 'Molecular Structure of Nucleic Acids. A Structure for Deoxyribose Nucleic Acid'. *Nature*, 171, pp. 737–738.

Williams, K., Woolliams, M. and Spiro, J. (2012). *Reflective Writing*. Basingstoke: Palgrave Macmillan.

Young, T. M. (2005). *Technical Writing A–Z: A Commonsense Guide to Engineering Reports and Theses*. British English Edition. New York: ASME.

Zinsser, W. (2006). *On Writing Well: The Classic Guide to Writing Non-Fiction*. 30th anniversary edition. New York: Harper Perennial.

Zinsser, W. (2009). 'Writing English as a Second Language.' *American Scholar*, Winter 2010. Available from: https://theamericanscholar.org/writing-english-as-a-second-language/ [accessed 8 August 2017].

# Index